THE VOLUNTEER

The

Volunteer

A CANADIAN'S SECRET LIFE IN
THE MOSSAD

MICHAEL ROSS
WITH JONATHAN KAY

McCLELLAND & STEWART

Library and Archives Canada Cataloguing in Publication
Ross, Michael
The volunteer : a Canadian's secret life in the Mossad / Michael Ross ; with Jonathan Kay.

ISBN: 978-0-7710-1740-7

1. Ross, Michael. 2. Israel. Mosad le-modi'in ve-tafkidim meyuhadim – Biography.
3. Espionage, Israeli. 4. Intelligence officers – Israel – Biography.
I. Kay, Jonathan, 1968– II. Title.

UB271.I82R68 2007   327.125694'092   C2006-904213-6

We acknowledge the financial support of the Government of Canada through
the Book Publishing Industry Development Program and that of the Government of Ontario
through the Ontario Media Development Corporation's Ontario Book Initiative.
We further acknowledge the support of the Canada Council for the Arts and
the Ontario Arts Council for our publishing program.

Typeset in Albertina by M&S, Toronto
Printed and bound in Canada

All persons who are identified by first name only have been given a pseudonym.
When first and last names are used, these are the actual names of real persons.

Epigraph on page 142:
Reprinted by permission of HarperCollins Publishers Ltd
© J.R.R. Tolkien 1954

Epigraph on page 236:
Load Me Up Words and Music by Matthew Good, Dave Genn, Ian Browne,
and Rich Priske
© 1999 EMI April Music (Canada) Ltd., Dunharrow Music and Publisher Unknown
All rights for EMI April Music (Canada) Ltd. and Dunharrow Music in the U.S.
Controlled and Administered by EMI April Music Inc.
All Rights Reserved   International Copyright Secured   Used by Permission

This book is printed on acid-free paper that is 100% recycled,
ancient-forest friendly (100% post-consumer recycled).

McClelland & Stewart Ltd.
75 Sherbourne Street
Toronto, Ontario
M5A 2P9
www.mcclelland.com

2 3 4 5   11 10 09 08 07

For Shannon, Moran, Sahar, and Tatum
You are all the redemption I could ever need

CONTENTS

| PREFACE

No nation on earth is as loved and loathed as Israel. To Jews, it is a sacred homeland; to Muslims, it is a neo-colonial tumour. But the conflict extends far beyond religion. As the twentieth century's various *isms* waxed and waned, history conspired to put the Jewish state at the eye of every ideological storm. Palestine Liberation Organization terrorists of the 1960s and 1970s dressed up their manifestos with Marxist jargon. Gamal Abdel Nasser preached pan-Arabism. The Baathists of Syria and Iraq traced their intellectual roots to Nazism. Then came the 1979 Iranian Revolution, and the worldwide awakening of militant Islam, which in turn inspired Hamas, al-Qaeda, Islamic Jihad, and Hezbollah. Name an ideology that embraces random slaughter, and Israel has been made to fight it. This fact explains the intense devotion exhibited by many Westerners – Jew and gentile alike – to Israel's cause: they instinctively see in the state a microcosm of the civilized world's struggle against a murderous ideology and the men who embrace it.

This sense of solidarity was only strengthened when the Twin Towers fell, for it became clear that the world's jihadists despised the "infidels" in New York and Washington as much as those in Jerusalem and Tel Aviv. In the decades leading up to 9/11, these jihadists were regarded as mere nuisances, a sideshow to more important geopolitical conflicts. Then the world discovered what I'd discovered two decades earlier: Israel's battle is everyone's battle.

From 1988 until late 2001, I had the rare privilege of serving in the Israeli Secret Intelligence Service, better known as the Mossad. My mission during that time was to protect Israel from exactly the sort of nihilistic killers who had struck the United States on 9/11, in the last days of my tenure. This book is the story of how I performed that mission.

I had a varied career. For seven and a half years, I operated as an undercover agent – a classic spy – deployed in a variety of hostile locales. Following that, I worked at headquarters for two and a half years as the counterterrorism liaison officer to the Central Intelligence Agency and Federal Bureau of Investigation. Though this position lacked the glamour of a foreign posting, it coincided with a period during which the CIA became involved in the Middle East peace process and Israel was experiencing a spate of deadly terrorist bombings. The events I witnessed during that time cast much light on the jointly fought war on terrorism that continues in Israel and the United States to this day.

My story continues with my redeployment to the field in Africa and Southeast Asia, where my mission was to recruit sources and conduct covert operations aimed at weakening terrorist networks and countering the proliferation of unconventional weapons. It was a period of odd, unconnected jobs. But many of them were memorable, and these have found their way into this memoir.

I wish the book you are holding were a slice of bygone history –
like the spy memoirs written by veterans of the Cold War. But sadly,
this is not the case. Israel is still an unwanted presence in the Middle
East. When Iranian President Mahmoud Ahmadinejad declared, on
October 26, 2005, that Israel must be "wiped off the map," he was
not delivering the opinion of a rogue hatemonger; rather, he was giving voice to the majority view in the Muslim Middle East.

During my time in the Mossad, I did my small part to prevent the
Ahmadinejads, Saddams, and bin Ladens of the world from getting
their way. In the chapters that follow, I will describe my role in
missions to foil attempts by Syria, Libya, and Iran to acquire
advanced weapons technology. I will also tell of my part in the
capture of three senior al-Qaeda operatives in Azerbaijan; a secret
operation by the Mossad and Israeli special forces to prevent Tehran
from assisting Sudan's government in its genocidal campaign
against the country's non-Muslim population; a joint Mossad–FBI
operation that uncovered a senior Hezbollah terrorist operating in
the United States; a mission to South Africa in which I intercepted
Iranian agents looking to expand their country's military arsenal; as
well as a bittersweet trip to neighbouring Zimbabwe, where I helped
rescue some of the country's few remaining Jews from Robert
Mugabe's brutal regime.

If you scan the list above, it becomes depressingly apparent that all
of the terrorist groups and rogue states I fought – with the singular,
contestable exception of Libya – remain enemies of the West. In the
case of Iran, North Korea, and al-Qaeda, the threat has only grown.

With my spying days now behind me, my goal is to provide
readers with what insights I can into the ongoing war against terror
and rogue power that I embarked on two decades ago. In so doing,
I will also tell my own story and describe some of the pitfalls of my
craft. As in John le Carré's *Circus*, the world of spies is a place of great

human drama, courage, and imagination. It can also be a place of banal human failings. Though I am proud of what I've done, and have few regrets, the fact is that the secret life I chose comes at great human cost. Estranged children, divorce, depression, anger, compulsive behaviours, post-traumatic stress syndrome, and general alienation are all too common among covert agents.

Few spies retire into money or fame. Speaking for myself, being a spy never got me a free beer anywhere. Aside from my collection of mementos – photos, military badges, and the odd newspaper clipping – memories are pretty much all that is left of my experiences. In the pages that follow, I will do my best to convey the smell, taste, and feel of the places and people I've seen around the world, and of the hollow men whose schemes I did my best to thwart.

A caveat: There have been other books written about the Mossad – some making broad, sensationalistic claims about the agency's means and mission. At best, such books are ill-informed claptrap; at worst, conspiratorial canards aimed at perpetuating the myth of global Jewish conspiracies. As in any intelligence agency, information is tightly guarded within the Mossad, even among active agents. Anyone who claims to know more than a small slice of what the Mossad does is probably lying. I therefore emphasize that *The Volunteer* is intended as a personal story, and not as a comprehensive history of the Mossad. If it didn't happen to me, it's not in this book.

A second caveat: Not every detail of every mission I performed in the Mossad is described here. That's because I have no wish to compromise "the Office" by disclosing sensitive information. Much of what I share on these pages is nominally secret, but I've left out anything that, in my judgment, would compromise my former colleagues or their allies in other intelligence services.

Before 9/11, I never gave a thought to writing a memoir. But now that the local conflict in which I willingly immersed myself two decades ago has become a global war, my attitude has changed. People everywhere now know that they are in a high-stakes war that pits civilization against a fascistic death cult. Having seen the enemy up close, I want to describe to the world the contours of its many faces.

If I am successful, I will not only arouse my readers' interest, but also impart a few grains of a retired spy's wisdom. The Mossad's much misquoted motto is not "By way of deception thou shalt do war" but rather a quote from the Book of Proverbs: "Where no counsel is, the people fall, but in the multitude of counsellors there is safety."

Amen to that.

1 | ARRIVAL

*Any man who afflicts the human race with ideas must be
prepared to see them misunderstood.*

H. L. Mencken

When I first came to Israel in 1982, it was not as a soldier or spy,
but as a tourist – a twenty-one-year-old Canadian fresh out of
the army looking to ease himself back into civilian life. After three
years of a strict military regimen in the Canadian armed forces, what
I really wanted was to see the world through the eyes of a typical
hedonistic backpacker – not through the crosshairs of a 7.62mm FN
assault rifle, or out of the Plexiglas window of a military helicopter.

Leaving my home in Victoria, British Columbia, I flew to Europe
and wandered the streets of London, Paris, and Rome, as well as
those of a slew of picturesque small towns in the European countryside. I tried to pick up some of the local languages, while earnestly
thrusting my own bad high school French, Italian, and German on
the hapless locals. It was the usual *Let's Go Europe* drill, in other words,

and it was great. I didn't have to answer to anyone, let alone salute them. I got drunk with all kinds of people in all kinds of places, and had the opportunity to learn a little about European women, and about their famously liberal sexual mores. In retrospect, those times were good preparation for some of the undercover work I would eventually be doing in Europe about eight years later.

By October, it was getting cold in Europe. My plan was to winter somewhere warm, then go back to Canada and rejoin my friends, who were by now slogging away in university. Through the youth hostel grapevine, I'd heard that Israel might be a practical choice. Especially popular at the time were the country's *kibbutzim* – collectives where visitors could work the fields or factories in exchange for room and board. I didn't know much about them, but it sounded fun. And when you're twenty-one years old, that's enough to go on.

I landed in Tel Aviv on a warm December evening. From the hurly-burly of what is now the old terminal at Ben Gurion Airport, I shared a taxi with a friendly British couple whose son was marrying a local girl. They dropped me off at a one-star hotel – noisy but clean by the standards to which I'd become accustomed. I was excited about my exotic new adventure. But as I drifted off to sleep, I also felt vague pangs of loneliness. Israel is a long way from Victoria, and I wasn't sure what to expect.

The next morning, I set out for the offices of the kibbutz volunteers agency on Hayarkon Street. Sauntering along, I took in the raucous action on Tel Aviv's streets. The scene resembled something like rush hour in Vancouver – except the drivers were a lot less polite. Everywhere I looked, I saw fat palm trees and lush green gardens surrounding low-slung apartment blocks – a strange combination of Santa Monica and the Italian Riviera. The language I heard around me sounded odd and entirely foreign. How amazed I would have been to learn that within a few years, I would become completely fluent.

From the sidewalk, I could see the sun reflecting off the Mediterranean. I watched a group of wetsuit-clad boys not much younger than me carrying their surfboards to the sea. You'd never have known that Israel was then at war, having invaded Lebanon in June to roust Palestinian terror groups from the southern part of the country.* Soldiers of both sexes were everywhere, their body language and manners casual. Military service is compulsory for Israelis between the ages of eighteen and twenty-one, and most men remain in the army's reserves until middle age, so people are used to carrying weapons and seeing others doing the same. The presence of armed men doesn't arouse the sense of anxiety it does in other parts of the world.

At the placement agency, I was met by a friendly man who spoke English well. As we gazed at the map of Israel that was pinned to the wall behind his desk, he asked me where I wanted to go. It was something I hadn't thought about, so I asked him to send me someplace warm that I could get to by bus. After thinking for a moment, he scribbled the name of a kibbutz in the Bet Shean Valley on a piece of paper. Then he handed me a transit pass and gave me directions to the city's central bus station.

Once the bus left Tel Aviv, I began to get a sense of the extraordinary natural and demographic variety that this miniature nation had to offer. Travelling roads once used by the Romans, Greeks, and a dozen other great empires, we passed through a succession of Jewish and Arab villages. In one of the latter, at Wadi Arah, we were greeted by a bloated, upended cow on the side of the road – dead as a doornail and full of flies. No one on the bus seemed much taken aback by this, and no one outside seemed in a hurry to remove it.

---

* On June 6, 1982, Israeli tanks rolled into Lebanon as part of Operation Peace for Galilee, in response to an attack three days earlier by Palestinian terrorists on Israel's ambassador to Britain, Shlomo Argov, outside London's Dorchester Hotel. By the time Israel withdrew most of its troops in 1985, about eighteen thousand people had been killed, 675 of them Israeli soldiers.

I closed my window and made a mental note to avoid restaurants in the area if I happened to return.

Then we turned into a fertile valley bordered by the Gilboa Mountains to the south and a set of low acacia-studded hills to the north. As we journeyed on, I saw the dun-coloured mountains of Gilead off to the east, property of the Hashemite Kingdom of Jordan. I was awestruck – not just by the physical beauty, but by the centuries of history in which I knew this land was steeped.

At the kibbutz, I was warmly greeted by the other volunteers – twenty-somethings from New Zealand, Australia, Brazil, Sweden, and South Africa. The place had something of a party vibe, complete with a pub that some 1960s-era volunteers had converted from an old poultry processing plant. The beer was plentiful and absurdly cheap. Whatever loneliness I'd felt the previous night quickly dissipated.

In recent decades, Israel's kibbutz movement has fallen into decline – along with the socialist political ideology that gave rise to it. But during the country's early years, the kibbutzniks were Israel's heart and soul. Most were stoical, avowedly secular Jews whose parents and grandparents had survived the Holocaust or other intense hardships. They'd arrived with a dream to forge a new identity for themselves and shed the dark cloak of Diaspora Judaism.

Though they always comprised a small percentage of Israeli society, kibbutzniks formed the core of Israel's founding warrior class – once staffing as much as eighty per cent of the country's top military jobs. To this day, whole special forces units are still composed of kibbutzniks. Getting up early, working the land, camping, and hiking were activities kibbutz children did practically from the cradle. They were tough and self-confident, and they knew how to work as part of a team.

I stayed on the kibbutz for several months and worked the cotton plantation while trying to learn Hebrew and exploring the country in my spare time. Like most tourists, I spent much of my time in Jerusalem. The city is a marvel to explore – particularly for a wide-eyed B.C. boy. Canada is not a religious country, and this was the first time I'd been to a place where people took their communion with God so seriously.

Of course, I knew nothing of the prayers I heard from the pious bearded men bowing before the Old City's Western Wall, but I could certainly appreciate the awe-inspiring historical significance of the site. This was the one surviving piece of the Jews' ancient Roman-era temple. The very idea that modern-day Jews could reclaim it two millennia later boggled my mind.

I was barely an adult at the time, at the stage in life when many of us begin to look for meaning – something beyond the quest for girls and peer-group acceptance that dominates the teenage years. For some, this search leads to identity politics, or to nationalism, or to a reversion to an ancestral religion. Looking back, perhaps it was fate that I found myself in Israel at this impressionable time of life. Born into an Anglican family, I'd never thought much about matters of faith.

But that began to change. As I traversed the country and drank in more of its history, I began to feel the stirrings of spiritual interest in Judaism. I felt something of a political awakening as well. Though I'd never followed foreign affairs closely when I was in Canada, I'd always felt a vague but oddly powerful sense of solidarity with Israel in its fight to survive amid hostile neighbours. Now that I was living in the country, learning more about its people and the threats they faced, this feeling grew.

We all have moments when we look back and think about the important crossroads in our lives. For me, the defining moment was in 1983, while riding a bus between Haifa and the pastoral fields and hills of the lower Galilee, near the sleepy town of Yokneam.

The spring sunshine was streaming through the old Egged bus windows, illuminating the crudely tattooed sequence of numbers on the upraised arm of an old man seated beside me. Despite the tattoo, the old man betrayed no evidence of previous trauma or past hardship in his life. He just looked old, wizened, and alive – and was seemingly living in relatively quiet obscurity. It dawned on me that this was the first person I'd ever seen whom I knew to be a Holocaust survivor. Despite the fact my knowledge of the Nazis' "final solution" didn't extend much beyond what I'd learned in school, the realization had a powerful effect. At a time when I needed direction in life, it awoke in me a reflexive need to protect and defend those who cannot protect themselves – the same reflex which, on a geopolitical level, led to the creation of the Jewish state itself after the Second World War. Many other factors and experiences influenced my desire to cast my lot in with the Jewish people. But this was the moment that I began to heed the words of Ruth 1:16: "Do not urge me to leave you or to return from following you. For where you go I will go, and where you lodge I will lodge. Your people shall be my people, and your God my God."

Other, less abstract feelings were at play as well. One of my fellow kibbutzniks had a one-eyed Irish setter named Pogey that I would take out for long walks. Occasionally I would bump into a certain German shepherd and her mistress, Dahlia, and we fell into the habit of walking and chatting together.

I spent so much time walking Pogey that he started sleeping in my room. And it was thanks to him that I mastered my first few words in Hebrew – "sit," "stay," and "come here." The winter passed, and then spring and summer and fall. By the time a year had gone by, any thought of returning to Canada was extinguished. Israel had become my home.

The kibbutz's leadership helped me stay in Israel. Through their auspices, I secured placement in an Orthodox conversion program that provided me with a year of intense study in Judaism and Hebrew. The application process said a lot about my new faith: while Christianity and Islam proselytize aggressively, Judaism almost seems eager to discourage new converts. During my interview with a representative of the ministry of religious affairs, which oversaw the program together with the Chief Rabbinate of Israel, the interviewer seemed downright confounded as to why I – or anyone else, for that matter – would want to join such an afflicted, downtrodden religion. He seemed to regard me as some sort of masochist.

But I would not be discouraged. I identified with the Jews and their struggle for a homeland and had met for the first time in my life people who had survived not only numerous wars, but attempts to "wipe them off the map" for good. I was never one to sit on the fence, and I felt in my bones that the Jews had not only a right to exist but a right to live in a country of their own as masters of their own destiny. I had fallen in love not only with an Israeli woman, but also with an entire culture and religion. They'd embraced me as one of their own during the past year, and the least I could do was demonstrate my sincerity by joining the tribe. Conversion wasn't a decision I took lightly, and I realized that, by taking Israel's side, I was embarking on a journey that had a deeper meaning than what I had intended when I left Canada.

My second year in Israel was very different from my first. As part of my conversion program, I moved to a different kibbutz. This one was run by Orthodox Jews, with nary a pub or merry New Zealander to be seen. I prayed three times a day, worked the fields in punishing forty-degree heat, and spent the rest of my waking hours hitting the books. It was at least as tough as anything I'd endured in the army.

But I survived – one of only three who completed the program out of an original twenty-eight. When the year was up, I had to write final exams, undergo an oral examination in front of three university professors, and sit before a quorum of rabbis from the Chief Rabbinate. Only when I'd demonstrated my learning to their satisfaction was I granted the privilege of entering the *mikveh* – a Jewish communal bath that symbolically washes away spiritual impurities. I'd officially become a Jew. (There is another step in the process, of course, but I was spared; mercifully, my parents had had the good sense to circumcise me at birth.)

Judaism blurs the line between religion and ethnicity, and so some Jews look askance on converts. But the scripture provides a rejoinder to such snobs: according to Jewish law, no person is permitted to remind others of a Jew's convert status for seven generations (after which the whole issue is guaranteed to be moot). As for me, I had an easier way of dealing with the issue. I'd simply remind the very few doubters I encountered that King David's Moabite grandmother, Ruth, was herself a convert.

After my conversion, my life moved quickly forward. In the space of a few months, I was granted Israeli citizenship and got married to Dahlia, the raven-haired German shepherd owner. Not long thereafter, I was drafted into the Israel Defense Forces (IDF). I was twenty-four when I received the letter from the government, the same age as my maternal great-grandfather when he was called up to fight in the Great War of 1914–18. Around this time, our first son was also born, and it was at that moment that I fully realized that my life had changed forever.

2 | SOLDIERING ON

People sleep peaceably in their beds at night only because
rough men stand ready to do violence on their behalf.

George Orwell

It was three o'clock in the morning on a warm September day in 1984. I was standing in a small, cramped barracks building in the Israeli countryside while Sergeant Yaron, a young Kurdish Jew, surveyed the thirty-odd soldiers who made up our newly formed platoon. He was that stock figure from many war movies: the tough-as-nails sergeant who breaks down recruits with an unending stream of verbal abuse. More than two decades later, I still remember Sergeant Yaron well. Never before or since have I met a man who could describe his contempt for you in such a wide variety of novel and entertaining ways.

This was my first day in an IDF combat engineer company, a unit tasked with assaulting and demolishing enemy positions. Having been up since five o'clock the previous morning, we were a tired lot.

I would have preferred to be sleeping, and I guess it showed on my face.

"Hey, look everybody, this guy seems really unhappy," Yaron said. He bounded over, stood about an inch from my face, and asked in a booming voice, "Where you from, pretty boy?" I gave him the name of my kibbutz.

"Not with that accent, you aren't. What candy-ass, UN-hugging country do you call home?" He continued without a pause. "Please don't be British, because Israel has its quota of homosexuals and we really can't handle any more." There were muffled chuckles in the background.

"Canada," I replied.

"Canada!" he exclaimed excitedly, instantly seizing on this fresh fodder. "And tell me, what does Canada produce besides snow, trees, maple syrup, and bears?" Without waiting for an answer, he riffed on. "Oh, I remember now. I've seen your peacekeeping countrymen in the Golan. Real fine fighting men – when they aren't fucking our girls in Tiberias!"

His words dripped with the derision that veteran IDF soldiers typically harbour toward "peacekeeping" forces and the foreign armies that staff them – troops whose idea of a casualty is a broken typewriter or flat tire punctured on a beer run.

In fact, I wasn't quite so green as Yaron thought.

Sitting on my dresser at home is a 1919 photo of my father's father, whom everyone knew as "Doc." Doc fought in some of the First World War's greatest battles, including the Somme, Vimy Ridge, and Amiens, the August 8, 1918 clash that began the Hundred Days Offensive, the decisive final campaign against Germany and its allies. The Canadian divisions that spearheaded these attacks managed to advance fifteen kilometres on the first day, an astonishing accomplishment at a time when gains were typically measured in metres.

Doc did not have a medical degree. But during one of his hunting and fishing trips with his friends in northern Ontario, he had managed to assist an Aboriginal man whose wife was undergoing a difficult birth. His friends called him Doc after that, and the nickname stuck until he passed away in 1973.

Besides slogging in the trenches as an infantryman, Doc was also a motorcycle dispatch rider. By his count, he managed to demolish five motorcycles in encounters with shell craters and other battlefield hazards. He may well have been the fastest-moving terrestrial target on the whole Western Front, and one that, luckily for my dad and me, German snipers never managed to hit. To this day, as I lie awake worrying about my own son – the third generation of my family in uniform – I dwell on the morbid fact that I wouldn't be here if Doc had been a tad less fortunate.

Doc's most notable mission was at Amiens, where he had to cross enemy lines to deliver a message to regimental headquarters. He was wounded by shrapnel in the arm and leg, but got the job done. For his bravery, he was awarded a mention in dispatches to the king, signed by Field Marshall Douglas Haig, commander-in-chief of the British Expeditionary Force and the Allied armies in France, and Winston Churchill, then secretary of state for war. Only 3,333 such honours were awarded to Canadian soldiers, out of some 418,000 who served overseas.

My great-grandfather on my mother's side, Herbert Burnett, also fought in the Great War, but I know little about his exploits: he never talked much about them and, like too many veterans, he left no artifacts that tell his story. His house on Joseph Street in Victoria, B.C., sits close to where I now live. When I pass by, I wonder what it must have been like for him to leave his wife and child in 1916 for a faraway war. He, too, returned safely, and he spent the rest of his working years in the employ of my great-great-grandfather, a contractor who built many of the old buildings and homes in Victoria.

Doc and Herbert both fought at Vimy Ridge. Perhaps they fought together, or even exchanged a few words. I have no way of knowing. But I often like to think about how their shared experience affected the destiny of what would eventually become our united family.

As for me, I joined the Canadian army after high school, my head full of adolescent notions of military glory. I served three years in an armoured regiment of Canada's Special Service Force, an elite airborne brigade designed for rapid overseas deployment. The unit was also tasked with defending NATO's northern flank in case of a Soviet invasion, and so we found ourselves doing a lot of winter survival and combat exercises in the frozen hinterlands of Ontario and Quebec – alongside visiting NATO troops from Norway and the other "UN-hugging" Nordic nations Yaron excoriated so stridently. Our brigade was distinguished from the rest of the military by our camouflage jump smocks and shoulder flashes that bore the emblem of the winged dagger, made famous by the British Special Air Service. The rest of the military hated us for these elitist trappings, and shed nary a tear when the brigade was disbanded in 1995 following revelations that some members had tortured and killed young Somali civilians during a peacekeeping operation in 1993.

When I was called up to serve in the Israel Defense Forces, I didn't tell anyone except the recruiting officer about my former military service in Canada because I knew it would have only been a target of mockery. During my training, I pretended that I didn't know what the business end of a weapon was.

The difference between the Canadian and Israeli militaries was startling. Israel is an isolated nation the size of New Jersey, which had gone to war with at least one of its Arab neighbours every decade since its founding. And so the IDF, then as now, was a combat-oriented force full of veteran officers experienced in military operations. The Canadian Forces of my era, by contrast, was a well-meaning but ineffective peacetime army stuck in a Korean War-era time warp. The country didn't invest in its military because everyone knew the United States would do the heavy lifting if things got hot.

Another difference: in the Canadian Forces, I rarely saw my troop commander. He was a remote figure, not really one of the fighting men. But in the IDF, the officer corps' motto is "Acherai," which means "After me." They lead from the front, and they don't stand on ceremony. Once basic training is over, everyone is on a first-name basis.

Lieutenant Tal, our twenty-two-year-old platoon commander, was the perfect embodiment of this IDF ethos. He was tough and taciturn, with dark piercing eyes, black curly hair, and a wiry, sinewy frame. Like Sergeant Yaron, he'd taken part in the 1982 invasion of Lebanon, where our unit had gone up against elite Syrian commandos in the eastern Bekaa Valley. These men had commanded soldiers in the field and seen some of them fall. Over time, I came to admire and respect Lieutenant Tal as I have few others in my lifetime. Today he's a full colonel in the reserves and a successful lawyer in Tel Aviv. He still looks the same as when I met him in 1984.

When he eventually appeared on that warm September morning in 1984 to relieve Sergeant Yaron, we'd all been up for about twenty-four hours. He told us to get used to it: the IDF fights primarily at night. I remember him telling us he'd "turn our days into nights and our nights into days." And he did.

My first days in the IDF were spent preparing my gear for combat and getting to know the other men in my platoon. Like me, a lot of my fellow soldiers were from abroad: the United States, Britain, Latin America, and a few guys from France (whom no one seemed to like because they complained a lot). Right from the start, I formed part of a tight-knit social group with three other transplanted Anglos: Peter, a funny Englishman from London who, like me, had gotten married and been in a kibbutz; Gary, a onetime New Yorker now living in Jerusalem; and Robert, a sardonic budding journalist from Minneapolis. I was lucky to fall in with these guys. As any soldier can testify, you need friends in the army to get you through the miserable times, and to look out for you when the shooting starts.

These ties endure once you're out of the army, as well. The IDF, and the three years most young people spend in it, are the social adhesive that binds Israeli society. Friendships and business contacts are made, jargon learned, patriotic values internalized. As I served, I came to understand why those Israelis who do not enlist – even for entirely valid reasons, such as medical problems – are sometimes treated as outsiders.

Peter, Gary, Robert, and I would sit together for hours and prepare our webbing – vests containing pouches for bullet magazines, grenades, and whatnot. It was a mundane task, but one that had to be done so our gear wouldn't jangle around once we were laden down with our kit and ammunition. We used fine wire to stitch it together and black electrician's tape to cover any shiny bits (this applied right down to our dog tags. Instead of leaving the metal tags exposed, we'd use shoelaces to bind them in a green canvas pouch). Once we'd tested our form-fitting webbing vests, we'd coat them with a special black matte paint. If you expected to be fighting at night, you had to be both quiet and invisible.

During our first week, we were issued our personal weapons. At the time, the gun of choice was the Israeli-made Galil assault rifle – a rough hybrid of a Russian Kalashnikov AK-47 and a U.S. M16. The rear sight had settings for three hundred and five hundred metres, and additional folding night sights with luminous inserts could be raised into position, allowing the gun to be aimed in low light conditions.

The barrel and the flash eliminator could also be used to launch rifle grenades. As well, the weapon featured a folding detachable bipod incorporating a wire cutter – very handy for getting through barbed-wire defences.

Though the Galil wasn't as accurate as the M16, it did the job when "zeroed" properly – that is, calibrated by firing a succession of test shots at the same target. That's one reason that people have their own personal weapon: no two rifles shoot the same.

A female soldier, Avital, taught us how to shoot straight. This was not unusual: the IDF doesn't put women on the battlefield in ground units, but they do serve a wide variety of combat roles as, for example, pilots and naval officers. And many others, like Avital, become instructors. Some Israelis argue the country should go further, fully integrating the forces right down to infantry platoons, tanks, and commandos. Based on my army experience, I oppose this suggestion. First, there is the usual argument that integrating women into combat ground units changes the traditional buddy-based social dynamic necessary for battlefield team-building. In Israel, there is another argument as well: any female soldier who becomes a POW in a Middle Eastern theatre cannot expect to be treated in a gentlemanly fashion. (For an indication of what I mean by this, read Andy McNab's Gulf War memoir, *Bravo Two Zero*.)

As well as teaching us how to shoot, Avital ran us up and down hills in full gear, and administered a course of gut-busting calisthenics. All this was conducted in the rough training grounds of Nachusha, an area in the West Bank selected because of its similarity to the rocky scrub terrain of southern Lebanon, where Israel was then fighting a counter-insurgency campaign. It was exhausting, though not so much that any of us failed to notice that Avital was drop-dead gorgeous. I think we all would have had an easier time concentrating on the live-fire exercises if she'd looked more like Yaron.

Having already received rifle training in the Canadian army, I excelled at the range, and my target groupings were often used as an example to my fellow soldiers, which resulted in my being the subject of some good-natured abuse. One day I had to shoot a bunch of balloons at long range while my whole platoon watched. Yaron, who'd made light of my Canadian roots just days before, dubbed me *Tsayad Hatsvayim*, or "Deer Hunter" – high praise, indeed.

Lieutenant Tal didn't witness that demonstration, but he must have heard about it, because he approached me a few days later and offered me a plum assignment: carrying the platoon's "MAG," a nearly two-metre-long Belgian-made belt-fed machine gun that spits out 850 rounds of 7.62mm ammunition a minute. It's highly effective at ripping up large concentrations of troops. In the right hands, it can also be used as an accurate long-range sniper rifle.

Being offered the MAG was considered a great honour in IDF combat units. It meant you had not only the skill to fire it, but also the strength to carry it and the enormous amount of ammunition it tore through. With the MAG and about 450 rounds of ammo, I was hauling some thirty-eight kilograms of gear – or about half my own weight. My ankles, back, and joints all took a pounding. But the heavy load was necessary: without an abundance of ammunition to feed it, the weapon is just a hunk of metal. (The need to carry such large loads is another reason women are excluded from combat units. For all her extraordinary abilities, I doubt that even as fit a specimen as Avital could carry thirty-eight kilograms on a long march.) The weeks we spent on infantry training in Nachusha were one of the physically hardest periods in my life.

I was one of three men issued MAGs in our 150-man company. We were instructed in their use by a certain Lieutenant Doobie, who'd been a MAG operator during the war in Lebanon. When we started, I couldn't hit the broad side of a barn, but after a few weeks I was shooting like a pro. I could even cock it with one finger on the run by using the tension of the carrying strap around my neck and shoulders.

My teammates were issued other weapons. Peter was assigned to carry a rocket-propelled grenade along with his Galil, and Gary was issued a 53mm hand-held mortar. Robert, the budding correspondent, was given the radio. I remember telling him that his career as a broadcast journalist was getting off to a promising start. "Go fuck yourself, Rambo," he promptly replied.

Over time, we were taught how to camouflage and conceal, patrol, move, and fight as a squad, platoon, and company. We learned the fine art of combat in built-up urban areas, ambushes, first aid, helicopter use, fighting in armoured vehicles, and demolitions. As combat engineers, we were also taught how to blow up everything imaginable. We learned the best place to plant explosives on artillery pieces, defensive positions, buildings, tunnels, bridges, and even an old helicopter.

Throughout all of this gruelling activity, not one member of the platoon dropped out. But that wasn't a surprise: in the Israeli army, you can't be placed in a unit without first meeting the appropriate physical standards. The testing is done well in advance – the logic being that you should not be placed in a combat unit if you have bad asthma, a bum knee, or are otherwise unable to deal with the challenges associated with being a *lochem*, or warrior. Indeed, there is a plethora of private clinics run by former Israeli special forces soldiers that cater to young men preparing for their conscription. Walk through any city, and you will often see cadres of high school students led by an older and very fit civilian. They are preparing for their *Gibush*, or official selection to the IDF's many special forces and regular combat units.

We ran all kinds of assault-and-defend exercises, until they were second nature. Most of the training was under live fire. This not only prepares you for the sounds and smells of combat, it takes the shock and awe out of it, so that when you are in a real firefight, you're not paralyzed by fear. That isn't to say that we ran around shooting our guns off like frat boys playing weekend paintball. We usually had to make many dry runs on an exercise before going through with live ammunition.

During our combined forces exercises, we also got the opportunity to participate in mixed-unit drills that required coordination with tanks, aircraft, and other infantry units. The sight of so many different cogs co-operating to achieve the same objective was impressive. I was equally awed by the sheer firepower of Israel's military. To this day, I am somewhat irked when the IDF is accused of being "heavy-handed" in its response to some terror attack or another. If the IDF applied a significant fraction of its firepower on a Palestinian area, it would be reduced to ash in an instant.

But the most impressive part of my experience in the IDF had nothing to do with the training or field operations. It was the way our trainers made us understand our role. On Friday afternoons, before we would head home for weekend leave (if we got any), we'd congregate in an informal circle on the ochre ground in the shade of an olive tree and talk with our platoon commander and sergeants about the ethics of soldiering.

These were open and frank discussions about when to kill and when not to kill. The format was essentially Socratic, with Lieutenant Tal presenting a moral dilemma and the rest of us discussing the best way to solve it. Examples: "Do you shoot someone who is unarmed but possibly carrying a bomb?" "How do you treat prisoners of war?" "What are the rules of engagement in such-and-such dangerous setting?" We were taught the IDF's official doctrine, which stipulates that "servicemen and women will use their weapons and force only for the purpose of their mission, only to the necessary extent, and will maintain their humanity even during combat. IDF soldiers will not use their weapons and force to harm human beings who are not combatants or prisoners of war, and will do all in their power to avoid causing harm to their lives, bodies, dignity and property."

Everyone took these lessons to heart. This fact helped explain a paradox I'd noticed since joining the Israeli army. No other nation on earth is more dependent on its military for its survival, or has, in living memory, fought so many fierce wars on its own borders. Yet Israeli soldiers are, by my first-hand observation, *less* militaristic in that gung-ho Marine Corps "hoo-ha" way that often characterizes other Western armies. While service in the military – especially in combat units – is a source of pride, fighting is still considered a necessary evil. By teaching its soldiers such lessons, the IDF ensures that it has not only a more effective military than those of its Arab neighbours, but a more ethical one as well.

Each phase of our advanced training was marked by a long night march in full gear. On the final march, we left Nachusha and covered seventy kilometres before reaching our destination the next morning. When we arrived, we had a torch-lit ceremony on a hill. Going from soldier to soldier, Lieutenant Tal placed a ceremonial beret on each sweaty head, coupled with a hard, but good-natured punch on the chest. It was one of the proudest moments in my life.

In the months that followed, we did what Israeli soldiers do. We patrolled the West Bank and did house-to-house searches for wanted terrorists. Sometimes it would dawn on me that Roman soldiers no doubt walked the same beat two thousand years ago. When I mentioned this thought to our company commander, he took a serious tone, reminding me that our little patrols were what prevented the whole territory from falling into anarchy. We also provided security on Christmas Eve in Jerusalem, and I guarded buses used to ferry international pilgrims to Manger Square in Bethlehem. People stared at me and my kit as I rode with them. Though I carried my Galil for such tasks, I tried not to alarm anyone. I remember an American boy, about six years old, staring at me during one bus tour. I smiled at him and asked if he'd been a good boy for Santa. His parents' mouths dropped open in shock. They seemed amazed that an Israeli soldier would know anything about Santa, let alone speak fluent English.

Another memory stands out vividly. An Israeli civilian had been shot at one night while driving to her West Bank home. Five of us set up an improvised roadblock to cut off the terrorists' escape. They never came by, but an older man in an Arab headdress came riding up. "Sabach al-hir (good morning)," he said. I gave him the standard reply, "Sabach al-noor," which means "good light."

It was almost dawn and we got word on the radio to stand down. The wizened Arab produced a coffee *finjan*, a single-handled pot for making Turkish coffee – known in Israel as *botz*, or "mud," because of the large amount of sediment left behind in the glass. We lit a fire and filled the *finjan* with water, and the visitor added scoops of cardamon-laced Turkish coffee. We added sugar, and when the brew started to boil over we poured it into some small glasses he'd brought. We sat around the fire Bedouin-style and drank the coffee.

I live on the west coast of Canada and, true to regional stereotype, am a premium-coffee addict. But nothing has ever matched the coffee we had that morning. When I look back, I see a quintessential Middle East moment: two cultures sharing a common pleasure without the fetters of politics and terror. The old gentleman knew we meant him no harm, and we respected him and his culture. His generation of Palestinians fought long and hard against the nascent Jewish state, but he seemed to know that we need to move on and make some kind of accommodation. Today's Palestinian youths have been hijacked by a Hamas-led death cult. You would be hard pressed to find any one of

them bringing coffee to an Israeli patrol. And if one did, he'd probably be treated as a potential suicide bomber. When I think of the
elderly Arab and his kind smile, I feel sad.

Though I conducted lots of patrols in the West Bank, I never
fired my weapon. In fact, my most dangerous moment in the army
had nothing to do with Palestinian terrorists. I was on a training
exercise in the Negev Desert. We were wheeling around in a
modified Zelda armoured personnel carrier (APC), a tracked vehicle
that typically carries about eight soldiers. We were following a ridge
line when the crew commander ordered the driver to pull a hard
right. Instead, he reacted by pulling a hard left and hitting the gas
pedal. We careened over the ridge and went on a roller-coaster ride
into the gulley below. When the APC skidded to a stop on its side, I
climbed out, shaking like a leaf. After that, I hated APCs.

Some nights, we went out hunting terror cells thought to be
operating in our area. But such missions were few and far between.
The Palestinian thugs feared us for the most part. Having not yet
been indoctrinated into fundamentalist Islam, they had no desire to
visit Paradise and its heavenly smorgasbord of virgins.

On one night I remember well, my group gave chase to a suspicious group of young Arab men we'd spotted while on patrol in the
West Bank. I was carrying the shoulder-crushing MAG and ammo at
full run when my foot went into a hole. I turned my ankle and fell flat
on my back. I looked up at the stars for an instant, only to see them
blocked out by the MAG coming down square on my face. Instantly,
my nose bled like an open faucet. The familiar hands of my friends
grabbed me and I was hauled to my feet. A whisper in my ear asked if
I was okay, and before I could answer we were off at full flight again.

Later, I went to see the medic – but only because Lieutenant Tal
told me to. Like most of the platoon, I avoided the medic like the
plague. He terrified us more than any officer. A sullen veteran of

the Lebanon invasion, and not overly sympathetic to our cuts and scrapes, he told us while teaching first aid that once you see a fellow soldier step on a mine and lose his sight, both legs, an arm, and his genitalia, other injuries fail to impress. His speech, delivered in an emotionless monotone, really scared the hell out of us, but such horror stories are a necessary wake-up call to anyone whose vision of war injuries is shaped by the bloodless battle scenes of Errol Flynn and John Wayne. Years later, I realized that I had been observing a victim of post-traumatic stress syndrome.

By this point, Israel had expelled Yasser Arafat and his PLO from southern Lebanon, but the void had been filled by Hezbollah, an Iranian-sponsored Shiite militia and terrorist group that pioneered the use of spectacular suicide bombings – including those against the U.S. embassy and marine barracks in Beirut in 1983. It was terrorism on a scale that had never been seen before in the Middle East.

After sending Western peacekeepers packing, Hezbollah focused its attacks on Israeli troops. In 1985, shortly after I joined the Israeli army, Israel withdrew the bulk of its forces to a newly created "security zone" along the border, and outsourced much of the fighting to the South Lebanon Army, a proxy militia staffed primarily by Lebanese Christians.

I became connected to the war in Lebanon in 1985, when I was transferred from my regular combat engineering post to a reserve unit of the Golani, Israel's most decorated military brigade. I was happy with the move; as well as having a reputation for bravery and extraordinary accomplishment, the Golani is also famous for its exceptional camaraderie. Soldiers call each other *achi*, or "my brother."

I joined the Golani ranks in a demolitions platoon, and was deployed to Lebanon with a unit tasked with securing Israel's defensive positions in the south of the country, and with keeping the roads free of ambushes and roadside improvised explosive devices (IEDs). It is no coincidence that this is exactly the type of threat that American forces have encountered in Iraq, and Canadian soldiers in Afghanistan. The insurgents in both countries learned their techniques from Hezbollah and their Iranian Revolutionary Guards advisers.

My single brush with Hezbollah in the IDF came after a military transport vehicle carrying our soldiers was blown up by a suicide bomber, right next to the border fence between Israel and Lebanon, a bombing that was conducted in retaliation for Israel having destroyed the Hezbollah headquarters in the town of Marrakeh. The suicide bombings were a new phenomenon in the region, and Hezbollah was particularly adept at using suicide truck-bombs to attack IDF units. We were going to retaliate with a technique of our own that didn't involve trucks or suicide bombs but would hurt Hezbollah nonetheless.

This engagement with Hezbollah would mark the first of my many encounters with the terrorist organization throughout my career in the Mossad. It was the making of a fateful relationship that would start on a dirt track in South Lebanon and end in a warehouse in Johannesburg, South Africa, some sixteen years later.

We were sitting around one sunny afternoon eating, sleeping, and talking trash as soldiers do when they are not soldiering. Then word came that we were going to run an ambush that night. When it grew dark, we congregated in a bunker where a whiteboard with an annotated map explained our mission. Intelligence provided by the IDF's Directorate of Military Intelligence indicated that Hezbollah militants would be driving vehicles on a road some ten kilometres away from our position in the northwest part of the Israeli security zone. Our mission was to hump out to a preselected position near the road, booby-trap the route with an antitank mine and additional explosives, then hose down (with lead) whatever was left of the Hezbollah vehicles and their occupants.

We organized our kits, talking little since there was much to do. After a few hours, our sergeants and platoon commanders checked our gear in an IDF ritual known as a *misdar*, or inspection. Afterwards, the company commander conducted his own inspection, not only checking gear but also making sure soldiers knew their assigned roles.

I was scared: I started to realize that I could die.

It may seem odd that such a basic fact of soldiering hit me only after several years spent in two different armies. But I was still young at the time – twenty-four – and like many soldiers, I'd glided along on an adolescent conceit of immortality. Until now.

We headed off in silence. It was about nine o'clock or so. Our target wasn't far, but we had to stop a few times to get our bearings and make sure we were on the right route. At the ambush point, the company commander made a reconnaissance of the road, a narrow dirt track with thorny scrub and rocks on either side. It was pitch black, and he moved with a small patrol and radio operator glued to him like a Siamese twin. My platoon commander, Gilad, took me and three other soldiers and we headed off in the other direction to see if any vehicles were approaching. Meanwhile, other members of my platoon started planting their remote-control explosives in the road. They got the job done quickly. All the materials had been prepared before we departed, so they really only had to pull the charges out of their rucksacks and bury them.

The spot was perfect, as there was a high ridge where the rest of the unit could set up – far enough away so as not to be affected by the blast that was to come. We lay in wait there for about six hours in the cool night air. I started to get cold.

The soldiers didn't talk to one another. But occasional whispered commands were passed from one man to the next as we sat in a big circle, each soldier with a leg overlapping the leg of the man next to him, to ensure that we would not be surprised by a roving Hezbollah foot patrol, no matter which direction it came from. This type of ambush defence is called a *ma'arav kochav*, or "star ambush." The circle is broken only when the enemy's direction of approach is determined, at which time the soldier who detects the attacker uses leg movements to signal to his neighbours, who then adjust their position to face the target. (The commander usually lines up in the direction that the enemy is supposed to approach from, so in most cases the soldiers know to line up on his position.)

Just when I thought we'd come out for nothing, we heard vehicles approaching. No one spoke, but instead we began to silently shift into a line on the ridge facing the road. I took my Galil off safe mode and waited.

In those days, Hezbollah would tear around the countryside in big dust-covered Mercedes-Benz sedans. They'd pile into them and drive hell-bent for leather on any kind of road. On that night, there was a convoy of two.

Suddenly there was a huge flash in my peripheral vision and then a solid *ka-thunk* noise. Flames shot up in a mushroom shape and then dissipated into the black night. Both cars had been damaged by the explosion, one more seriously than the other.

The next thing I heard was Gilad's ferocious shout of "ESH!" (Fire!). The sudden spasm of violent activity was unnerving after hours of stillness and enforced silence. Bullets and streaks of white light began raining down on the two Mercedes. I took aim at the less damaged vehicle and let loose with my Galil, firing single shots in semi-automatic mode. I got off thirty rounds – my last two being phosphorous flashing tracer, an indication that I needed to change magazines. I had just put in my second magazine and released the action when I heard a succession of voices in our company repeat the word "CHADAL!" (Cease fire!).

Some of us secured the ridge while the company commander descended to the wreckage. After a minute or two, we were commanded to get into formation for the return hike. My adrenalin was pumping, and I was on a high that I imagine is the sort of thrill you get from crystal meth or crack cocaine. The only disappointment was that I never even got a single look at the enemy. We returned for our debriefing, and word was that we'd killed eight Hezbollah militants.

The next day, I had time on the long bus ride home to my kibbutz from the border town of Kiryat Shemona to reflect on the night's events. It was my first, and last, taste of real combat. I suppose that I was a lot closer than modern warfare allows most combatants these days.

After my army service ended in 1985, I received a discreet letter from an obscure department of the Israeli government inviting me for an interview. It was my first contact with the Mossad and thereafter my military service would turn into another kind of service.

3 | INTO THE BREACH

> Tom Bishop: *"It's not a fucking game!"*
> Nathan Muir: *"Yes, it is. That's exactly what it is. It's no kid's game, either, but a whole other game. And it's serious, and it's dangerous, and it's not one you want to lose."*
>
> From the movie *Spy Game*

It was mid-afternoon on a warm day in December 1989, and I was driving around Tel Aviv with no belt, no shoelaces – and little composure. My hands were shaking as I struggled to guide my tiny four-speed Subaru through traffic. I'd just suffered forty-eight hours of humiliating, painful interrogation. My emotions were a mix of relief and fear. I was happy to see the sky and feel the fresh air on my face after spending two days in a tiny cell. But I was also terrified that the ordeal might not be over – that I would be re-arrested and subjected to the same Kafkaesque scenario all over again.

I was looking for a pay phone, glancing nervously in my rearview mirror every few seconds to see if I was being followed. From the parking lot of a gas station, I called Oren, my Mossad supervisor.

Speaking in code, I told him that I needed a "crash" – an emergency meeting with him at a pre-arranged location. Once the arrangements were made, I hung up, drove to a nearby hotel, and tried to clean up in the washroom. The staff and passing guests eyed me with distaste, probably thinking I'd woken up in a nearby alley after a bender. Having gone several days without a shower, I'm sure I smelled the part.

Once I felt halfway presentable, I made my way to a lounge overlooking a restless blue Mediterranean. While I waited for Oren, I calmed myself by watching the waves break against the rocks. As a young boy growing up in Oak Bay on Vancouver Island, I'd enjoyed a similar scene walking along Beach Drive and Dallas Road. Not for the first time, I thought about the circumstances that had conspired to make me trade that view for this one.

After a few minutes, I was awakened from my dazed reflections by a hand on my shoulder. It was Oren, accompanied by a Mossad psychologist named Elan. Almost before they'd taken their seats, I started pouring out everything that had happened. My voice broke here and there, but I managed to get through it without tears. They watched me with solemn expressions as I spoke, never interrupting.

When I'd signalled I was done, Oren looked at me and said, "I know all about it. I was in the next room while you were being interrogated. So was Elan. You were always within range of one of our cameras."

I froze for a minute. Then my mind flashed back to my cell and the odd wall coverings placed throughout the room: the oil painting of a cornfield and the travel posters – one of Greece, the other of Croatia – opposite one another on the far sides of the rectangular room. I started thinking about that stock scene from a hundred TV dramas, in which a team of cops work over some poor sap while men in suits, casually drinking coffee and exchanging jaded wise-cracks, watch from behind one-way glass. The roles were clear: these were the men in suits and I was the sap.

By this time, I was six months into my training as a Mossad agent. When I'd been arrested by narcs a few days before, I thought I'd stumbled into some sort of random snafu – an embarrassing screw-up that might get me labelled a druggie and kicked out of my training program. Now I realized this *was* my training program. The cell, the interrogation, this seaside debriefing – they were all part of a test to see if I could maintain my cover under duress.

Up until this point, I'd put up with everything that had been thrown at me. But arresting a guy, putting him in jail, knocking him around until he resembled a barely continent lowlife – this was too weird, too demeaning. My reaction to Oren's cool confession was that I wanted out.

"I don't think I'm cut out for this sort of thing," I told him. "I'd like to go home."

The journey to this moment began three years earlier, shortly after I'd finished reserve service in the Israeli Defense Forces. At the time, I was living with my wife and infant son on the kibbutz. Between working the land and taking care of my family, the kibbutz was my world. This was the era before the Internet or cheap international phone calls, so my communication with family and old friends was restricted to the blue aerograms that occasionally made it from Canada.

Then, one day, I received an odd piece of mail from the Israeli government. The brief letter was typewritten, unsigned, and composed in the formal style that typifies Israeli official correspondence. (Since I began learning Hebrew, I had observed that it is almost two separate languages, one spoken and one written. The written form is very formal, and uses words that are never used in the spoken form.) Yet something about the document stood out: the phrasing was cryptic and obfuscated by bureaucratic jargon. The upshot seemed to be that I'd been selected to interview for a vaguely defined job in the domain of "international co-operation."

At the time, I was working on the kibbutz's cotton plantation. The job had its benefits – namely, tear-assing through the fields of the Bet Shean Valley on a dirt bike or in a dusty Jeep. My most vivid memory of life in the field was whiling away the hours spotting Dorcas gazelle, striped hyena, and the dreaded *tsepha*, or Palestinian viper, a snake so feared that it's used as a symbol for one of the IDF's paratroop battalions. On one occasion, I killed a *tsepha* in the field. When I proudly brought its carcass back to the plantation's offices, I was scolded for killing such an effective rodent hunter.

Notwithstanding such pleasures, however, I was beginning to realize that irrigation, fertilization, and pest control were not where my heart lay. I had been considering taking a leave of absence from the kibbutz and heading back to British Columbia with my wife and son, so that they could meet my family and experience life in Canada.

But I decided to at least see what this new opportunity might offer. I made arrangements to head to Tel Aviv – two bumpy, winding hours away on an Egged bus. After tracking down the address on the letterhead, I found myself in a nondescript office with a small waiting room filled with other young people. Eventually I was ushered into an equally generic office, where I met a fellow named Ari. After mechanically repeating some of the jargon I'd read in the letter, he explained that I'd been selected as a candidate for an overseas Israeli government "function." His manner was reserved and bordered on obtuse. Indeed, the whole exercise was surreal. But I played along.

Ari handed me a questionnaire with a series of twenty questions, each requiring a one-word response. For example: "When attacked, the young man _____?" or "The boy _____ his parents?"

I did my best to produce sensible answers and handed Ari my completed questionnaire.

He gave a cursory glance at what I'd written, then put down my test and suddenly changed his tone. Dropping the jargon, he asked me all kinds of probing questions about my life, ideals, goals, and experiences. The interview lasted about an hour, and he took notes throughout. In many cases, he repeated questions, or otherwise revisited subjects he'd already covered. (I learned later that the point of the interview was to test an applicant's honesty. Telling a lie is easy. Telling it the same way twice is more difficult.)

There was also a test in which I was sent into a room with a pencil and a piece of paper. I was told to close my eyes and make X's in a series of circles printed on the page. The ostensible purpose was to test my "spatial" response, but I found out later that it was another honesty check. (A candidate who successfully puts all the X's in the circles is clearly cheating.) I didn't know that, however. So when I handed in my test – some X's in and most out – I thought I'd failed.

I finally got up the nerve to ask what this was all about. Instantly, Ari retreated to the land of Kafka: "If you are interested, and we find you suitable, we will send you on a training course for about a year and then put you to work." Despite Ari's evasions, I had an inkling of what was going on. Only one employer was this secretive about recruitment: Israel's famous intelligence service, the Mossad. When the realization hit me, I could feel a slight tug in my gut.

To this day, I'm not one hundred per cent sure why the Mossad specifically recruited me, but I can assume that my nationality and Anglo-Saxon background were contributing factors in their decision. By the same token, I had many foreign-born Israeli friends who never received an invitation from the Mossad, so perhaps in their mysterious method of separating the wheat from the chaff, they saw a few grains of possibility in me that could be trained and indoctrinated for their purposes.

At the end of the interview, I told Ari that I was planning on returning to Canada for a year or so, and he gave me a plain white business card with a telephone number on it. He told me to call when I returned to Israel if I was still interested. I kept the card – all through the time I was in Canada.

I spent two years with my family in beautiful Vancouver. Upon my return to Canada, I quickly lucked into a decent-paying federal government job. I never had to take work home with me, and had every weekend and statutory holiday off. But despite the long lunch hours and slacker work schedule, something told me I needed to go back to Israel. I hadn't put in hard time during my conversion and army duty so I could stroll down Robson Street or lie on Kits Beach.

On this point, Dahlia didn't need much convincing: she was homesick. And so in the summer of 1988, we boarded an El Al flight and returned to Israel.

Once back, I didn't waste a lot of time before calling the number Ari had given me, and I was granted another interview. I had thought a lot about the opportunity the Mossad was presenting me and my family and, to be frank, didn't see myself growing cotton on a kibbutz for the rest of my days. I'd converted and made Israel my home for a higher purpose – and the Mossad seemed the perfect vehicle to put my ideals to the test.

The address they gave me this time was different, and when I arrived I noticed that many of the recruiters were new. I later found out that had I waited another week or so, the phone number on the card would also have been changed – all part of the Mossad's normal security procedures – and the opportunity might have been gone, and I'd still be working the cotton fields.

In 2006, years after I'd left the Mossad and was trying my hand at writing, I had the good fortune to meet the renowned Canadian writer and iconoclast George Jonas – author, most famously, of *Vengeance*, upon which Steven Spielberg's Oscar-nominated film *Munich* was based. During lunch in Toronto, George told me a story about Austrian Archduke Franz Ferdinand, whose assassination in Sarajevo ignited the First World War. On the fateful day in June 1914, his vehicle had made a wrong turn. But his assassin, Gavrilo Princip, had also been diverted. Somehow, they both turned up at the same street corner. Within four and a half years, fifteen million people would be dead on the battlefields of Europe.

George made the point that when something is fated to be – for good or ill – nothing will stand in its way. Immediately, I thought back to that plain white business card Ari had handed me twenty years ago.

My recruitment was a drawn-out affair. I understand that the process is more streamlined these days, but in my time, it involved months of waiting and uncertainty.

I first underwent casual interviews with people who identified themselves only by their first names. They asked me about my ambitions, what I thought about the situation in the Middle East, and how I felt about being separated from my family.

No one ever admitted that they belonged to something called the Mossad. In fact, the word *Mossad* was never used until the first day of my training course – and the only place it appeared was in one of my training manuals. Instead, we always used the expression *hamisrad*, which means "office," even later when I was a veteran working in HQ. (Similarly, CIA agents have traditionally called their outfit "The Company.") Running around calling ourselves "Mossad agents" seemed silly and made us feel self-conscious. To this day, I am uncomfortable using the actual name of the organization that once employed me – it just seems corny.

Along with the interviews, there was a medical exam that measured just about every aspect of my physical health. Then came a battery of psychological and psychometric exams. These were real – nothing like the bogus honesty tests Ari had put me through a couple of years earlier. They lasted an entire day, and were conducted by an austere psychologist straight out of the movies. (He even had the requisite German accent. I half expected him to ask me, "How long haff you vanted to kill your Father zo you can sleep vis your Mother?")

I had to make the two-hour commute from my kibbutz to Tel Aviv for each stage of my testing and interviewing. I must have made ten such trips. It was gruelling and tedious. And unlike my army experience – during which I at least could rely on camaraderie to buoy my spirits – I had to go through the process on my own. If they were testing other candidates at the same time, I never met them. It was a lonely affair, in other words. As I would learn years later, it was just a taste of the loneliness that awaited me.

As a twenty-seven-year-old who'd spent much of his adult life in the Canadian and Israeli armies, my personal history was hardly mysterious. But my background was complicated by the fact that, unlike just about every other Mossad agent, I wasn't born Jewish, and therefore had no pedigree that could be easily checked. The Mossad is an exclusively Jewish outfit: no matter if you have Israeli citizenship and serve faithfully in the military, if you are of another faith, you can't be recruited as a serving officer. There are no exceptions.

I'd learned something about Jews since my conversion: their communities are usually tightly knit, and the six degrees of separation that are said to link any two people in the world often shrink to two or three degrees when both of them are Jews – even if they're from opposite ends of the globe. If someone isn't related to you in a distant fashion, then his great-grandfather and yours prayed at the same synagogue in the same *shtetl* in Lithuania. Or Poland. Or Romania. Tell people you're from Canada, and they'll recite lists of friends you might know – or their favourite kosher delis. If your face doesn't light up with a flash of recognition at least once – well, that's suspicious.

Having lived in Israel for a few years, I'd been through this sort of conversation many times before. So rather than have the truth flushed out of me, during one of my early interviews I confessed to a fellow named Maor that I'd converted.

I half expected to be bounced then and there. But Maor, a kindly old fellow, looked at me and said, "We already know about your conversion. And we make no distinction – you are as Jewish as any of us." I remember being moved by his simple declaration of acceptance. It made up for the various small-minded Israelis I'd met who clearly thought otherwise.

Next, I had to undergo a polygraph exam – commonly (and inaccurately) known as a lie detector test.* I was asked whether I was a mole working for a rival intelligence service, a criminal on the run, a drug user, or a homosexual. In each case, I truthfully said no.

Today, sexual orientation is no longer a subject of inquiry for Mossad recruits. In my day, however, being gay was seen as a negative because it was believed enemies could use it as a source of leverage against an officer. Thankfully, attitudes have changed – at least in countries such as Israel. (Homosexuality is still a capital offence in many less enlightened nations.)

---

* From professional observation, I learned during my career as an intelligence officer that polygraphing is an art, not a science. Its effectiveness is limited by the skill of the polygraph technician. Some subjects can fool even a highly proficient technician, which is why polygraphs are generally seen as just one tool in an investigator's arsenal.

As for the drugs, they didn't care whether I'd toked up as a student, but they wanted to know if I was going to tell the truth about whether I had or hadn't: the sort of person who tells small lies is also the sort of person who tells big ones. As a matter of fact, I never did toke up in school, and told them so. On this and everything else, the polygraph backed me up. And so did the many friends and relatives who were later questioned regarding my background.

Once I passed the tests, my training began. I was told to present myself with personal effects suitable for a two-night stay in Tel Aviv. The address turned out to be a well-appointed apartment, where I was met by a half-dozen men and women who looked me over with bemused detachment. After some basic introductions, their apparent leader, a tall, dark-haired man with piercing blue eyes named Halleck, told me to go into the next room and devise a cover story for both my identity and my reason for being in Israel. "Let your imagination go wild," he told me. "The only rule is you can't be Canadian. We want to make this challenging."

After fifteen minutes or so, I came up with what I thought was a winner: I was a U.S.-based journalist doing a background story on Tel Aviv for the *Los Angeles Times*. Once I worked out the biographical details, I came out of the room quite pleased with myself, and presented my invented identity to Halleck and his colleagues.

Unbeknownst to me, this was a stock exercise in the intelligence business. I was being asked to create something that every covert intelligence operative must have: a bogus but believable cover story about who you are, where you come from, and what you're doing. In intelligence parlance, this assumed identity is known as a legend. It sounds easy, but it's not, as Halleck demonstrated to me in about thirty seconds.

"Nice to meet you, Fred Porter," he said in a casual tone after I'd introduced myself. "Welcome to Israel. May I ask where you're staying? The Hilton you say? Nice place. What's your room number? I'd like to call you later in the day."

After I stammered who knows what unconvincing nonsense, he went to work on the rest of my cover story. "You sound disoriented," he said. "Why don't we call up your editor in L.A. I bet he's worried. You must know the number off the top of your head, right? What's that? You don't know your own *area code*?"

I felt the eyes of Halleck's entourage on me, but they didn't interrupt the conversation. I was unnerved, and I couldn't help but feel that I was failing an audition of sorts – a kind of *American Idol* for spies, if you will – and at that particular moment, I was warbling hideously. After enduring some constructive criticism, I was sent back into the next room with my tail between my legs. Creating a convincing story is not the hard part, I realized. The challenge was in concocting a convincing story that is also virtually impossible to check out.

It took me several tries, but I eventually hit on something that held up under Halleck's preliminary probing. I was still a journalist, but for a small Christian community college with a generic-sounding name (this was the era before Google, remember). I was staying at a youth hostel. No, I couldn't remember its name and there are hundreds in Israel. And I'd checked out that morning anyway. Once my identity and raison d'être had been established, I was bundled into a van with Halleck and some of his retinue, and we drove into the epicentre of a bustling Tel Aviv afternoon.

There is a scene in the film *Spy Game* in which Robert Redford, the old CIA hand, takes his protégé, Brad Pitt, onto the streets of Berlin and runs him around to test his smarts. This was more or less what I was doing. I had to appear on a randomly chosen apartment balcony after convincing the tenant to allow me access; get the first three names from a hotel register; start a conversation with a complete stranger and hold his attention for twenty minutes; put a device in a public phone mouthpiece in the heart of the Hilton Hotel lobby without being noticed; and a whole host of other odd but challenging tasks.

In each case, I had to rely not only on an invented identity – my legend, or "status cover" – but also on what I later learned to refer to as my operational cover, that is, my fictional motive for being in a particular place and doing a particular thing at a particular time. A legend stays with you for years, but an operational cover is often invented on the spot.

One thing they don't show you in the spy movies: what the agents do at night. No, I'm not referring to bedding beautiful women with names like Plenty O'Toole and Pussy Galore. When the sun goes down, spies morph into paper-pushing bureaucrats. (I suppose that Canadian government job was good for something.) There is a saying in the Mossad: "If you complete a mission and don't report it, the mission never happened." I was instructed to write reports about all of my activities during the day in any format I saw fit (this being 1988, I recorded everything in longhand). By the time my head hit the pillow, I was exhausted.

As I performed my various tasks over the next couple of days, Halleck and his colleagues sat in cafés and watched me. On the odd occasion, one of them would ask me why I did what I did, and I'd try to explain my thought process. These were not puzzles that had any correct answer. Rather, the idea was to test my judgment and ability to improvise. There was no going back to the office and thinking about it. I had to solve problems then and there.

In some cases, the tasks seemed plain impossible. But more often than not, I surprised myself. Hotel staff, I knew, would not make a guest registry available to anyone who asked. So I simply told the desk clerk that I had the camera of one of their guests, and that the young lady had given me her last name but I had forgotten it. "Look," I said in a pleading tone, "it's a very expensive camera and I'd like to return it to her . . . and truth be told, I really like her and would like to see her again . . . ."

I found that, with a good story and a hint of personal disclosure, most people will try to meet you halfway – say, turning the registry in your direction so you can scan it, without actually handing it to you. In other cases, where accomplishing the task just wasn't in the cards, I had to realize as much and back off rather than force matters and cause a security problem. The adage that smart agents live to fight another day is an important principle in intelligence work.

The tests varied, but they all had the same goal: to see how far I could be pushed before I broke cover. In the spy business, I was gradually learning, you simply never break cover. A spy's cover is the most important weapon in his or her professional arsenal. These tests don't have a high pass rate because many promising candidates break cover at the first hint of a threat. It's a natural response: reverting to your true self feels like a safe move. It's an instinctive way of saying "I'm not playing anymore." Those who can resist are highly valued by intelligence services.

I don't know what it says about me – that I'm a good liar or a decent actor, or that I just don't like to fail a test – but I never broke cover, not once. After two days, Halleck and the anonymous ringleaders who'd been putting me through my paces told me I'd passed. No, I was not a Mossad officer yet – nowhere near, in fact. But I'd made it past the first big hurdle. They told me to go home. They'd call me when the next stage was set to begin.

It was now spring of 1988, and I admired the wildflowers growing in the Jezreel Valley as I rode the bus home to my wife and son. I had been away for longer than usual this time, and was glad to be back in the warm embrace of family. We had dinner together, and then Dahlia and I had a serious talk. I described a little of what I'd been through, and where I thought it was all leading. I was still riding the wave of pride that came from making the grade in Tel Aviv. But she was worried, and she told me so.

My mood changed quickly. Until now, I hadn't seriously considered the rather obvious fact that Dahlia wouldn't be thrilled about the prospect of my taking on a dangerous profession. She also reminded me that since we'd been married, we'd spent little time under the same roof. This training would keep me away from my family for months more. And if I got through, then what? Possibly a career that would make me an absentee husband permanently. Our child was then four years old. Did I want him to grow up without a full-time daddy?

Over hours of kitchen-table conversations with Dahlia, I decided that family life was more important than whatever awaited me in Tel Aviv. The next day, I called the Office. I couldn't reach my handlers, but spoke to a secretary and left a message: "Can you please let them know that I've thought things over, and would like to quit? Thanks." Then I hung up, feeling comfortable with my decision.

It was back to the cotton fields for me. I quickly fell back into a life that couldn't have been more remote from the world I'd briefly tasted. I was out in the countryside, wearing nothing but shorts and sandals. I swam in the pool with my son and had barbecues with my buddies. Just an average Israeli kibbutznik.

I was not the first recruit to get cold feet. The Mossad, I now know, has established procedures for dealing with such situations. A few days after I'd come back to the kibbutz, one of the recruiters phoned and invited himself up for a chat. To be polite, I acquiesced. He would have his say, I expected. All I'd have to do was hear him out and then let him know my decision was final.

And so Benny appeared at our doorstep, and a lifelong friendship with my family was formed.

If the Office had dispatched a slick desk jockey with a canned sales pitch, I would have found it easy to recite back to him my prepared rejection. But Benny, himself a former "combatant" (as Mossad agents are called), took a different approach. He was over six feet tall, slim, with a shock of grey hair and blue eyes. His Hebrew was French-accented, and he had an easygoing manner. My son liked him instantly, and so did my wife.

He came into our small bungalow and we put a cup of coffee in his hand. Once my son was out of the room, he proceeded to give me a detailed picture of what awaited me should I change my mind and make it through the training program. Far from promising me roses and sunshine, he told me that my work would involve operating in hostile countries, often alone, while under foreign cover. He also outlined the risks of torture, long confinement, and even execution that I would face if I were caught.

Dahlia was in the room throughout the whole conversation. Benny wanted her there, because he knew she would probably be the one who needed the most convincing. He assured us that joining the Office was like joining a family, and that it takes care of its own. Speaking plainly to a morbid issue that both Dahlia and I had thought about, he told us that she would be looked after financially no matter where I was sent, or what happened to me.

As I watched her reaction, I could tell she was impressed that he was telling us the unvarnished truth – that he was leading us to an informed decision rather than trying to dazzle us with false assurances. The fear of the unknown is a powerful force, and contending with it had put both of us on edge. Benny gave us a clear indication of what lay ahead, and reassured us that we'd be able to navigate it together.

One of the questions that I am asked most frequently about my former career is how much a spy's spouse gets to know about what happens in the field. The Mossad's policy is unequivocal: the spouse has to know what his or her partner is doing, because more often than not, she (or he) is integral to the spy's ability to operate. The spouse keeps the family together during the other's absence, and has to face the inevitable prying questions from friends and relatives about the husband's (or wife's) occupation and long disappearances.

I never told Dahlia specifics about ongoing operations, but she knew the big picture. The truth is, she never pried, and I gave her the details only when I was stressed out and needed to talk. There are many incidents in this book that she didn't know about, and many that she knows more about than the reader will learn here.

Finally, after about two hours of conversation, I told Benny I'd go ahead with the training. When he saw his job was done, Benny stood to leave, and we shook hands. I then spent the next two months waiting for a phone call. In the meantime, it was back to the cotton fields.

When my phone rang, it was October. I was told to present myself in a Tel Aviv hotel lobby, where I would meet my instructor. (Spy agencies, I've concluded over the years, are what keep the hotel trade afloat.) Once again, I kissed my wife goodbye and hopped on a bus to the big city.

I remember sitting in the hotel with butterflies dancing in my gut, not knowing what hoops I'd be made to jump through this time around. Eventually, I was approached by a young man in his thirties who sat down and introduced himself as Oren. We spoke Hebrew, and it was only later that I discovered he spoke fluent English with a slight accent that made him sound like a cross between a Brit and a South African. (I never did find out where he actually came from.)

Oren was tall and fair, with light brown curly hair and blue eyes. He wore glasses, jeans, a white dress shirt, and Timberland loafers. In fact, he looked and acted like a kibbutznik – fit, self-confident, and informal. "So, are you ready to start?" he asked me with a smile.

We walked to Oren's van, and drove to an apartment in Ramat Aviv, an upscale part of North Tel Aviv that houses professionals, diplomats, and the odd political figure. (Yitzhak Rabin lived a few streets over from where I was ensconced.) The place had a modern look – by 1980s standards, at least – with a glass-topped dining room table and contemporary furnishings, along with an incongruous combination safe. I was told this would be my home during training. Oren set the ground rules: "Everything you write or read goes into the safe. Anything you wish to discard goes into this bag, and you give it to me. I'll see it gets destroyed." ("Destroyed" was accurate. Years later, when I was at Mossad HQ, I saw how they got rid of paper: it was reduced to a powdery pulp in a gigantic processor.) He continued: "When you write, it's on a single sheet of paper on a glass-topped surface. Otherwise, it leaves an imprint on anything under it."

Oren gave me a clunky camera – a chrome-finish Pentax Spotmatic. He also produced a low-tech typewriter of the kind Hemingway must have used to bang out his stories while covering the Spanish Civil War, saying, "Give me the ribbon when you wear it out." I was confused, and then remembered that whatever I typed would be left on the ribbon.

These were my first and basic lessons in spy tradecraft, a term that covers the entire gamut of how intelligence agents speak on the phone, walk, talk and interact with others, treat documents and identities, take notes, drive, and dress.

Oren left me a huge pile of reading material to go through – basic primers on tradecraft. He also gave me an assignment: type out my autobiography, or at least as much of it as I could produce in a single night's typing. "On the basis of your real life, we're going to construct a fake one," he said. He then left me to my writing, but not before giving me strict instructions on phone use and the importance of keeping the apartment secure. This included locking the doors and windows, storing my papers securely in the safe when I left the apartment, and leaving the radio on to give the impression that the apartment was occupied and to mask my conversations with Oren and any other visitors from HQ.

As he turned to go, Oren stopped and looked at me. "Oh, yeah, you are no longer 'Michael' to any of us," he said. "Your new name is 'Ridley.' That is how you will sign all your reports and identify yourself when you call me on the phone." I understood. If my real name were bandied about, it could find its way to the wrong people. By using my code name from an early stage in my training, I helped to ensure that even most Mossad colleagues wouldn't discover my real identity. (And indeed, they didn't; throughout my entire career in the Mossad, from the day those words came out of Oren's mouth, I was known as Ridley. For all my colleagues knew, my real name was Murray Schwartz.)

"Write up your life story and get some rest," Oren said. "I'll be back tomorrow and then we really get to work."

During all the hundreds of hours of training I received, I don't think there was an assignment I threw myself into more enthusiastically than this one. I sat at that glass-topped table and wrote and wrote. The hours slipped by, but I didn't get sleepy until well after midnight. By the time I was done, I'd banged off a double-spaced tome.

The next morning, Oren appeared with a slight bearded man named Shalom. I gave Oren the assignment, and he seemed impressed by its bulk. "I expected about ten pages – what have you got here, fifty?"

When I look back on it, my enthusiasm for the project fore-shadowed my later interest in writing. But at the time, I just enjoyed the experience of going down memory lane.

Shalom would be my photography instructor, Oren explained. In the spy game, photographs really are worth a thousand words. But taking good ones, he told me, is about more than just point-and-shoot. Combatants are well trained in the art of photography – including covert practices. I cannot disclose the Mossad's methods in this regard, but suffice it to say that a combatant could photograph you up and down from three metres away without your noticing. For a week, Shalom instructed me on the Pentax's features and sent me out onto the streets to take hundreds of shots of all kinds of things – cars, apartment buildings, people, shops, street signs. I learned how to take panorama photographs and how to cut them and process them into one folded image as long as your arm. After each assign-ment, Shalom developed and screened the photos on the spot.

Photography never became a hobby outside of work, but I did take pride in it as part of my tradecraft. Over the years, I took some beauties when I was in the field: a panorama of a ship docked in Hamburg; terrorist safe houses in Khartoum; various landscapes and people from Africa – all of which, regrettably, are now just gath-ering dust in files somewhere.

Next, Oren brought another expert from HQ: Yosef, a mild-mannered type who taught me clandestine radio communications. He also taught me some old-fashioned skills, like deciphering embedded messages using graph paper.

For his part, Oren taught me something more fundamental: the art of human observation. He took me out into the city and asked me to assess all manner of things: the height of buildings, types of antennae on rooftops, cars, people, junction boxes, entrances, hotels, security systems. He'd ask me later what was written on a

T-shirt worn by a random passerby. I was taught to *notice* the sort of mundane things that usually slide by us.

The drill worked: I started to look at the world in a different way and to retain more of what I saw.

As the days wore on, the exercises grew more elaborate. He would give me the photo of someone who worked somewhere within a specified neighbourhood. I had to memorize the image, then head out and find the person. If I located him or her, I had to call Oren from a pay phone and tell him I'd seen "our friend," providing the exact location.

The targets were unwitting workers and residents – a cashier, an art gallery attendant, a barmaid, an office worker. I always picked out a combination of features on the faces in the small photos that was unique and easy for my eye to recognize, maybe the jaw line and hairstyle, or the way the nose and mouth were configured. I always scored one hundred per cent on this exercise.

One day, after a few weeks of this expert training, Oren appeared and handed me a *Teudat Zehut*, a national identity card that all Israel's citizens carry. There was my face on the card, but the name was different. Oren instructed me to make up a cover story for this fictional Israeli, and he'd return in a few days to hear it.

Thinking about what I'd learned from Halleck's demolition of my *Los Angeles Times* persona, I carefully worked out a legend that couldn't be exposed, and that was simple enough that I wouldn't get tripped up in the details. When Oren returned to test my story, it was with Elan, the psychologist, who asked only the occasional question about my thinking. It was clear that he was there to observe and assess me. Even though I knew this was part of the standard Mossad training protocol, something about Elan's presence bugged me. Clearly, he wanted to see if I could take what Oren was dishing out. As it often did during my training, my competitive instinct helped me: I wasn't about to give this shrink the satisfaction of seeing that I was bothered by anything.

I had memorized the ID number on the *Teudat Zehut* and made up a story that relied somewhat on my real life. (This is the preferred practice; just as a good novelist ensures realism by sticking to the world he knows, so too does a spy.) My alter ego was a student auditing courses at Tel Aviv University. In preparation, I'd actually visited the campus and hung out at the library and registrar's office, getting to know the place and what courses I was supposed to be taking. I'd sat in on the odd lecture and class and I had even been invited to a student party! The experience had given me the confidence and knowledge I needed to lay out my cover in a convincing way. Oren looked pleased.

"What I like to see is that you are not some delusional egomaniac living in a complete fantasy world," Oren said. "The problem in building a legend is that you have to walk a fine line between reality and fantasy. Stray too far in either direction and you have a security problem. You have to believe your story because it's based on truth, but you have to keep it far enough from the truth so it can't get back to you."

We fine-tuned my tale, with Oren pointing out some potential problems I hadn't thought of (for example, where was my student card?). And with that, my legend was established – a momentous step in the career of an intelligence agent – even if this legend was merely for training purposes.

Without further ado, Oren produced a file. In it were the details of what the Mossad calls an "object," a person about whom the agency wants to know more, through physical surveillance and other means. The object was a Tel Aviv-area doctor who kept odd hours and swam in the sea each day at dawn. I had two days to observe him and perform intelligence collection tasks related to his daily habits and work. Oren and Elan left, and I got down to work.

I lacked operational cover – that is, a story about what my alleged motivation was for being at the object's hospital, his apartment block, or even the beach at dawn. I was quickly learning about one of the Mossad's basic teaching philosophies: no one tells you how to do things. You have to figure it out for yourself, and only later are the mistakes analyzed and corrected. In training, as in the field, nobody holds your hand. I set myself to preparing possible operational cover scenarios: if I was taking pictures at the beach, I was a photography hobbyist. If I was in the hospital, I had shooting pains in my back that needed to be checked out, and so on.

For the next forty-eight hours, I ran around after the doctor. I had to find his car and apartment, take pictures of him while he was swimming, and find his office in the hospital. To this day, I don't know whether he was a witting participant in the exercise or not, but I had to perform my tasks without arousing his or anyone else's suspicion. It was exhausting and difficult. I felt as if I was botching it, drawing attention to myself and standing out in every crowd.

To my knowledge, the object never spotted me, but I was questioning my operational cover choices. Some were weak, and I doubted anyone would believe them – thankfully, I never had to use them. In one case, for instance, I crafted a convoluted story about a girl that I met at a bar who gave me an address in the same apartment building as the doctor.

Making matters more difficult was the fact that I was going about this exercise in a particularly challenging environment – Israel. For good reason, Israelis are a nosy and paranoid lot. They watch for anything out of the ordinary and are not skittish about reporting odd behaviour or simply asking a complete stranger, "What exactly are you doing?" To most Israelis, a guy with a camera is just a tourist or hobbyist. But a not insignificant portion of the population will look at you and think you're collecting intelligence for a terrorist attack. The Mossad has never felt compelled to do their training outside of Israel; it's easy to turn Israel into hostile territory for novice spies.

When the gruelling two days were over, I returned to my apartment, wrote up my reports, and waited for Oren and Elan to return. When they did, Oren asked me if I had had any security problems. I told him I hadn't and walked them through the two days.

We went over my operational cover stories, and I came to understand one of the reasons I'd felt uncomfortable at times: my stories were overly complex. It always sounded as if I was trying too hard to justify myself. As if reading my thoughts, Oren provided me with a simple rule of thumb that I never forgot.

"Ridley, if you are crossing the street and someone asks you why, you only have to say you are going to the grocery store," he told me. "You don't have to tell him what you're going to buy there, or how you plan to cook it." He continued, "Better yet, say nothing. If you're going to walk to the beach at dawn and you're worried about the cops checking you out, buy a cheap fishing rod and throw it over your shoulder. You don't even have to speak to them because the fishing rod has already answered their questions."

I gave him the reports I had spent all day typing on that museum piece of a typewriter. He tucked the documents under an arm without glancing at them.

"Aren't you going to read them?" I asked, perplexed and a little annoyed.

"Maybe, but the exercise wasn't about the doctor. It was about you. It was about how you felt about being undercover. The rest was just to keep you busy."

During this phase of my training, I learned that I was being groomed to be the ultimate operational weapon in the Mossad's arsenal: a combatant in the division known simply as "the unit." The unit has many names, but its most widely known cryptonym is "Caesarea." It is legendary in the intelligence world, not least because of its oft-celebrated (and decried) mission to bring justice to the perpetrators of the Munich Olympics terrorist attack in 1972.

Originally, Caesarea was a unit of the Israel Defense Forces charged with intelligence missions in neighbouring Arab countries, but in 1953, after it met with a number of disasters that killed some of its members, Prime Minister David Ben-Gurion transferred it to the nascent Mossad. Caesarea now operates as a completely compart-mentalized "Mossad within the Mossad," and its combatants do not enter or interact with Mossad HQ except through their controlling intermediaries. Their identities are kept secret, and they are told only what they need to know. (Think CIA agent Jason Bourne, of *The Bourne Identity*.) If a combatant is captured, you don't want him to be able to reel off the Mossad's personnel database to his interrogators. (Everyone talks when tortured. It's only in the movies that they don't.)

Eventually, I moved on to more advanced training, and was outfitted with a foreign passport for lengthy exercises that more realistically simulated deployment in a foreign country. During this phase, I operated as if in hostile territory, with all the associated constraints and difficulties – maintaining strict communications protocols and hewing carefully to status cover. While on exercises, I was not permitted access to the apartment either.

As in a computer game, each series of exercises contained a num-ber of separate missions that I had to complete before advancing a level. Unbeknownst to me, I often was being observed by Mossad per-sonnel. In many cases, they tried to trip me up through seemingly accidental mishaps, just to see how I'd react. In the most dramatic episode, a motorist insisted I'd hit his car with my rental and delayed me while I was en route to a tightly scheduled rendezvous.

Throughout it all, my family back on the kibbutz might as well have been a million miles away. Both my wife and I suffered emotionally for my absence. Yet we knew that this was nothing compared with the far longer periods of separation that awaited us. I missed my son, too, and I hated the fact that he was growing up fast without me. When I dwelt on this aspect of the experience, I felt like quitting. But I also remembered the commitment I'd made to Benny. He'd warned me about the downside; I hadn't been tricked. I kept moving forward with my training.

About six months into my training, events took a traumatic turn – so traumatic that I tried to quit for a second time.

I was on a mission in the old port of Jaffa, taking photos of boats in the marina as part of a tour group I'd joined for operational cover. A creepy little man walked up to me and asked if I wanted to buy some drugs. He was shifty and kept rubbing his nose. I brushed him off, but he wouldn't take no for an answer. He kept following me, and I finally hissed at him between clenched teeth, "Piss off." Eventually I left on the tour bus, and I forgot about the incident – but only for a short while.

I was in my hotel later that night when someone knocked at my door. It was two plainclothes detectives. All business and unsmiling, they had a warrant for my arrest. I asked on what charge and they told me "drug smuggling." I protested my innocence, but they put me in cuffs all the same. I decided to ride with it, sure that a simple, rational chat would clear the whole thing up. They collected all my belongings and then led me in handcuffs through the hotel's packed lobby – quite the spectacle for my fellow guests.

At the police station, I was processed – fingerprints, mug shot, the works. They even took my belt and shoelaces. Then they put me in a cell with a huge steel door with a small eye slot. I was freezing; it was December and even Israel gets cold at night. The toilet was a foul-smelling hole in the floor. I had no window and the only light came from a single bulb overhead. I went over my cover story in my head and tried to rest, but couldn't close my eyes. This seemed serious, and I wondered where it was going to lead.

Early the next morning, a uniformed cop led me up to a chamber about the size of a standard office conference room, where I was met by two men. One was boyish with short brown hair. He looked like Kevin Bacon. The other was heavyset with glasses and thinning hair. He reminded me of Jack Nicholson. I called them Kevin and Jack in my head.

I tried a friendly approach, and said "good morning" with the best smile I could muster. Spread on a table in front of me were all the articles from my bag and suitcase. My photos were developed and scattered in plain view. My small shortwave radio was in pieces, and so was my camera.

I was shoved into a chair; Jack kicked its legs out from under me and I tumbled to the floor. He hauled me up and sat me back down. He then cracked me a good one across the face.

"Who are you?" Kevin demanded. I told him my spiel. My status cover story had changed since those early days in training: I was now a businessman on Mossad-fabricated foreign documents.

They told me that they had seen me interact with a drug dealer in Jaffa, and were sure that I was a smuggler. I pleaded my innocence and insisted that the dealer was a stranger to me. I don't know how I did it, but I stuck to my story – even though I was sorely tempted to tell them that this was all a big mistake and that I was on a Mossad exercise. The questioning went on all day, and then I was sent back down to my cell.

I was now able to sit in silence and ponder my predicament. I felt sick with fear. I was thinking endlessly about my family and started to feel my resolve weaken. I wanted to break cover and make it stop, but something inside my head wouldn't let me. I was on a bucking bronco and wanted to see how long I could stay on the horse without falling. I remember thinking, if I can just endure this a little longer, someone will realize that I'm missing and start to look for me. I felt alone and completely out of control. I went over my cover story in my head and worried until my stomach ached. I didn't sleep a wink.

The next day, they roughed me up a bit more. They humiliated and mocked me. They made me sit and stand for long periods at their whim, and on many occasions forced my head down between my knees while I was being questioned. They slapped me (far more humiliating for a man than a punch) when I gave less than satisfactory answers, and kicked me at random intervals. They asked why I was unmarried and why I never took pictures of pretty girls. They made all kinds of comments about my manhood and sexual preferences. When one stopped, the other one started in on me. One tried to appear kind and the other was mean – classic good cop, bad cop.

After about eight hours of this, they started taking things up a notch. Jack put a hood over my head. They stripped me naked and cuffed my hands behind my back. I then heard electronic buzzing. Over the din I could hear Kevin saying, "We're going to run some high-voltage current through your balls and see if that makes you talk." All I could see was a thick cable through the bottom of the hood. I really started to panic at that point, and pleaded with them to believe that I was who I said I was, and not a criminal.

I never got the shock. All of a sudden, they stopped what they were doing and told me to collect my things and get dressed.

One of the cops who'd arrested me forty-eight hours earlier took me out to the parking lot. Someone had brought my rental car from the hotel. He handed me my car keys and told me, "Get the fuck out of Dodge." I looked at him blankly and he snarled at me, "You're free, idiot!" I was euphoric and would have hugged him had I not remembered that he arrested me in the first place. He also didn't look like the hugging type.

And so there I was, a little while later, with Oren and Elan in the lounge of the Sheraton Hotel, looking at the waves crash on the beach and sipping a ginger ale.

"How do you think you did?" asked Elan. It was one of the rare moments when he actually talked to me, as opposed to merely staring at me.

"Terribly," was all I could answer.

Oren regarded me with compassion. "We thought you did well. You stuck to your story and have earned the right to get on with the next phase of your training. Only a small percentage get this far." So it was a training exercise after all. It was so well-staged that I hadn't a clue – like something you'd see in *Mission Impossible*. I felt a confused mixture of anger and relief.

"I'd like to go home and stay there. This is not a life for me," I told them. I was horrified by the reality of what could happen to me in this job. It was all great when I was taking pictures of boats on a beach or whatnot. But being captured and subjected to genital electrocution – that was a different story.

Oren said matter-of-factly, "We can't let you go home like this. You need a couple of days to decompress – then you can go home." They probably thought I wouldn't return if they let me go right then and there. They were right.

I found out a few days later that I had undergone an interrogation by two of the Shin Bet's finest (Shin Bet is Israel's domestic security service, and one of its mandates is counterintelligence – hence they have the capability to weed out spies.) Oren told me that one of the two would be coming over later with a videocassette of the interrogation, and we would discuss it.

When Oren showed up with Jack, I was cool in my reception, wearing my injured pride on my sleeve. Jack took it all with a grain of salt. He'd probably been through this dozens of times.

I was embarrassed by the tape, and it was hard to watch. To his credit, Jack kept things on a professional level, and the experience turned out to be very instructive. Once again, I learned a lot about myself. Some of it wasn't pretty. I was a mess and looked like hell. Maybe we should never see ourselves in such situations. But that was me on the TV screen, and I couldn't hide from what had happened.

When Jack left, he shook my hand and told me that I had done well. "Don't feel bad," he said. "It's nothing personal. You should see how many people break cover before they even get to us."

When I got home to the kibbutz, I didn't tell Dahlia about what had gone on in the cell. She wasn't in love with the Office to begin with, and I didn't want to sour her view further. As for my son, he probably didn't understand why I couldn't stop hugging him: while being interrogated, I'd had visions of being locked up until he was a teenager.

In the end, I decided not to quit, so I went back to Tel Aviv and embarked on more advanced training – firearms, martial arts, and complicated exercises involving special forces units, helicopters, and boats. I learned about commercial cover (how to travel to foreign locales undercover as a businessman), and did an intensive course in international commerce. In all, my training took a full year.

Then one summer afternoon in 1989, I returned to my apartment to find a good-looking man in his early fifties sitting in my living room. "Hi, Ridley," he said. "I'm Avi, the head of Caesarea, and the fact that you are meeting me is a good sign." Being the head of the unit, he knew all about me although I had never met him before.

I stood dumbfounded, with a look that probably said "how's that?"

"I'm the man who not only accredits you as a combatant, but also authorizes your deployment overseas," he said. "You've finished your training. Welcome to Caesarea."

4 | DEPLOYMENT

A brave heart and a courteous tongue. They shall carry thee
far through the jungle, manling.

Rudyard Kipling

Cover is an intelligence agent's air and water. Without a credible
alternate identity, an agent simply cannot operate in the field.
An agent's identity documents receive the same reverential treatment that devout Jews give to Torah scrolls. Passports are the most
valuable specimens, but driver's licences, national ID cards, and
credit cards are also useful. The more documentation a spy has – even
a library card or gym membership can help in a pinch – the more
legitimacy and protection he or she will enjoy. Mossad field personnel are trained to be obsessive about their documents. To this day, I
often get an uncontrollable urge to stop what I'm doing and run a discreet physical check to make sure my wallet and personal effects are
in the appropriate pockets. Getting your wallet snatched is traumatic
whatever the circumstances, but for an intelligence officer, it can spell

disaster. When I was working for the Mossad in Africa, I carried two wallets. One contained about thirty dollars and some throwaway identification – a decoy to be hauled out if I was mugged or shaken down by a crooked cop. The other was my real wallet, safely tucked in a Velcro-sealed compartment attached to my clothing.

But documents are just the beginning. They may tell people who you are, where you live, and what you do for a living, but eventually you have to open your mouth and talk. And the personality you project has to match your supposed identity. That means getting the vocabulary and diction right, as well as the clothing, food preferences, mannerisms, and grooming.

Even a single wrong word choice can betray you. I once heard a story about a German spy clad in a U.S. army uniform who'd infiltrated Allied positions during the Second World War. His downfall came when he drove his Jeep up to a U.S. fuel depot and asked for a tank full of "petrol." Urban legend? Perhaps. But there's a lesson in it either way.

Refining your cover to the point where you can fool true experts means becoming something of an anthropologist, or at least a connoisseur of national stereotypes. If a spy's adopted identity is British, he may tend toward politeness and a reserved persona. If Irish, he might spin his drinking companions a soulful tale or two while quaffing a Guinness (served warm, if he can bear it). If American, he might be slightly louder and less bashful than everyone else in the room.

Once Avi had welcomed me to Caesarea, I was made to attend what can only be described as a sort of finishing school for Mossad agents. My instructor was Doron, a former combatant of some renown. Meticulously dressed, tall, with blue eyes and sandy-blonde hair, he was self-possessed, almost haughty. Doron spoke English, German, and Hebrew (as well as several other languages he didn't reveal to me, I'm guessing), all without the trace of an accent. He looked like a poster boy for the Aryan Nation, yet he was as Jewish as they come. Israelis refer to such specimens with the somewhat derogatory term *yekke*, used to describe Jews of German origin who exhibit the fastidious habits attributed to that country. Those who know me will say that I answer to the same description. But when I was in the same room as Doron, we were like the Odd Couple of movie fame, with me playing Oscar Madison to his Felix Unger.

Appearances aside, Doron was a perfect instructor for an agent looking to blend in among Europe's urbane business class. He gave me primers in finance and put me through an accelerated program in international commerce and trade. He would appear at my doorstep with copies of the *Financial Times, Fortune,* and various European and Middle Eastern business reports. He taught me how to read the financial pages and decipher the arcane codes contained in the stock market listings – the FTSE 500, NYSE, Hang Seng, Nikkei, CAC 40 – until I could discuss stocks and bonds with all the casual panache of someone who made six-figure investment decisions with the click of a mouse.

The studying took place mostly at night. During the day, we ran SDRs, or "surveillance detection routes," which are pre-planned journeys that spies take to detect if they're being followed. The art of the SDR is to make it look as if you're going about your normal business – browsing in shops, visiting restaurants, taking taxis, riding the bus – without giving the appearance that you're trying to detect a "tail." SDR drills are to a junior combatant what scales are to a piano student. Even veteran agents often do refresher courses.

"Tail" is a misleading term (albeit one used commonly even by intelligence agents). In truth, any surveillance team worth its salt – and I trained against the best – doesn't follow you around like a bunch of hounds on the scent. Its members dance around their targets with a practised choreography worthy of the Bolshoi Ballet. Far from the menacing, chisel-featured spies you see in the movies, the good ones resemble everyday schleps who can blend into the urban landscape. Their cat-and-mouse sport is played out every day on the streets of every major city in the world.

Any intelligence operative heading out for a meeting with a source or colleague has to make sure he is clean when he arrives at his destination. If an agent with a tail doesn't abort, he risks letting in the "locals" – that is, domestic counterintelligence – on whatever mischief he's up to.

On my SDR drills with Doron, I did my best to implement the detail-recognition skills Oren had taught me. Moving from one section of Tel Aviv to another, I scanned the people around me. If the same person kept popping up, I knew there was a good chance my movements were being monitored.

As is often the case in the field, I had help – teammates who watched from a series of "choke points," which are places where spies could easily observe without drawing attention to themselves, like an outdoor café. This is known as countersurveillance, or watching the watchers.

The critical moment comes when the SDR is complete, and the countersurveillance team must send a signal to the agent telling him whether he's clean or dirty. Before spies entered the era of cellphones and pagers (and even after, in many cases), this was accomplished through coded physical messages: a countersurveillance agent sitting in a café at the end of the route with a hat, scarf, or rolled-up magazine. All of the elements have to be timed and coordinated properly, of course, or the signal may be missed.

Doron also helped me take the new identity I'd devised – one that I cannot divulge in this book – and develop it into a three-dimensional persona. We devised plans whereby I would live undercover in a European nation for an extended period. I would study the history, culture, literature, language, and regional idioms. I would rent an apartment, open a bank account, join a gym, follow the local sports team. I'd form opinions about the country's politics and become a regular at bars and restaurants. But my relationships would all be superficial: I'd become known without being known about. If people asked me where I'd popped up from, I'd tell them I'd been living overseas for many years.

I'd start my own commercial trading company and build myself a life as a European national – an operational infrastructure that would allow me to come and go in places where Israelis were normally *personae non gratae*, and where, if they were discovered, they would become fodder for the torture chamber and the executioner.

Over the years, the Mossad has sustained abundant criticism for its agents' practice of using foreign passports. In 1973, for instance, Canada complained when it emerged that the Mossad assassination team that had mistakenly killed an Arab waiter in Norway was on fake Canadian passports. A similar tempest erupted in 1997, when two Mossad agents, also using fake Canadian passports, were caught in Jordan trying to assassinate Hamas leader Khaled Mashaal. And in 2004, New Zealand went so far as to impose diplomatic sanctions against Israel when a suspected Mossad-run passport-forging operation was discovered in that country.

But it is naive to assume that Israel is the only culprit; all national intelligence services break international rules when necessary, to protect their agents. If Israel is a more frequent offender, it is because the Jewish state is in a unique position: even ordinary Israeli citizens are denied entry in many Muslim nations simply for the sin of carrying their country's passport. (Some countries won't let you in if you even have an Israeli *stamp* in your papers – which is why many intelligence officers and journalists carry two passports, one that is

61

stamped by Israeli border agents and the other that is kept diplomatically *judenrein*.) This is a problem with which the CIA, MI6, and other foreign intelligence services do not have to contend.

On the more mundane matter of clothing, Doron was insistent that I convey the image of a successful businessman. Nothing flashy or ostentatious, just tasteful and expensive. He managed to secure some extra money in my clothing budget and directed me to a number of high-end European tailors and clothiers he knew from his days on the Continent.

When I was ready, we drew up the operational order for my deployment, a document known in the Mossad by its Hebrew acronym, *pakam*, which stands for *pekuda l'mivtza*. No operation in the field is conducted without one. It contains all the relevant details about personnel, objectives, communication methods, logistics, security, timing, codes, itinerary, documents to be used, and so on. There is also a section called *Mikrim v'Tguvot* ("occurrences and reactions") designed to set out expected responses to contingencies that may arise. Once everything is written into the *pakam*, the contents have to be memorized: for obvious reasons, the Mossad doesn't want its agents carrying comprehensive mission catalogues.

When the *pakam* was complete and arrangements for my departure were set, I had one final meeting with Avi, so he could ensure that I understood my mission and its parameters before signing off on my initial deployment. I later learned that Avi did this every time a combatant was deployed on foreign soil. He felt responsible for us.

People like Avi are the main reason that the Mossad is considered one of the best intelligence services in the world. Ultimately, intelligence work isn't about satellites, budgets, oversight committees, or high-tech gadgetry. It's about the motivation and skills of your people.

As in other organizations, leadership in the Mossad is about making decisions. By this standard, Avi was one of the most impressive bosses I've ever met. In situations where most people would need to know seventy-five per cent of key variables to make the right call, Avi could do it with twenty-five per cent. Lives depended on this ability: the decisions he made weren't about his stock portfolio or what colour would be in this fall. He sent people into some of the most dangerous places on earth. And to my knowledge at least, he never lost any of them.

As a bonus, Avi had a great sense of humour. He was a delight to work with and (on rare occasions) socialize with. Unlike most brilliant people, he didn't have an outsized ego or antisocial quirks or strange emotional baggage. As the years went by, he and I developed a close relationship, and I came to see him as a father figure.

During that final meeting with Avi, the two of us sat in my safe house in North Tel Aviv, and Avi grilled me about my mission. Once he was satisfied I knew my stuff cold, he set the *pakam* aside and gave me a few life lessons. "Ridley, we are all human and everyone makes mistakes," he said. "The key is to learn from those mistakes, and make them only once. I am forgiving of a mistake, but I am not forgiving when it is repeated. It means you didn't learn from it, and that is deadly.

"One more thing," he said. "Before you do anything – regardless of how mundane you imagine it to be – think it through before you act. God gave you a brain. Use it." He smiled warmly and shook my hand. "You're ready," he said. "Good luck."

I rented a car and returned to the kibbutz to say goodbye to my wife and sons. Dahlia had given birth to our second son in July, and here I was heading off to Europe a scant two months later. I knew they would be in good hands on the kibbutz, surrounded by family and friends, but it was a hard parting nonetheless. The kibbutz had come to terms with the fact that I would no longer be managing the cotton plantation. Kibbutzniks are a patriotic lot, and they understand better than most the sacrifices that have to be made to ensure Israel's security. While my friends and neighbours didn't know the specifics, they knew that I wasn't going to work for the ministry of transport.

That night, I was booked on an early flight out of Ben Gurion Airport. In the wee hours, I was picked up by a unit driver, who was to take me to the VIP departures area (one of the rare perks of the trade). My chauffeur was a diminutive, balding guy with soulful eyes, and he collected me in a plain white van. As he helped me load my bag into the car, he said in a matter-of-fact voice, "You have some shaving cream behind your ears." The way he said it, I thought he could have been telling me that I was wet behind the ears, and he'd have been perfectly correct in his assessment. As we drove to the airport, I thought about how far I'd come, and how much my life had changed. The last time I'd been in Europe, it was as a carefree Canadian backpacker in jeans and a T-shirt. Now I was returning in a suit and tie – with a new religion, a different name, and a secret job. Just eight years had passed, yet everything was different. If these two versions of me met one another in a departure lounge, they'd have little to talk about.

I was nervous. In some ways, being an intelligence agent undercover is similar to being an actor. I was about to go on stage with my character and play my part as a different person. I was going to construct a new life piece by piece and live it as if it had always been my own. The difference was, if I didn't give a credible performance, I might never be heard from again.

When I arrived in Europe, I met Effi, the first of three Caesarea controllers I was to work with during my career, in a café and went over my *pakam*. He gave me money and I gave him my travelling Israeli passport (an alias) in exchange for my foreign operational papers. Controllers are the unit's representatives who operate under diplomatic cover overseas and act as intermediaries between the Office and the combatant in the field. They are usually on official Israeli documents and have access to diplomatic missions. A combatant without a controller is, to put it simply, an expensive piece of equipment without someone to run it. Controllers convey the details of missions, bring funds, provide direction as per HQ commands, and are the combatant's only contact with the "real" world outside of cover.

Effi was one of the Mossad's old hands – a short, affable polyglot who always looked tired, with dark circles under his eyes and unkempt hair. He made sure I signed for the money he was giving me. While movie spies are forever exchanging large stacks of bills as if they were restaurant matchbooks, the handling of currency is not nearly so casual within real intelligence agencies. In fact, accounting is a huge part of the spy trade. While the Mossad is generous in reimbursing field expenses, like all other bureaucracies, it is careful to keep track of who spends what.

Despite my initial stage fright, developing my cover and ensconcing myself in the local community came surprisingly easy. I'd never had a problem getting people to like me, and my charm had survived my identity shift: within a few months, I had a network of acquaintances and casual friends. It was a fake life, but a comfortable one. (When I entered HQ as a staff officer in 1996, six years later, many of my non-operational colleagues were impressed that I was able to stick it out under deep cover for so long. Six years may not sound like a long time, but years in the field are like dog years: multiply by six or seven.)

I bought a wardrobe that would make Doron proud, and established myself as a respectable commodities broker. I kept an office in Switzerland as my business address, and even hired someone to answer the phone in the name of the cover company I'd devised. The people I met during that period of my life would be shocked to learn

I was an intelligence agent – let alone in the Mossad. By all appearances, I was a profit-driven twenty-nine-year-old yuppie juggling any number of deals from Hong Kong to Madrid.

After two months, when I was done establishing my cover in Europe, I flew back to Israel and basked in the praise of Doron and Avi. More importantly, I was able to spend some quality time with my family. Unfortunately, our reunion was to last only a few days. I had a life awaiting me in Europe, and the Mossad was ready for me to begin doing the real work of a combatant in the field.

Too soon after I'd arrived back in Israel, Doron called me at the kibbutz. The time had come, he said, to meet Charles.

5 | CHARLES

Nothing truly valuable arises from ambition or from a mere
sense of duty; it stems rather from love and devotion towards
men and towards objective things.

Albert Einstein

When two combatants meet for the first time, they don't just walk up to each other in a darkened corner of the local souk and introduce themselves. As for a lunch date between two nervous singles, an abundance of protocols must be followed. Foremost among them is the information-guarding principle known as "compartmentalization."* Like other combatants, I didn't know the real names of anyone I worked with, or where they lived, or if they were married or had children. The more a Mossad agent knows, the more he will tell Israel's enemies under interrogation.

---

* Actually, the term I more often heard thrown around was "compartmentation." I tried to convince my Mossad peers that no such word exists in the English language, but no one believed me. The principle of compartmentalization was applied assymmetrically: every

My first meeting with my future field partner, Charles, required extensive preparation. We had to conceive a mutually viable cover story that explained not only the circumstances of our initial meeting, but also the rationale for our continued working relationship. Moreover, our handlers had to decide what we could know about one another without compromising that important line separating cover from reality.

Doron had trained both Charles and me, and thought us a good match. Coincidentally, it turned out that during one of my training missions, I'd completed the second half of a two-part operation that Charles had set up. The training operation consisted of my clearing a "dead letter box" that Charles had selected.

(A "dead drop," or "dead letter box" [DLB] as we called it, is not an actual mailbox, but a secret location for leaving items out of sight for pickup by another operative. The idea is to facilitate the transfer of an object between operatives without their having to meet in person. Widely used during the Cold War, DLBs allowed the transfer of things like documents, film, codebooks, and cameras. Selecting a suitable DLB is a fine art, as the drop site must be located in an area where the persons planting and clearing have sufficient cover to be present, yet not so public that every Tom, Dick, and Harry out walking the dog can find it. It also has to be somewhere that can be explained easily to a person who's never visited the location.)

After several weeks of back-and-forth meetings with Doron, arrangements were made for Charles and me to have the supposedly

---

* person from Caesarea's HQ with whom I worked knew everything about me, but I often knew nothing about them. At the time, I didn't even know where Caesarea's HQ was, or the range of activities performed by my own operational division. Compartmentalization is never implemented perfectly. Humans are social creatures and, over time, agents working closely together inevitably let some of their secrets out. This is why a Caesarea security officer would interview me and other combatants every few months, to find out what we knew (or had figured out on our own), so that they could prepare security risk assessments.

"chance" encounter that would blossom into our ongoing professional partnership. We met during the fall of 1990, at a Savile Row tailor in London – one of the many high-end sartorial establishments Doron had patronized during his time in Europe. Both of us were having suits made to order. During our fittings, we began to chat. In no time, Charles and I realized that we had overlapping business interests in various parts of the world. Our conversation was a charade, of course. But I like to think that to a third-party observer – say, a tailor – we convincingly appeared to be strangers enjoying a random social encounter.

My first impression of Charles was that he was a man of contrasts. On the one hand, he had the air of a tough guy, with a nose that had clearly been broken more than once. I wasn't surprised when I later learned he was a karate champion who'd served in Israel's special forces. But he also spoke English with a refined accent and precise diction. I guessed he'd attended an elite private school in Britain or one of its former colonies.

I never learned which corner of Queen Victoria's world Charles had originally called home. Regardless, I felt some sense of cultural kinship, having grown up in a sleepy onetime colonial outpost best known for its English-style gardens. Victoria is now a more cosmopolitan – and less overtly Anglophile – place than it was when I grew up there in the 1960s and 1970s. But in my era, it maintained many of the Mother Country's quainter traditions. At school assemblies, we sang "God Save the Queen" before "O Canada." We called our male teachers "sir" and played rugby. My district of Oak Bay, the most old-fashioned of the city's neighbourhoods, is often referred to as the "Tweed Curtain." Charles, I guessed, came from a similar sort of place.

Despite his intimidating persona, Charles was of average build – maybe five foot eleven inches and 180 pounds, with dark hair, light brown eyes, and a square, dimpled jaw. As a fussy, effeminate tailor took our measurements, we bantered for our Savile Row audience. Charles seemed glib and relaxed. But even during our first superficial pleasantries, I detected an edge to his personality: he was clearly a man used to being in control.

As our contrived session of male bonding played out, we "discovered" that we were both planning to visit the same Middle Eastern trade conference, scheduled for later that month in another European city. We agreed to meet for a drink during the event and then, after our suit fittings, went our separate ways.

The conversation may have been phony, but the conference was real. Charles and I both attended, and we used the opportunity to establish a commercial partnership between our respective cover business's operations. Soon after, we began meeting at Charles's apartment – a comfortable two-bedroom flat on a bustling commercial street.

Combatants select their apartments with care. Multiunit buildings in upscale areas, far from prying eyes, are preferred. So are buildings with plenty of exits, and a secure main entrance equipped with a camera and coded entry. Such precautions are aimed as much at thwarting common criminals as rival intelligence agents. Combatants often find themselves carrying large amounts of cash. (Credit cards are eschewed where possible because they leave a paper trail. Know a spy by this sign: he may make a hotel reservation or car rental with a credit card, but when he shows up, he'll pay in cash.) In one unfortunate case, a courier carrying Charles's and my operational passports and operating funds was robbed on a train. Luckily, the thief took only the money – about twelve thousand U.S. dollars – and dumped the rest of the pouch, which was recovered unopened.

In time, Charles and I got our first assignment – a mission to Tunisia to verify the address of a Palestinian involved in the 1972

Munich Olympics massacre. During our preparations, we received a visit from Uzi, the head of our Caesarea unit, a tall professorial ex-combatant with spectacles and a hairstyle that reminded me of a mad professor.

Until now, Charles and I had gotten on rather well – at least superficially. But the presence of an authority figure brought out an unattractive quality in him. From the time Uzi arrived, Charles needed to show he was the smartest person in the room. As he did at numerous subsequent meetings, Charles would not stop arguing a point until everyone gave up and agreed he was right.

His manner that day struck me as petulant and bullying. From the deferential way Uzi treated him, however, it was clear he could get away with it. Charles, I would learn, was extremely gifted – probably one of the best combatants Caesarea had ever produced. The fact that he was willing to take advantage of his status made my life during the next six years extremely trying. But for Charles's exasperating presence, I might well still be a Mossad combatant today.

Charles's opinions went beyond operational matters. He also tried to impose his judgment on my personal life – even including the manner by which I observed my faith. Both of us took our Judaism very seriously. But unlike Charles, I thought that while living undercover it was best to dispense with Jewish rituals and blend into the secular European world. He professed to be appalled by my attitude, and upbraided me several times for my lack of adherence to Jewish dietary laws. On one occasion, which I still remember clearly, he got angry that I put croutons in my soup while out for lunch during Passover, when Jews are forbidden to eat any form of leavened bread or grain product. I probably should have cut him short then and there. But since Charles was apt to turn every disagreement into an endless debate (or, if I wasn't participating, a sanctimonious harangue), I kept my mouth shut.

Several years later, I had my revenge – if you want to call it that – while taking my family to the Burger King on the Champs-Élysées in Paris during Passover. Sitting there right in front of us was Charles munching on a very unkosher Whopper with cheese. The episode was especially indefensible from his point of view since we were on Israeli documents at the time, and therefore had no professional excuse for not keeping kosher.

Another time, Charles and I had an unfriendly encounter with some young drug dealers while in Europe. Sadly, many North African youth in Europe sell hard drugs on the streets. Young Moroccan men, in particular, often deal cocaine and hashish. Charles was making a call from a pay phone one evening while I stood nearby gazing at a shop window in mock interest when a young man tried to entice him with his product.

Charles didn't appreciate the interruption: calls from pay phones were the only way we kept in touch with our families and, for one reason or another, opportunities to use them had recently been hard to come by. He shooed the dealer away while holding his hand over the mouthpiece. Angry words were exchanged before the young man headed off to summon his buddies, two other young dealers standing on a corner nearby. "You're making a big mistake," I thought.

The youth approached the pay phone again, gesticulating theatrically, with his buddies standing some five metres behind him in what I thought to be a half-hearted show of solidarity.

I knew how this episode would end. Charles was a former special forces soldier with a good knowledge of karate and a short temper. Sure enough, he hung up the phone, walked over and, without breaking stride, crouched down and punched his fist up into the Moroccan's solar plexus. He crumpled like an aluminum can.

I had read Charles's body language before he hung up the phone, and had moved to back him up. The fellow on the ground moaned and tried to get up, but fell back down again when I gave him a solid kick to the thigh. (Anyone who's had a bad charlie horse knows how that feels.) The other two, not quite committed to the encounter in the first place, ran off. We stood there in our business suits breathing hard, feeling somewhat self-conscious. Charles said something to break the tension like, "I don't think we'll be using those phones again."

We reported the incident to our controller, Effi, when we met up with him a week later. HQ was furious: engaging local hoods in fistfights was a pointless misuse of our training. No good was going to come to Israel because some local drug dealer had been given a licking – it merely put our health and cover in jeopardy. Effi puffed on his cigarette and said, "Imagine if the cops had shown up – that guy could be dead for all we know."

"They'd probably thank us for helping out with the war on drugs," I said, but Effi was not amused.

Professionally, however, Charles was extraordinarily competent. As exasperating as his personality may have been, he knew enough to keep his attitude in check during missions, so we enjoyed a highly productive working relationship. In fact, we were the team Caesarea often turned to when they needed to staff a dangerous, difficult job with a minimum of preparation time. Charles may have regarded me as an overpaid factotum but, ego-jousting aside, we got the job done – and that's what counted.

For the most part, Charles was a workaholic. He drank copious amounts of black coffee, and seemed to sleep no more than four hours per night. But in the moments when he allowed himself to unwind, Charles could display a cutting sense of humour. Sometimes, for instance, we would thumb through the Yellow Pages and make prank calls to Europe's fetishist bordellos. Charles would pretend to be a shy British civil servant on vacation and make inquiries about the rates for the most outrageous acts on offer. It was juvenile stuff, but it helped us unwind – and probably kept the two of us from killing one another.

When the time came to execute the Tunisian mission, HQ decided that only one agent would go, and that agent would be Charles. Perennially short on manpower, the Mossad obeys the principle that the minimum of assets be used in any operation – never two men when one is enough.

I remained in Europe, where my task was to build cover for Charles's trip and manage logistics and communications while he was there. I was disappointed at not going, but knew it really was a one-man job. All Charles had to do was pass by the Palestinian's residence, discreetly take some photos, and note the plate numbers of any vehicles on the premises.

It sounds like child's play, and by the standards of many of our later missions, I suppose it was. But it is important to remember that the Palestinians in Tunis were a fearful, violent lot. Many were senior members of Yasser Arafat's PLO, and several assumed they'd been targeted by the Mossad, and were accordingly hyper-conscious of personal security.

In the end, Charles pulled off the mission successfully. I had played my first supporting role in a real Mossad operation, and all had worked out fine. Professionally, I was gaining confidence. In fact, my main concern now was whether I could continue coexisting with Charles during our off hours.

But in the coming months, events took an unexpected turn. The same month, August 1990, that Charles and I embarked on our Tunisian operation, Saddam Hussein invaded Kuwait, a move President George H. W. Bush vowed would not be allowed to stand. During the ensuing Gulf War, Israel faced a new threat. And with my family at risk, my anxiety over Charles's antics became the least of my worries.

6 | TWO IF BY SEA

I never was on the dull, tame shore, But I loved the great sea more and more.

Bryan W. Proctor

I wanted to go home. It's one thing to be away from your family for months at a stretch. It's another to sit in front of a television screen and watch your country being bombed.

Operation Desert Storm began on January 17, 1991. I was in Europe when I first heard the news, eating breakfast in my hotel dining room while watching the large-screen TV the manager had thoughtfully wheeled in so guests could see the bombs drop as they sipped their cappuccinos.

The next day, Saddam Hussein fired a dozen Scud ground-to-ground missiles at Tel Aviv and Haifa as part of a desperate effort to rally the Arab world to his side. Though I was terrified for my family, I couldn't show it. After all, why would a European businessman be overly distressed about events in the Middle East? I was supposed to watch the war unfold with the emotional detachment of one whose interest lay primarily in how the conflict would affect oil futures.

I'd been living like this for almost two years since beginning my training in early 1989. During that time, I'd felt the strain between my two competing identities – the real and the fake. But it had never been as bad as now. One problem was that I didn't have any kind of social network to rely on in Europe. Though I had numerous local acquaintances, I'd deliberately avoided anything approaching true friendship. All the parts that made me a real person – my wife, my children, my friends, my real name, my national identity – had been put in boxes and stored in another country.

This is one aspect of intelligence work that rarely gets portrayed in movies and books. It's lonely – especially when you don't have the stress of a mission to distract you. I exercised a great deal and joined a local martial arts club, but the majority of my time in between missions was spent developing cover opportunities that could grant me access to just about anywhere on the globe. It's the type of loneliness you feel when you're surrounded by millions of strangers. (I imagine that salespeople who spend a lot of time on the road exchanging fake smiles with clients and airport bartenders probably know this feeling well.) Perhaps this explains why overseas combatants are the only operational personnel in the Mossad who undergo a psychiatric assessment in addition to in-depth psychological testing. Don't misunderstand me: I'm not complaining. Benny had warned me about this aspect of the job during that fateful visit to my kibbutz in 1988. But there's no denying that this anomie was a large part of my life as a combatant.

The onset of war added a new sense of powerlessness. Notwithstanding the soothing updates of Nachman Shai, the IDF's wartime spokesman, I knew it took just 180 seconds for a Scud to travel from western Iraq to Israel. I also knew my wife and six-year-old son were sitting in a sealed room with gas masks donned, doing their best to soothe a newborn.

Saddam and the moustachioed yes-men who surrounded him in Baghdad were hoping to elicit an Israeli counterattack that would bring a ring of truth to his claims of a joint Zionist–American conspiracy. Given that Israelis weren't known for turning the other cheek, it wasn't a bad bet. But George H. W. Bush had leaned hard on Israel to sit this one out. Prime Minister Yitzhak Shamir was a wily pragmatist. He did the smart thing and held his fire.

Iraq's Scuds turned out to be ineffective. The forty missiles Saddam lobbed at Israel during the Gulf War killed a total of one person. But at the time, we didn't know whether the Iraqi leader might be crazy enough to attack us with chemical or biological weapons, and rumours that the Scuds would be full of Sarin or VX nerve agents seemed credible. Just a few years earlier, during the late 1980s, Saddam had waged a genocidal campaign against Iraqi Kurds, killing about two hundred thousand people. In one village alone, Halabja, an estimated five thousand innocents were slaughtered with poison gas. If Saddam was willing to do this to his own Muslim citizens, why wouldn't he use the same weapons on Israeli Jews?

As I watched the war unfold in that hotel dining room, I began to hate my job. It occurred to me that I could go home: just walk out the door, hop on a plane, and bus it back to the kibbutz. My family was now sitting in what had overnight become part of a war zone, and all I could do was tut-tut along with the other hotel guests. The frustrating irony was that *I* was supposed to be the one in harm's way, not my wife and children. This was the ultimate test of an agent's ability to maintain cover: sitting impassively in front of a television while your family, friends, and home are under attack.

When my anxieties got the better of me that morning, I made a circuitous surveillance-detection route and found a pay phone. But thanks to the war, the lines to Israel were jammed. After several unsuccessful attempts – each punctuated by obscene outbursts on my part – I finally got through to Dahlia. She put on a brave voice, but I could tell she was worried.

Eventually, I was granted leave to fly home, where I spent a week with my family, experiencing the Scud missile attacks first-hand. I spent long hours in a sealed room, listening to news reports on a battery-powered radio while I helped my wife put our infant son into what resembled an incubator (his head was too small for him to don a gas mask). The most disturbing image I retain is of my older child sitting calmly in a chair with a gas mask on his head, as if this were a perfectly normal thing to do. Not for the first time, I questioned my fitness as a parent. In what sort of world was I raising my family?

But before making that trip back to Israel, Charles and I were going to do our small part to make that world a little safer. And by coincidence, we would be targeting exactly the sort of weapon system and rogue tyranny that were attacking Israel. It felt good to know that, at least indirectly, I would be doing something to protect the people I loved.

In John's le Carré's legendary spy novel *Tinker, Tailor, Soldier, Spy*, the director-general of the British Secret Intelligence Service, known cryptically as "Control," states that "good intelligence work was gradual and rested on a kind of gentleness."* So it normally is in the nonfictional intelligence world. But there are exceptions, and our mission to Casablanca, Morocco, was one of them. My Mossad

* The "Scalphunters" (the fictional British equivalent to Mossad combatants) were, of course, the exception to this rule.

commanders had ordered Charles and me to identify a ship whose contents – Scud missiles of the type being launched at Israel – needed to be diverted to the bottom of the ocean. The mission would be neither gradual nor gentle. A ship would be sunk and its crew would likely die in the process.

The missiles were destined for shipment not to Iraq, but its neighbour, Syria, another country ruled by Baathist tyrants. And there was little doubt what Damascus planned to do with them: aim them south at the hated Zionist enemy. Israel has defeated Syria in several wars – including the Six-Day War of 1967, in which the IDF seized the strategic Golan Heights. In 1973, Syria invaded northern Israel, but ultimately was pushed back. Since that time, Syria has given up on the idea of assaulting Israel with a conventional ground attack – especially following the break-up of the Soviet Union, Syria's onetime military supplier and benefactor. Instead, Damascus has sought to build up a large missile force with the power to rain death on Israeli cities in the event of war.

Syria's attempts to expand its ballistic missile capabilities were stalled in the late 1980s by the limitations imposed by the Intermediate-Range Nuclear Forces Treaty, which prevented the Soviet Union from selling its sophisticated solid-fuel SS-23 missiles to Damascus. Frustrated, Syrian President Hafez Assad turned to North Korea, which had on offer a simpler, liquid-fuelled missile, the Scud-C.

The first signs that the two rogue states were doing business came when North Korean Prime Minister Yi Chong-ok travelled to Damascus in the spring of 1990. His visit resulted in the signing of an agreement that ensured "mutual co-operation" in unspecified "technical and scientific" fields – a euphemism for weapons transfers. And thanks to a two-billion-dollar (US) windfall Syria received from the Gulf States in return for participation in the Desert Storm campaign against Iraq, Assad would soon have the funds to go on a missile-buying spree.*

By the end of 1990, Syria had entered the final stages of secret negotiations with North Korea for the purchase of Scud-C missiles, which were improved versions of the Scud-Bs Saddam was using. Naturally, the business relationship between the two nations had gotten Israel's attention.

Of course, North Korea had nothing in particular against Israel. Had Tel Aviv come knocking, Pyongyang gladly would have sold missiles to the Jews, too. Then, as now, North Korea was the global equivalent of the neighbourhood drug pusher. Its leaders couldn't care less about who gets blown up; they just want their money.

The first shipment of Scud-Cs was scheduled to leave North Korea in January 1991 aboard a Syrian–Jordanian co-owned ship called the *Al-Yarmouk*. Our intelligence indicated it was carrying at least twenty-four Scud-Cs in kit form, including twenty Scud launchers.

From North Korea, the ship was to chart a circuitous path to the Syrian port of Lattakia on the Mediterranean, via the Cape of Good Hope, thus bypassing the Suez Canal. In order to avoid the possibility of detection by the U.S. naval armada sailing in the Persian Gulf region in support of the war against Iraq, the *Al-Yarmouk*'s captain had declared to Lloyds of London that the ship's destination was Cyprus.

The Syrians had overestimated U.S. omniscience: the Americans were fixated on Saddam and didn't have a clue what the Syrians, their nominal allies, were up to. But the IDF's military intelligence

---

* In actuality, Syria's military contribution to the Gulf War consisted of sending a token collection of ragtag soldiers and aging armoured vehicles to bask in the sun well behind the frontlines. One report had the Syrians stating that they would not participate in the actual fighting. I also found it more than a little ironic that Syria's payback money from the Gulf states was being used to purchase Scud missiles similar to those that Saddam rained down on the Saudis. The episode seems to encapsulate the mind-bending logic of the Middle East and of the despots who rule the region.

branch, Aman (a Hebrew abbreviation for the Israeli Defense Forces Directorate of Military Intelligence) and the Mossad's counter-proliferation department were carefully monitoring the shipment.

Caesarea had dispatched teams of combatants from Southeast Asia to Africa in a bid to keep a close eye on the boat. We were to be the final link in the chain of Israeli intelligence contacts that would track the *Al-Yarmouk* before it reached its final destination. Our role would come when it made its last stop in Casablanca for bunkering (refuelling and resupply) before entering the Mediterranean via the Straits of Gibraltar.

Charles and I met at one of our safe houses in Europe for a briefing on the mission. These safe houses are actually apartments rented by "helpers" who are local agents, for clandestine meetings and to provide a place for combatants to hide from the local security service. The helpers didn't know for whom or what purpose they were renting the premises and merely handed the keys over to a HQ representative, who also gave the helper money, to make sure the rent was paid. Being local citizens, the helpers didn't fell under suspicion nor have to provide extraneous documentation like passports.

Charles and I were apprised of the *Al-Yarmouk*'s journey and cargo via a briefing from a Tel Aviv-based intelligence officer whose beatnik appearance was enhanced by sandals and an abundance of facial hair. Struck by his unusual appearance, I made a snide crack about the possibility that the boat might be an LSD-induced hallucination.

He promptly told me that he had a doctorate in comparative literature from a prestigious U.S. university. He was something of an expert on Jack Kerouac, it turned out. Politely passing over my sarcasm, he explained that he admired the icons of the Beat generation because they rejected traditional social and artistic forms long before the hippies came onto the scene. Comparing his area of study to various Eastern religions, he told me that he appreciated beatnik culture because it encouraged expression through intensely felt personal experiences and something called "beatific illumination." It was a serious lecture – albeit a surreal one, coming in the midst of a discussion of a missile interdiction mission. I behaved myself after that.

Beatnik philosophy notwithstanding, the intelligence officer – I'll call him Kerouac – came equipped with an arsenal of maps, photos, and satellite images of the ship. All we had to do was pick out our target in port and attach a homing device (or "beacon") so the Israeli air force could track her and sink the vessel in the middle of the Mediterranean. There are a lot of ships in the Mediterranean, and we didn't want to make a mistake.

The mission may sound simple – the sort of thing James Bond could do between cocktails – but in real life, there are a million and one details that have to be worked out. As usual, cover was the main consideration. How would we gain access to Morocco, let alone to the port area of Casablanca, on short notice? How would we get close to the ship without arousing suspicion? How would we attach the beacon so that it went undetected and wouldn't fall off?

I've always loved the sea. I used to sail with my friend Chris McDonald, on his Cal20 sailboat after school. We'd head off to the marina on our bikes and within minutes be barefoot sailors on the blue Pacific around the Gulf Islands. Even as a small boy, I loved watching my older brothers sail a scale-model sloop around a pond off Dallas Road. I loved watching the wind take her, and was always amazed at how difficult sailboats are to capsize. And so to calm myself, I did my best to think of my new assignment not as a dangerous mission, but as an opportunity to revisit my nautical roots.

Days before the *Al-Yarmouk* was to arrive, Charles and I made the uneventful flight to Morocco and checked into our hotel – a modernish effort with a lot of white tile. Charles called headquarters and uttered a prearranged code word that let the worrywarts know we'd arrived. Then we set out for some meetings we'd arranged before leaving Europe, with shipping companies that had operations in Casablanca's port. The meetings would not only help us develop our cover, but also give us a chance to check out the security arrangements around the docks.

Because I quit fieldwork before the Internet took off, I can't comment on how it's revolutionized tradecraft. But the effect, I imagine, must be enormous. Had an operation like this been performed in the post-Netscape era, Charles and I would have been able to access an abundance of information – including satellite photos of the dock area, chat rooms devoted to mariners and security experts, even video snippets from tourists. Thanks to Google and the like, your average backpacker has access to more background information on short notice these days than the spies of 1991 did.

The story we'd concocted had us looking for warehouse facilities to process goods en route from Southeast Asia to southern Europe. In particular, we were looking for a location near the port that would permit storage, repackaging, and redistribution.

Commercial enterprises in the Arab world were always eager to solicit business from Western business representatives. Not only would they do their best to meet your needs, but they'd try to interest you in unrelated business ventures that required outside financing or a Western distribution partner. I did my best to follow up on these proposals, since they often provided golden opportunities to develop business cover for future intelligence operations. I could only take these relationships so far, of course. Since I didn't have any real business operations – in Southeast Asia, southern Europe, or anywhere else – I had to be deliberately vague as to my commercial activities.

Casablanca, a port city on the Atlantic coast, is a nervous, chaotic place mythologized by travellers and Hollywood movies. It is a city of desert air, blue skies, and heavy scents. Open-air markets are piled high with rugs and handmade woodcarvings, and the strong smells of spicy North African cooking are pervasive. It's the smells that stir my memory: each neighbourhood seemed to have its own.

We met with a garrulous shipping agent who spoke French-accented English and gave him our spiel. He was friendly and we drank tea in his office while the hot Moroccan sun poured in. We asked him if we could see the port facilities, and he agreed. In fact, he offered to take us to lunch and we happily accepted. North African cuisine is outstanding, and Morocco's is, in my opinion, the best of the genre. There are few nations on earth where food is prepared more artfully, served more proudly, or consumed more enthusiastically.*

After lunch, the three of us walked to the port, where Charles and I immediately spotted our quarry docked among a line of freighters. She was right where Kerouac, bless his beatnik soul, had told us she'd be: tied up against one of the long quays that stretch out from the port. Charles and I had memorized her lines and features, but a five-year-old could have picked her out: the ship's name was written on the bow in the Roman and Arabic alphabets.

As we had hoped, security was light, and we realized we would have little difficulty slipping into the port area that night. It was fenced, but with gaps. This was before 9/11; many port officials barely even read the ships' manifests or checked them against the boats' contents.

Later, we returned to the hotel and called our HQ to report our sighting. We got the green light and started planning our incursion

---

* Israel is home to a large community of Jews expelled from Morocco in the 1950s, and their descendants. Thankfully their culinary influence remains strong. They've given the country a million and one different kinds of salads, to say nothing of delectable dishes featuring couscous, meatballs, lamb, and chickpeas.

and cover options. I suggested we bring a small bottle of Scotch (which we had purchased earlier in Europe) in the hope that, if caught, we might pass ourselves off as a couple of drunken crew members. We could splash our clothes with whisky and take a swig for good measure. Being a single malt Scotch man, Charles agreed, and even suggested we buy a good bottle since it was on expenses. "I mean, I don't want to have to spit it out," he added.

After another cover meeting with a second shipping company, we made our final preparations and set out from the hotel for the port at around ten o'clock at night. We were both attired in dark clothing, and Charles carried a small knapsack containing the Scotch, a towel, a change of clothes, swimming goggles, eight metres of blackened rope attached to a grappling hook, a small underwater flashlight, and the beacon itself, which had been painted to blend in with the ship's surface. The beacon had been hidden away. The tricky part was the slow-dissolving adhesive that we planned to use to attach the beacon to the ship. It would last for a few days in sea water before loosening so that the beacon would fall off if the mission were aborted. We didn't want the thing discovered months or years later when the ship was in dry dock.

Carefully, we walked to the port-access point closest to the ship. We avoided the lights and moved quietly. I felt almost as if I was in the army again and my unit was approaching a town held by hostile forces.

We edged up to the rail line that trains used to transport cargo and supplies to and from the ships, and followed it out to the *Al-Yarmouk*. We stopped when we reached the point where the stern was tied, some fifty metres from the end of the ship. We crouched behind some railcars and prepared the beacon and adhesive. When it was ready, Charles put on the swim goggles, grabbed the flashlight, and headed off for the stern line.

Cover has its limits; in many operations, there comes a point where cover is useless because there simply is no credible innocent explanation for what you're doing. On the other hand, the plain truth – "I'm a Mossad agent. We're helping to blow up this here boat." – is never an option. And so I always made a point of having some kind of tall tale ready. In this case, Charles and I were going to claim that we'd been drinking with some sailors on board the *Al-Yarmouk*, and that Charles had fallen in the water as we were trying to get back to shore. Not particularly believable and easily debunked. But many people – including security guards and cops – are lazy: if you give them a half-decent pretext to end their investigations, they'll take it.

As Charles edged out to the stern line, I could see interior lights on the ship, but nobody on deck. Like all freighters, it reeked of salty diesel. With an audible splash, Charles lowered himself into the water. I kept watch and held the knapsack. He was gone for what seemed a long time, but then I heard him resurface quietly. I edged over to the water and lowered the blackened rope into it, attaching the hook to the lip of the quay. If anyone showed up, I'd unhook it and let it sink, and Charles would have to get out another way.

Charles is a strong guy as well as a good swimmer and diver. And from what I know of special forces training, they spend a lot of time climbing ropes. He grabbed hold of the rope and was out of the water in seconds. Immediately, we retreated to an inconspicuous spot near the rail line.

"The beacon's attached under the stern," Charles whispered in between gasps. "But I had a bugger of a time. It's all crusty with barnacles and crap."

"Good job," was all I could think to say.

He quickly towelled off and changed. Then we each took a swig of the Scotch – for purely professional reasons, of course. It burned gloriously all the way down.

Our retreat from the port was uneventful, and we made it back to the hotel well before midnight. We called in and reported that the mission was completed and that the beacon was on. We were both wired, but retired as soon as we could to rest up for the long flight home the next day.

After breakfast, we headed out to the airport and made our connection to Paris, relieved to be out of the operational arena. We reported in to HQ and were told we'd be meeting a representative from HQ after we arrived at one of our safe houses.

I was glad to have the mission behind me. The Gulf War was still on, and I was looking forward to the chance to fly home and see my family. The U.S.-led coalition's relentless air campaign wasn't lessening the Scud launches, and we were still worried that Saddam, in his desperation, would go into genocide mode.

A week or so later, we were told abruptly that the mission to sink the ship had been cancelled. When I asked why, somewhat miffed and disappointed, I was told that Prime Minister Shamir himself had made the call. He'd decided that blowing up the *Al-Yarmouk* might be construed by the Syrians as an act of war. Under normal circumstances, that might not be a deal breaker. But given the sensitivities at play with the Gulf War still on, he wouldn't chance it. The Americans would have been furious.

I think Shamir also didn't like the fact that innocent lives would have been lost. And I have to admit that this would have bothered me as well. The crew of the ship – impoverished third world men trying to make a buck or two to send home, no doubt – couldn't have known what the ship was carrying. And Shamir himself had cancelled less important missions in the past on the grounds that there was even a slight chance innocent bystanders might be killed.

I'd run into this scenario before during an aborted operation to assassinate the leader of the Palestinian Islamic Jihad, Fathi Shiqaqi.

He was the first terrorist leader to publish a booklet that – in his own mind at least – legitimized the justification of suicide bombings to further the cause of jihad. In 1995, Shiqaqi was assassinated in Malta outside the Diplomat Hotel while breaking his journey from Syria to Libya, but that wasn't the first operational scenario conceived to ease his way into premature "martyrdom."

I played an integral part in a plan to assassinate Shiqaqi as early as 1993, and the mission was only aborted after an assessment of the situation determined that his assassination would have probably left a lot of hats on the ground and possibly civilian casualties. We were very close to getting the green light to launch the operation, and I have to admit that I was somewhat relieved when it was decided to wait for a better opportunity – even if that meant years. One of the guiding principles that carried me through my work, and convinced me that the Mossad was both moral and ethical, was respect for civilian life, no matter how hostile to Israel's existence those civilians seemed to be.

So, though I was angered that Syria would now have a couple dozen more Scuds to aim at Israel, I was relieved that I would not have any "collateral damage" on my conscience.

Unless they read this book, the captain and crew of the Al-Yarmouk may never know how close they came to being sent to Davy Jones' locker. As for the Scuds, on March 13, 1991, the Al-Yarmouk docked in Lattakia. The ship arrived the exact same day U.S. Secretary of State James Baker arrived in Damascus to meet with Syrian President Hafez Assad for the first time.

I'll bet they never discussed it.

7 | PRINCES OF PERSIA

I would rather discover one true cause than gain the kingdom of Persia.

Democritus

"That's not an EEI. That's a black hole!"

As Charles announced this, he took out a pen and, with a dramatic flourish, scrawled "black hole" across the Iran dossier the three of us were studying. Effi sat impassively, absent-mindedly fiddling with his cigarette lighter. He seemed annoyed by Charles's usual drama-queen antics, but said nothing.

"He's right," I added. "The first question here really should be, Where *is* Iran? We haven't had an agent in the country since the days of the Shah."

Every intelligence service in the world produces some version of an EEI, a document that catalogues "essential elements of intelligence" – in other words, the things your government needs to know about a particular target, but doesn't. In the case of Iran, that meant, most crucially, the country's first-strike capability and the state of its advanced weapons programs.

It was 1993, two years after Iraq's defeat in the First Gulf War. Though Saddam Hussein was a menace to the region, Israel had relied on him to supply a military counterweight to Iran. With Saddam's army and air force decimated, that counterweight was now gone.

In fact, it was becoming obvious that Iran was emerging as Israel's main threat. The country's current president, Mahmoud Ahmadinejad, may have grabbed headlines with his recent threats to wipe Israel off the map, but he is merely rehashing established policy set down by Iranian leaders going back to Ayatollah Ruhollah Khomeini himself. To find out if Tehran had the know-how to make good on its long-standing creed of exterminating Israel, the Mossad needed to restart its dormant Persian operations. Charles and I were the two agents picked for the inaugural foray.

According to the plan Effi laid out for us, Charles and I would fly into Tehran together under our usual commercial cover, then split up to investigate designated industrial sites in the Iranian hinterland. My task was to travel 250 kilometres southwest, to the environs of the now-infamous Natanz Uranium Enrichment Facility (or, as it is known in the Israeli intelligence community, Kashan, after a nearby city), take some photos and soil samples, and then return to Europe. It was a brief mission, but at least it would help put an end to the Mossad's Iranian "black hole." Charles's assignment involved individuals who still play a valuable role in ongoing Israeli intelligence operations, and I cannot disclose details of his mission. Suffice it to say that, between the two of us, he got the more important and complicated task. This was par for the course, and I did not begrudge him. We'd been working as a team for three years now, and it was clear to all concerned that Charles was simply the better combatant.

Charles and I knew we were in for an interesting experience when the pilot's voice came on the cabin speaker during our descent. After perfunctory instructions advising us to restore our trays to the locked position and buckle up, he added: "All women are kindly requested to don headscarves and adopt a moderate manner of dress so as to avoid any unnecessary difficulties with local authorities."

Unnecessary difficulties was a euphemism for "being arrested." The women seated around me needed little reminder; as is the custom among well-travelled Iranians, they'd already discreetly used the lavatories to effect the transformation from jet-setting sophisticates to shrouded Muslim matrons.

Tehran is a sprawling metropolis of closely packed buildings set in the shadow of the beautiful Alburz Mountains. The volume and speed of the morning traffic astonished me. I've driven in some crazy places, but Tehran may take the prize for sheer white-knuckle insanity. Breathing can be a challenge, too. Most of the cars you see on the road are old-fashioned jalopies, and the air is thick with pollution.

Like many royal dynasties, the Pahlavi family who ruled Iran up until the Islamic revolution in 1979 had a fondness for grand architectural design. The most prominent example we passed on our way from the airport was the Azadi Tower, a marble structure built by the Shah in 1971 to commemorate the 2,500th anniversary of the Persian Empire. Azadi Square, where the tower is located, was the site of the popular demonstrations that led to the 1979 revolution. Along with Enghelab Square (literally, "Revolution Square"), it carries the same symbolic value in postrevolutionary Iran as did Red Square to Soviet Russians. In its propaganda, the government exploits such symbols relentlessly. Like many radical third world tyrants, the mullahs of Tehran try to get as much mileage as they can out of their aging revolutionary bona fides.

On the streets, the heavy hand of the theocracy was very much in evidence: Everywhere, we saw paramilitary forces cruising in pickup trucks, looking for any outward displays of libertine decadence. In our hotel, as outside it, posters of a glaring, Big Brotheresque Ayatollah Khomeini (who'd died four years earlier) were a common sight.

Our hotel lobby also featured a rug made to look like the U.S. flag. Its central position encouraged guests to wipe their feet on the Great Satan – a terrible insult in this part of the world. (Rather than draw attention to myself by steering clear of the Stars and Stripes, I reluctantly passed directly over the rug, offering a silent apology to my American friends as I did so.) Whether such petty gestures are a symbol of the mullahs' genuine antipathy or a demagogic ploy to keep people riled up against a foreign enemy is hard to say. Most experts would tell you it's a combination of both.

But despite the obscurantist world view espoused by the country's clerisy, many Iranians are well educated (often in good Western schools), sophisticated, and knowledgeable about world affairs. Most roll their eyes at the propaganda emitted by Tehran, and hold a sympathetic attitude toward Westerners, including Americans.

In fact, if you want to avoid unpleasantness when speaking with an Iranian, remember this: Iran may be located in the Middle East, but it is *not* an Arab country. While they share the same religion and much of the same geopolitical world view as Arabs, Iranians have their own language, culture, and history. As many Iranians are quick to point out, by the time Mohammed rescued Arab nomads from their pagan backwardness, the Persians had already been building empires for two millennia. Unlike their tradition-bound Arab neighbours, ordinary Iranians are eager to embrace modern technology. Even in the early 1990s, it took me hours to place a long distance call from Damascus. Iran, on the other hand, long ago adopted a state-of-the-art European-designed telecommunications system. The trend continued with the Internet, which young Iranians have embraced en masse. (Farsi is now the fourth most popular language of bloggers.)

After unpacking, Charles and I had lunch at a nearby restaurant. Our pale skin and Western clothes made us stand out, but no one regarded us with more than passing curiosity. While enjoying lamb and rice, we played a game: as women dressed head-to-toe in black sailed past, we tried to guess their age, based only on their gait and speed. Like the infidel I am, I imagined there were beautiful women buried beneath those chadors.

Once we'd eaten our fill, we headed off to a scheduled cover meeting at an office of the Bonyad-e Shahid (Martyrs Foundation) – one of several government-subsidized tax-exempt trusts that answer directly to Iran's supreme leader. In the aftermath of the Islamic Revolution, these entities were established to redistribute oil income to families of the country's war dead. But as anyone might have predicted, they were quickly co-opted by corrupt regime apparatchiks, and now function as bloated, overstaffed dispensaries of patronage. Their dominant place in the nation's economy is one of the leading sources of resentment among ordinary Iranians.

During our cross-town taxi ride, it was all I could do to fight off the nausea induced by the carbon monoxide fumes and our driver's erratic driving style. Charles, on the other hand, was in his usual fine form, bonding with the man using his rudimentary Farsi. By the time the trip was over, they had become best friends. With his self-assured manner, Charles had a superficial charisma that worked on everyone from minor Arab royalty to fish sellers in Lattakia. (Only I seemed immune to the spell. As is often said, no man is a hero to his valet – nor to those they *treat* as their valet.) Annoying as it was, Charles's slick personality was a major professional asset, allowing him to cultivate intelligence sources by the bushel. Sometimes I thought the man would be able to rule the Levant if he were somehow able to keep his ego in check.

We met with the Martyrs Foundation executives in a dingy conference room. They all wore neatly trimmed beards, navy blue suits, and white Chinese-collared shirts done up to the neck. Ties are considered symbols of the West, so no Iranian man wears one. Knowing this, we went open-collared so as not to offend.

The meeting was courteous and professional. Charles and I discussed the usual commercial concerns – quality, price, delivery schedule – as if our outfit were just a normal shipping company looking to gain a commission. For their part, the Iranians showed themselves to be shrewd negotiators. When it was over, they presented me with a huge paper bag of pistachios – which made a fine gift for Dahlia when the trip was over. Such was the surreal nature of my job. One day, I was glad-handing with a bunch of Islamists on Tehran's payroll. A few days later, my Israeli family was munching on their finely wrapped pistachios while we sat watching a rerun of *Seinfeld*.

After the meeting, Charles and I retired to our hotel, where we were scheduled to receive a shortwave radio message from HQ authorizing the next phase of our operation. Like all such public-broadcast transmissions received from the Mossad, this one required the use of a "one-time pad" to decode.

Essentially, a one-time pad is an algorithm that has been widely used to transmit encoded information since the Second World War. (Study the history of intelligence tradecraft and you will find that many of the techniques still in common use date to this period. If you could pass one over on the Nazis' counterintelligence apparatus, chances are you were on to a good thing.) Each one-time pad provides a unique code that maps the text you want to encrypt to seemingly random alphanumeric characters and back again. Only two copies of any one code exist – one held by the transmitting entity (in my case, Mossad HQ) and the other by the field agent. Each combatant is assigned his own one-time pad, which means you can't hack an entire network merely by seizing a single code.

Armed with our pads, all we had to do was tune in to a specified shortwave radio frequency at the appointed time, wait for the appropriate call-sign (mine was Victor-Lima-Bravo), note the sequences transmitted by the computerized voice, and decipher the messages.

There are lots of things that can go wrong when using the one-time pad system, such as radio interference and bad reception. And because the method relies on a one-way broadcast, the transmitting party has no way of knowing if his message has been received. Which invites the question, why use such an old-fashioned, laborious method in an era of instantaneous digital communication? Wouldn't it be simpler to use the sort of devices every ten-year-old now takes for granted – cellphones, text messaging, e-mail, or an Internet chat room?

The answer is simple. Unlike all of these rival methods, short-wave radio broadcasts provide an eavesdropper with no means of identifying the person receiving the message; or, indeed, of determining if *anyone* is receiving the message. Moreover, the communication leaves no electronic residue and requires no specially configured gadgets; all you need is the sort of shortwave radio you can buy for fifty dollars at your local discount electronics store. Contrast this with e-mail and telephone lines, which are an open book to any counter-intelligence service worth its salt (including, we now know, America's National Security Agency). Even in the case of anonymous pay-as-you-go cellphones, government snoopers can use voice recognition, calling patterns, and signal tracking to zero in on a suspect user, especially in a totalitarian state such as Iran.

Once Charles and I had received authorization from HQ, he left to take a second flight to a smaller Iranian city and I hopped in a rental car and set off for Natanz. My cover story was that I was visiting a picturesque oasis town south of Tehran. To back up my tale, I brought along a European tourist book with the town's entry circled and annotated with enthusiastic scribblings. The hotel kitchen staff had packed me a lunch, and I made sure I blabbed to the concierge and desk clerk about my purported destination.

As for my true target, the Natanz area, the truth is that I knew little about it at the time of my mission. I hadn't even been informed that the site was connected with Iran's nuclear program. All Effi gave me in his rudimentary briefing were a set of coordinates and a bare-bones geographical description.

It may seem odd that a spy would be provided with so little background information about his target. But in the intelligence trade, this is hardly unusual. During my career as a combatant, I often was sent to photograph a house, collect a soil sample, or visually confirm the coordinates of a set of antennae on a building – but for what rhyme or reason, I was seldom told.

It's not that we were treated as brainless drones incapable of understanding complex projects; it was simply a matter of operational security. The expression "need-to-know" describes an important principle of intelligence work.* Given the ruthless nature

---

* In spy novels and movies, this principle is often ignored; spies are told not only every detail of their mission, but operationally irrelevant information about how their mission fits into their paymaster's schemes. *The Bourne Identity* (2002) is a notable exception. Having seen all too many cheesy spy films, I was impressed that the "Treadstone" assassins were portrayed as operating in complete isolation and were told of their missions only through intermediaries who knew only their first names. Like all Hollywood films, this one contained a variety of credulity-stretching plot devices, of course. But in this particular respect, art imitated life to a T.

of Israel's enemies, this adage is particularly appropriate to Mossad operations. Terrorist outfits and rogue nations such as Iran have sadists on their payroll who can extract information from the most stoic combatant with ease. The key, therefore, is to ensure the agent has nothing sensitive to divulge in the first place.

As I later found out, the Natanz complex was just one part of a larger Iranian nuclear enrichment program. The oldest facility is the Bushehr Nuclear Power Plant, on Iran's southwestern coast. Construction began with the assistance of the German government in the 1970s, when Iran was a stable Western ally under the control of the Shah. But after various stops and starts, the project was eventually mothballed by the leaders of the 1979 Islamic Revolution. It was restarted in earnest with Russian help in 1992 thanks to two factors, Iran's expanded regional ambitions and Moscow's need for hard currency.

Tehran acted in secret; it wasn't until 2002 that a dissident Iranian group blew the lid off Tehran's uranium enrichment program, thereby setting the stage for the lengthy high-stakes confrontation between Iran and the West that persists as of this writing. But farsighted Israeli intelligence analysts knew something was up a decade earlier, which is why Charles and I had been dispatched.

After some wrong turns and a few near-misses with maniacal local drivers, I eventually found my way out of Tehran. The traffic thinned and the scenery became more rustic – as did the people who occasionally waved at my passing car. Following the instructions I'd been given by HQ, I took photographs, including several panorama sequences, at prescribed locations along the route.

When I reached the Natanz area, I parked the car and checked to make sure I hadn't been followed. It was a flat, arid, isolated landscape. Aside from the two-lane road I'd travelled on, there was no sign of any human presence. Iran is a huge country, most of it empty, and my little solo adventure into the outback made me feel like a British explorer from the nineteenth century.

I took some more photos, then slipped off a loafer – for speed, I'd avoided wearing laced shoes – and used it to scoop a large sample of sandy topsoil. I put it back on my foot, returned to the car, and drove to a second designated location. There, I took some more shots and filled the other shoe. Taking care to remember which shoe was which, I got back in the car and dutifully proceeded to the oasis town that was my ostensible destination. During my visit, I made sure to take a bunch of cheesy tourist photos: I had a cover story to protect, after all.

Packing for home, I stuffed socks in my loafers and then sealed them in a plastic bag at the bottom of my suitcase. I told myself the soil I was bringing back was as precious to the analysts at the Mossad's counter-proliferation department as the soil of the Holy Land is to Christian pilgrims.

During Charles's far more eventful trip, he happened to drive right into the largest military exercise held in Iran since the end of the Iran–Iraq war of the 1980s. You can imagine how much fun it was for him, a lone Westerner stopped at a military roadblock in the middle of nowhere with the Iranian military running about. But naturally he finessed the situation easily: he immediately adopted an imperious manner (hardly a stretch), and demanded to speak to whoever was in charge. In no time, he had an Iranian army general eating out of his hand. I could imagine the scenario: the two of them sitting in the shade of a drooping pomegranate tree, drinking tea while Charles gave the general some pointers on how properly to deploy the forces under his command.

As for me, I departed Iran without incident. Once my plane hit cruising altitude, I celebrated the successful completion of my modest mission with a drink. As I emptied my miniature bottle of Beefeater into a plastic glass half full of tonic, I noticed a parade of chador-clad women making their way toward the bathrooms. Each of them, I noticed, was carrying a small garment bag.

8 | KHARTOUM: TERROR CENTRAL

The bush fowl saw the chicken being carved up and laughed.
The chicken told the bush fowl to stop laughing, for the same
hands now carving up the chicken would be used to carve up
the bush fowl.

Sudanese proverb

Over the course of Israel's short life, the country has endured thousands of terrorist attacks. Most Israelis, even the lucky ones who have not been directly affected through the loss of a friend or family member, retain the memory of at least one encounter with a victim.

In my case, that victim is Yael. When she was introduced to me at a dinner party in Paris, it had already been several months since Hezbollah blew up Israel's embassy in Buenos Aires, but her face was still swollen and marked by stitched lacerations. Though Yael was unable to produce a full-blown smile with that wounded face, her eyes conveyed a strong, mirthful spirit. It was obvious she'd once been – and would become again – a beautiful woman. Her husband, Ronen, doted on her as she spoke. Together, they told me the tale of their ordeal.

Yael and Ronen both worked at the embassy. On March 17, 1992, she was at her post when a pickup truck packed with high explosives smashed into the front of the building and detonated. The blast destroyed not only the embassy, but also a nearby church and school. Ronen, who'd briefly left the building on an errand at the time of the explosion, returned when he heard the blast. He searched frantically until, miraculously, he found his badly wounded wife amid the debris. Twenty-nine people died that day. But thanks to the life-saving medical intervention she received, Yael was not among them.

My thoughts turned immediately to Yael and Ronen two years later, when I learned of a second Hezbollah truckbombing in Buenos Aires. On July 18, 1994, a terrorist had driven a van full of ammonium nitrate through the front gates of the Argentine Israelite Mutual Association (AMIA), the heart of Argentina's Jewish community, reducing the seven-storey building to rubble. As with the 1992 attack, the victims were innocent civilians. The AMIA building housed everything from social welfare offices, where the elderly collected pensions, to the city's Jewish burial society.

The AMIA attack produced outrage in Israel, but also a sense of helplessness. Israel is remarkably effective at protecting itself from large-scale terrorist attacks, but it can do little to defend the many vulnerable Jewish communities scattered throughout the world, which are spiritually connected to the Jewish state but lie beyond its military protection. Iran, which through its proxy, Hezbollah, follows the terrorists' cowardly course of attacking the most defenceless targets available, is well aware of this. By such means do the ruling mullahs hold a sword of Damocles over Jewry's collective head.

Following the AMIA bombing, Israel opted to let Argentina prosecute the matter as a domestic crime. But the subsequent investigations were severely bungled – perhaps intentionally so. Numerous leads pointing to the complicity of Iran and Hezbollah were ignored. According to a lawyer for the AMIA victims, rubble and human remains from that blast were carried off and used as landfill before anyone could inspect them for clues. Meanwhile, the investigating judge, Juan Galeano, was impeached for paying a witness to change his testimony and burning incriminating evidence. There have even been allegations that the former Argentine president, Carlos Menem, was bribed by the Iranian government in return for sabotaging the investigation. Whatever the truth of these claims, it was clear Argentina could not, or would not, bring the architects of the plot to justice. And so Israel, to punish the Iranians, devised a plan involving targeted killings of the Iranian intelligence cadres in Sudan, an operation in which the Mossad was expected to play a key role.

My life had changed since my initial deployment to Europe. First, my family had moved from Israel to France. Although I was stationed in a different European city, I was close enough to visit regularly. For the first time since my basic training, I could take a meaningful role in the lives of Dahlia and the children.

There had been changes in my professional environment as well. Effi, my chain-smoking controller, had finished his three-year stint and had been replaced by Kerouac, the beatnik who'd briefed me and Charles prior to the *Al-Yarmouk* operation. Stick around for a few years in the Mossad and you start to see the same faces pop up over and over again.

When he took up his post in Europe, Kerouac had the same hippie manner I remembered from Tel Aviv. But that soon changed. Like many large cities in Western Europe, his new base of operations had a growing and culturally assertive Muslim population. On his way to one of his first meetings with Charles and me, a group of Arab men spotted him and waved to him as one of their own. While we all savoured the irony of a Mossad officer receiving such a warm welcome from the local Muslims, Kerouac took it as a sign that it was time to lose the extensive facial hair and dress in slightly more fashionable Western attire.

I got along well with Kerouac, but he had a few cultural differences that complicated our relationship. For one thing, Charles and I were foreign-born Israelis with Anglo roots. Kerouac, on the other hand, was a native-born Israeli sabra. And so a lot of the jokes, idioms, and euphemisms Charles and I threw around in casual conversation escaped his Mediterranean antennae.

Secondly, Kerouac was maddeningly risk-averse. During the planning for any operation, he tended to divert our attention from important mission details to fret needlessly over implausible worst-case scenarios. For instance, he had a rule that Charles and I weren't permitted to meet with the same target separately, lest one of us say something that was inconsistent with the other's cover story. So if Charles met with a Syrian businessman in Damascus, then I couldn't meet him in Zurich the next month unless Charles was also present, or vice versa. (When Doron took over as our handler a few years later, he said this policy was ridiculous and deep-sixed it immediately.)

It was while I was getting to know Kerouac that the AMIA bombing occurred. Not long after, he presented me with my first mission under his stewardship – one I would have to perform on my own, since Charles was occupied with another assignment. During a meeting at my apartment, Kerouac emptied a diplomatic pouch from Mossad HQ onto my dining room table. As I sifted through the maps and documents, I quickly noted that all related to the Sudanese capital of Khartoum – or, as many of us then called the city, Terror Central.

By 1994, forces from Israel and Hezbollah had been engaged in regular combat in southern Lebanon for more than a decade. But the Argentina bombings seemed to require retribution beyond that daily attrition. Khartoum provided the perfect venue: it was one of the few places in the world where Hezbollah maintained an official presence. Yet, unlike Iran, it was also sufficiently chaotic that a team of Israeli commandos might penetrate undetected, attack targets within the city, and escape quickly.

As Julie Flint and Alex de Waal demonstrate in their outstanding book, *Darfur: A Short History of a Long War* (2006), modern Sudan is beset by a bewildering welter of conflicts: Arabs versus Africans, herders versus farmers, Muslims versus Christians, riparian elite versus hinterland peasants and, suffusing everything else, tribe versus tribe. Even by the standards of other African nations, the country is poor, unstable, and fragmented.

Since 1989, Sudan's government has been controlled by an Arab-supremacist cabal led by Umar Hassan al-Bashir and Hassan al-Turabi,* fundamentalist Muslim ideologues who've done their best to exterminate the country's religious minorities in the south and central parts of the country. In Darfur, Sudan's government has applied the same brutal methods against fellow Muslims, hundreds of thousands of whom lie dead as a result. Yet few Islamic nations or organizations have spoken out against the Darfur genocide. Oddly, the same loud voices that ring out when a handful of innocent Palestinian Muslims are killed fall mute when the death toll is multiplied by several orders of magnitude in Africa.

In search of oil money and military aid, Sudan reached out to its fellow radical Islamist government in Tehran during the 1990s. Khartoum

---

* In 1999, Bashir successfully moved against Turabi, and consolidated power in his own hands.

also put out the red carpet to the world's leading terrorist organizations. Osama bin Laden himself lived in the city from 1991 to 1996. At around the same time, Khartoum was home to Imad Mughniyeh, a Hezbollah leader who personally involved himself in some of the group's most notorious crimes. Though the name Mughniyeh is little known in the West, I consider him a more skilled and influential terrorist than bin Laden. Mughniyeh got his start in Lebanon in the 1970s, when the PLO ruled the southern part of the country. He was then enlisted in Force 17, the elite security apparatus charged with protecting Yasser Arafat and his closest cronies. When the PLO was ousted from Lebanon by the 1982 Israeli invasion, he stayed behind and, with the assistance of the Iranian Revolutionary Guard Corps (IRGC), formed and ran what we now know as Hezbollah. Mughniyeh has a twenty-five-million-dollar bounty on his head – though, interestingly, it was put in place only after September 11, 2001.

Hassan al-Turabi deliberately set out to make his country a unifying force in the terrorist war against the West. According to the 9/11 Commission Report, he "sought to persuade Shiite [Muslims] and Sunni [Muslims] to put aside their divisions and join against the common enemy. In late 1991 or 1992, discussions in Sudan between al-Qaeda and Iranian operatives led to an informal agreement to co-operate in providing support – even if only training for actions carried out primarily against Israel and the United States. Not long afterward, senior al-Qaeda operatives and trainers traveled to Iran to receive training in explosives." Since 9/11, many have wondered how a ragtag bunch of Afghan veterans and hounded Egyptian Islamists coalesced into a terrorist confederacy capable of bringing down the World Trade Center. A large part of the answer, I believe, lay in the dusty alleys of Khartoum.

Kerouac was candid about the purpose of my mission. "The prime minister wants to strike back at Iran," he said. "And he's decided that it's going to be in Khartoum." I was surprised at this blunt talk and even more surprised when he handed me my travel itinerary. Before flying into Khartoum, I was going to Tel Aviv. This mission, Kerouac told me, would require the sort of specialized preparation that a combatant couldn't get in Europe.

Once in Israel, I had a round of meetings with some serious-looking fellows from Caesarea's operations department. My mission to Khartoum had several objectives. First, I was to collect intelligence on the Iranian embassy in Khartoum. Second, I was to survey the environs of the city in search of a landing area for Israeli Special Forces troops. Third, I was to study a neighbourhood where most of the world's Islamic terrorist organizations kept their offices. As I learned, Hamas, Hezbollah, the Egyptian al-Gama'at al-Islamiyya (also known as Islamic Group, or IG), and the Algerian Armed Islamic Group (also known as the GIA) all operated openly in Khartoum. In fact, their offices were clustered together within a few blocks of one another – a sort of one-stop shop for mass murder.

Khartoum is more than fifteen hundred kilometres from the southern tip of Israel. But the Israeli military had launched this sort of long-distance special forces operation before. In 1973, for instance, seaborne Israeli troops – escorted by my Mossad forebears, operating locally – assassinated members of the PLO leadership in Beirut following the Munich massacre, an operation known as "Spring of Youth." Three years later, Israeli special forces rescued 103 passengers of an Air France airliner hijacked by Palestinian and German terrorists to Entebbe Airport in Uganda. The Entebbe raid was a particularly complex operation, requiring the Israel Air Force (IAF) to transport two hundred soldiers, Jeeps, and a black Mercedes-Benz (intended to resemble Ugandan Dictator Idi Amin's vehicle of state) thirty-two hundred kilometres into the heart of Africa. That mission was a complete success, with only one Israeli soldier being killed: commander Jonathan Netanyahu, the older brother of former (and perhaps future) Israeli prime minister Benjamin Netanyahu.*

In the Ugandan operation, Israeli planes simply flew into Entebbe International Airport – albeit under cover of darkness. For a variety of reasons, that would be impossible in Khartoum, and so something less conventional than a paved tarmac would have to be used. This is why I'd been brought to Israel: to fly in a Lockheed C-130 Hercules troop transport, and learn first-hand from Israeli pilots what kind of real estate the plane needed to land and take off.

My boss for this part of my training was a Mossad veteran named Arik. He drove us out of Tel Aviv in a white Mitsubishi sedan, both of us wearing standard Israel Defense Forces combat fatigues. There were no markings on our uniforms except the IDF acronym over the breast pocket and rank badges on our epaulettes. I was designated a major, with one oak leaf, and Arik a lieutenant colonel, with two. (The oak leaves are referred to as "falafels" in the IDF. More morbidly, the three bars signifying a captain are termed "coffins.")

Arik was a tough old nut with a bald head and a nasty scar on his cheek. He looked familiar. And as we drove, it gradually dawned on me that I'd seen him once before, during my Mossad basic training. For some reason, he had come into my Tel Aviv apartment unannounced when I was still under the wing of my instructor, Oren, and, without a word of greeting or explanation, began rummaging through my wastebasket. At the time, I assumed he was checking to make sure I hadn't discarded classified material in the regular trash

---

* The IAF has also performed its share of long-distance humanitarian missions in Africa. Aside from several times bringing relief supplies to wartorn African nations, Israel's air force, assisted by Mossad agents on the ground, brought fourteen thousand members of Ethiopia's beleaguered Jewish community to Israel in the early 1990s – likely the only time in human history when whites have brought legions of blacks from one continent to another for any reason other than enslavement.

but had disposed of it in the burn bag, as required. But neither he nor anyone else ever said a word about it to me one way or another, and so I'd always remained mystified by his odd cameo appearance.

After we arrived at the base, Arik and I were introduced to two pilots, Ayal and Ronny. They were your typical Israeli air force types: young, tanned, fit, good-looking, confident, with matching Ray-Ban sunglasses and smiles. In Israel, pilots are seen as the crème de la crème of the military. It's unfair, but true: the pilots get all the girls. Wings are the ultimate chick-magnet.

Ayal and Ronny got us strapped into a C-130 Hercules, then put on an amazing demonstration of the craft's flying abilities. With its four propeller engines and massive cargo capacity, the C-130 is a far cry from a fighter jet. Among Israeli military types, in fact, it is known as *Karnaf*, which means rhinoceros. But in these pilots' hands, it seemed quick and nimble. (I'd actually flown in C-130s plenty of times in the Canadian army – under more conventional flying conditions. But I kept my mouth shut about that because, even among fellow Israelis, Mossad agents are never supposed to volunteer gratuitous background information about their own lives.) They flew the plane low, under the radar line, giving us an exhilarating ride. Though the pair never identified their unit, it was clear from their flying style that they were part of the elite corps of pilots who work with Israel's special forces and Caesarea units on long-range covert operations.

Fortunately, I got a seat in the cockpit. From experience, I was glad not to be seated in the Hercules' large cargo "seating" area within the fuselage, which consists of nothing more than a mass of thick netting. Travelling long distances requires you to sit hunched over for hours at a time, practically in the lap of the soldier beside you. You can't really sleep, and you can't converse because your words are drowned out by the noise and vibrations.

After wowing us with their flying skills, Ayal and Ronny briefed me on the plane's technical specs. The most important of these, for my purposes, were the minimum dimensions of a tactical landing strip that could accommodate the plane: about sixteen hundred metres long and twenty metres wide. To help me appreciate what a patch of barren turf that size looks like, they turned south and flew Arik and me deep into the Negev Desert.

After an hour's flight, we flew over a ridge and then the aircraft banked. I held tight and we descended hard onto a flat plain in the desert valley. Once the wheels hit the ground, we decelerated rapidly. Then the pilots spun the plane around, kicking up a small dust storm in the process. For my benefit, everything was being done to mimic the methods used in a real covert ops fly-in.

Once the plane stopped moving, the back ramp opened. Ronny told Arik and me to get out and sprint away from the landing area. As we scrambled off, the plane accelerated toward the other end of the runway. The noise from its engines and prop wash was deafening. Within seconds, the *Karnaf* was airborne again. As Arik and I waited for the aircraft to return, we walked the length of the landing strip and I paced off the distance.

The plane came back after twenty minutes and we hopped on board. In no time, we were already starting to ascend for the short flight back to base. (With Israel being so small, in-country flights never take long.) We had a mission debrief and then retired for an excellent air force lunch. With my training now complete, my next stop was Sudan.

As I walked down onto the Khartoum airport tarmac a week later, I was hit with a blast of hot air that seemed instantly to turn my hair into straw. I prayed that the air conditioning at the hotel wouldn't be on the fritz. I also hoped the car I'd rented would have enough gas to get me there. Despite Sudan's cozy relationship with oil-rich Iran, the country was then suffering from a shortage of refined gasoline.

In fact, Sudan seemed to be suffering from a shortage of just about everything – except AK-47s and the skinny, vacant-eyed young men who held them. Even around the capital city, many of the roads were little more than windswept tracks of reddish-brown dirt and sand. The heat was so oppressive, the human landscape so destitute, that the city's poor shantytowns carried an almost apocalyptic quality – as if the surrounding desert, sensing the misery of Khartoum's residents, were seeking to close itself around this failed human experiment and return the land to its natural state.

I arrived at the hotel and cleaned up using the trickle of water I could coax from the shower head. Then I called HQ's Europe-based answering service and let them know that I was okay. (The telephone system wasn't as bad as I'd expected.) There are only two decent hotels in Khartoum, and I was lucky to be in one of them. Despite the third world atmosphere, it wasn't cheap – about eighty dollars a night, which is more money than your average Sudanese wage earner sees in a month.

I had a meeting with a local businessman named Mustafa, a contact I'd cultivated through my commercial front operation in Europe. In Sudan, I couldn't rely on my usual cover as an international shipping broker looking to close a deal. Private business opportunities for foreign companies are simply too scarce in Sudan to make the ruse credible. And so I'd told Mustafa and his country's visa-issuing authorities that I was actually on my way to Kenya, and merely sought to visit Sudan en route to evaluate the country's business climate in general. (To support the tale, I flew on to Nairobi from Khartoum – a scary trip that involved the same sort of white-knuckle flying that I experienced with Ayal and Ronny over the Negev Desert. I hope never again to fly on Kenya Airways.)

Mustafa was a lot of help. Without any apparent concern for the position of his car's fuel gauge, he gave me a driving tour of Khartoum. He also took me to Omdurman, a suburb on the western side of the Nile that contains the tomb of Muhammad Ahmad, a legendary Sudanese Islamist who led a revolt against Ottoman and British forces in the late nineteenth century. In some ways, Muhammad Ahmad was a man ahead of his time. A century before political Islam came to full bloom with Iran's Islamic Revolution and the rise of Sunni fundamentalist movements, he was holding himself out as al-Mahdi al-Muntazar, the Muslim saviour of prophecy who would create a perfect Islamic society based entirely on the teachings of the Koran. The pathetic squalor I saw in the city, not to mention the two million lives that had been lost in the country's religious civil war, bore silent testament to the inevitable endpoint of such eschatological fantasies. But Umar Hassan al-Bashir and Ahmad's other ideological progeny don't seem to have noticed.

On the way back from Omdurman, I asked Mustafa if we could stop at the Tutti-Frutti ice cream parlour in Khartoum, a well-known hangout among the few Western travellers Sudan attracts. I wanted him to take me there not because I had a craving for authentic Italian gelato, but because it provided cover to access the terrorists' bazaar that I needed to photograph. With Mustafa's help, I got a roll of great tourist shots featuring the two of us posing at various points of strategic interest with other accommodating locals.*

By now, Mustafa and I were best friends. (I guess I'd learned a thing or two from watching Charles.) When we got back to the hotel,

---

* I'd learned during my years on the job that photography truly is a spy's best friend. And I imagine it must be an even more useful tool in this age of digital cameras. I recently purchased one for my son's birthday, and the thing was only slightly larger than a credit card. Yet the photos were just as good as those I took with my clunky film camera. It's the sort of gadget I really could have used in Khartoum – and a hundred other places.

I insisted on giving him some U.S. currency for the gas he used, and he thanked me profusely. I extended a sincere invitation for him to visit me in Europe, where I promised to show him a good time. (During my time as a combatant, my conscience would occasionally bother me about the way I would deceive people like Mustafa for my own purposes, and I looked for ways to help them out when I could.)

The next day, I picked up my rental car – with a full gas tank, I was happy to observe – and set out to a tourist-spot cover point close to the possible landing zones HQ, Kerouac, and I had identified on the maps before my departure. The key to the planned operation would be picking a spot that was far enough out of town not to arouse the interest of locals, yet close enough so that a force of special operations soldiers could get in and out of the city quickly without having to drive for miles.

Within a few hours, I was able to inspect a variety of potential landing strips. Using the low-tech but relatively accurate means of my car's odometer, I marked out their coordinates on my map. They were every bit as smooth and flat as the makeshift runway I'd seen days earlier in the Negev. Ayal and Ronny would have been proud.

The next morning, I held meetings at my hotel with a few local contacts I'd managed to meet through Mustafa. In order to make it plain to any observers that I was actively engaged in commercial pursuits, I conducted these in the lobby. As I drank coffee with businessmen, I was able to make a casual survey of the hotel's clientele – an interesting mix of NGO representatives, diplomats, foreign teachers, and journalists, many of them presumably waiting on permits to travel to the parts of the country that Sudan doesn't want appearing on the nightly news.

Then it was on to the last phase of my intelligence-gathering mission: taking photos of the Iranian embassy's environs. I drove my rental car to a cover point near the Iranian embassy, then proceeded on foot. My knapsack had a mesh sleeve into which I had inserted my camera with the lens facing outwards. A remote control I carried in my pocket allowed me to snap photos without exposing the camera to public view. Such subterfuge was necessary: I remember Oren telling me that reconnaissance photography is essentially an aggressive act. Pointing and shooting a camera in the spy trade is like pointing and shooting a gun on a more conventional battlefield – it gets you noticed and brings down return fire.

I was sweating profusely, in part due to the thirty-five-degree-plus heat, in part due to nerves. The Iranian embassy would be employing any number of countermeasures against surveillance, and I was worried about getting too close. From the lobby of a nearby office building, I fired off a number of shots. After visiting the adjacent bank to ask some inane questions about the commercial finance services on offer, I exited the building, snapping photos as I walked back to my vehicle. The sweat was now pouring down my back, and I recalled another one of Oren's sage sayings: "Al rosh HaGanav bo'er HaKovah" (A hat burns only on a thief's head).

I put the pack on the roof of the vehicle facing the embassy and took more shots. Pretending to fumble with the keys in my pocket, I pressed the remote over and over, listening to the *whir-click* of the shutter. When I was finished, I put the bag in the car and drove back to the hotel, all the while checking that I was not being followed. I then headed straight for the airport to catch my flight to Nairobi. Once I'd returned safely to Europe, my reports and developed photos were on the first diplomatic pouch back to Israel.

In the end, however, nothing came of my efforts. Shortly after getting back, I learned that Prime Minister Yitzhak Rabin had scuttled the mission on the grounds that it would only provoke more Hezbollah attacks against other overseas Jewish communities. According to one theory, the Argentine bombings themselves had been acts of purported revenge. (In February 1992, a month before the Buenos Aires embassy attack, Israel's air force had decimated a Hezbollah motorcade, killing the group's secretary general, Abbas al-Mussawi. Likewise, shortly before the 1994 AMIA bombing, Israel caught and jailed top Hezbollah leader Mustafa Dirani.) Rabin concluded that a large-scale attack on Hezbollah or its Iranian paymasters would likely bring more of the same, and so called off the Sudan mission. How ironic that a prime minister so concerned with the lives of his fellow Jews, regardless of where they lived, would fall victim to a Jewish assassin a year later.

Although part of me was disappointed that the mission – like that against the *Al- Yarmouk* – had been cancelled, I recognized that such caution is the price Israelis must pay for the humanitarian ethos that informs their society and government. While killing a few terrorists and Iranian apparatchiks would help even the score on the geopolitical chessboard, eye-for-an-eye retribution ultimately cannot deter an enemy that treats innocent human lives, Muslim and Jewish alike, as expendable fodder to be slaughtered in the name of Islam's glory. Such are the frustrations of those who cast their lot with a civilized nation locked in a fight against extremism.

9 | THE ROAD TO ANKARA

Mercy but murders, pardoning those that kill.

William Shakespeare

It was one of those moments you remember as much for the music you were listening to as what you were doing. It was October 1995, a year after my trip to Khartoum, and I was driving a hardtop silver Mercedes 500SL, doing about 220 kilometres per hour on the Autobahn somewhere between Stuttgart and Munich. On this rare instance, I thought, my career truly did resemble a James Bond movie. Except I doubt Sean Connery, or even Roger Moore, would have been secure enough with their manhood to have had Depeche Mode's *Violator* in their car stereo system. I had the volume cranked up, but the roar from the engine was so loud I could barely hear David Gahan belting out "Personal Jesus."

In a special magnetic compartment under my car was stashed a container of high explosives. Had it gone off, the explosion would have left a crater in the middle of the Autobahn, and the car's fine appointments, along with my body parts, would have been strewn all over the Bavarian countryside. But I wasn't particularly worried. The Mossad's science and technology division had assured me I would have to drive the car off a cliff or into an oncoming truck to risk blowing the thing – in which case, the lethal effect of the blast would be redundant. As flying bombs go, I was fairly serene. Most people don't realize that military-grade explosives such as Semtex typically will not detonate without a smaller ignition charge from a blasting cap or detonation cord. Heat itself is not enough: you can hold a match to the stuff and it won't light up. To demonstrate that point, one of my IDF instructors had done just that in front of a group of terrified cadets.

The explosive device was earmarked for a second Mercedes heading from Germany to Syria, via a ferry from Venice to Izmir, Turkey. Kerouac didn't tell me who was driving the car; I'd guessed it was someone nasty – probably a member of Hezbollah or of a radical Palestinian outfit with a significant amount of innocent blood on his hands.

The only thing marring my glorious 007 experience was the fact that I was recovering from pneumonia. And so I had a small bottle of antibiotics in the car, which I was supposed to take once a day. I mention this boring fact not to garner pity, but because that container would play an important part in preventing what almost became one of the most colossal screw-ups of my career. To this day, I'm a big believer in fate, and that little bottle is one of the reasons why.

Under a clear, bright sky I sped southwards into Austria, then through the Brenner Pass and on into the Italian Alps. Every turn in the road brought a new postcard-quality vista. When I got to Venice, I felt disappointed. In all my life, I'd never enjoyed a driving experience so thoroughly.

I checked into a Venetian hotel across the causeway from the working-class suburb of Mestre. It was Thursday, and I was booked to sail on Saturday night aboard a Turkish Maritime Lines vessel that would arrive in Izmir early Tuesday morning. At some point during the voyage, I would have to transfer the explosives sitting under my car to the target. I wouldn't detonate the device – that was a job for my operational colleagues at Caesarea and the Israeli military. My only job was to put it in place.

Why do this at sea? There were two reasons. The first was that we didn't want to blow him up on European soil. The event would make front-page headlines across the Continent, a professional police investigation would be opened, and – who knows – the Mossad might even be implicated. Instead, we wanted the bomb to go off in a remote part of the Middle East, where exploding cars (and people) are a more common and accepted phenomenon.

The second reason was that doing the job this way meant the target car would be at my disposal in the dark bowels of a long-distance ferry, away from prying eyes, for two full days and nights. This was a lot less risky than taking my chances in the parking lot of a European office complex or apartment building.

While in Mestre, I visited a tiny family-run restaurant to meet with a representative from Mossad HQ. Neil was an unassuming, cherubic polyglot with glasses and curly brown hair. Notwithstanding his Ewok-like appearance, I knew him as a brilliant man who'd risen to high office in the Mossad after serving in just about every operational role the agency offers. After discussing our cover story for the meeting (business associates), we talked about the mission in a relatively open fashion, as combatants do when meeting in public places; we don't speak loudly so that others can hear and, given the technical nature of the job, few would understand what we are talking about anyway. Not all briefings can be conducted in safe houses, and it's quite common to meet in cafés and hotel lobbies, as they provide the needed cover for clandestine conversations.

Being a gourmand of the first order, Neil made a superb dinner companion. We ate a five-course meal with gusto, enjoying not only the fine food but the endearing sight of the owner's young children scampering underfoot. I can't remember everything we ate, but I do remember the pasta was out of this world, and that we finished off with delectable chocolate profiteroles. To this day, I think back longingly to that charming place. The French can keep their fancy cuisine – the Italians just know how to make good food.

I can't say I enjoyed every mission I received, but this one was turning out to be great. I particularly liked the fact that I was working alone, as I had in Khartoum. It was nice to get a break from Charles's hectoring presence. I would have enjoyed that fine meal a lot less if he had been there lecturing Neil and me about how we should stick to bread and water lest we disobey the rules of *kashrut*.

The next day, I did the sightseeing drill – including sipping an exorbitantly priced coffee in the Piazza San Marco among the pigeons and the tables they'd befouled. Then, decked out as a tourist, complete with gelato and camera in hand, I visited the port to collect intelligence, with a particularly keen interest in the security procedures for vehicles.

I spent a few hours checking out the embarkation area and watching cars roll onto the docked boats. Nothing I saw suggested there was any chance that a discreetly camouflaged package attached to the underside of a vehicle would be discovered by anybody. I wandered over to a bank of pay phones near the cruise-ship terminal building and called an HQ relay to let them know I was good to go. Then I returned to my hotel, went out onto the terrace, and watched the controlled chaos of gondolas and small boats plying the canals.

At night, I went out for dinner. Without Neil's culinary guidance, I stumbled on a rather less worthy restaurant. As I ate an ordinary plate of pasta on a terrace in the candlelit darkness, I noticed the waiter had deposited a side dish at my left elbow. When I held the candle to my plate, there appeared a plump, ungarnished octopus split down the middle. I lost my appetite and ordered a beer, followed by a few more.

A large table of eight Australian men in their twenties spied me drinking away and, recognizing a fellow traveller in need of company, boisterously invited me to join them. A few beers later, we all decided to embark on an ad hoc pub crawl – which is hard in Venice, since, as we discovered, the city has little night life to speak of.

Undeterred, my new Aussie mates eventually found a young Italian fellow who, in crude English, anxiously volunteered to take us to an "exciting" bar. We walked on the Venetian cobblestones until our feet ached. Finally, when we were all about to throw in the drinking towel, we tumbled into a gloomy, darkly lit subterranean lair. As we sat down and ordered a round, something just didn't feel right to me. I started casing the place out carefully – or as carefully as I could given my state of inebriation – and then I put my finger on it: the complete absence of women. We were in a Venetian gay bar. More amused than annoyed, I calmly described the situation to my rather more drunken Aussie friends, at which point one of them stood up and shouted, "Crikey, we're in a fucking poofter bar!"

The clientele may not have understood the Australian idiom, but they got its insulting gist. And these weren't the effeminate hairdresser types of stereotype. Whatever their sexual orientation, they looked beefy and angry enough to put us in hospital. Without further ado, I grabbed my new mates and we headed for the exit. I didn't want my family to read in the papers back home that the person whom they knew to be a married, heterosexual Jew had died under unexplained circumstances in a Venetian gay bar with a group of drunken Australian tourists.

I eventually made my way back to my hotel, fell into bed, and woke up the next morning with a whopping hangover. Groggily, I began my preparations for that evening's trip.

A few hours before the ship's scheduled departure, I parked my car just outside the embarkation area, and waited. Eventually, I saw the big Mercedes 560SEL with the licence plate number I'd memorized. As it passed, I got only a brief glimpse of the driver in silhouette. There were no passengers. This was a relief: I don't know what I would have done if this anonymous bad guy had been travelling with his kids in the back seat.

The toughest question, of course, is how I would have reacted had my quarry been travelling with passengers. I would have had two options. The first, which is the prerogative of every combatant in the field, would have been to abort the mission based on my own good judgment. Avi had told me on several occasions that when faced with operational dilemmas in the field, I was the commander and had to act on my own accord. I couldn't pass the buck, and while I could consult with HQ, I didn't always have the time or the means to do so.

The other option, which I would have been more inclined to adopt, would be to attach the explosive device and inform HQ of the fact that he was not alone in the car. While that may seem as though I would have been shirking the tough decision and fobbing the burden off to other shoulders, I can say with some authority that HQ probably would have scrubbed the mission and waited for a clearer (and less morally obstructed) shot at the target. Besides, who was to say that he wasn't going to drop his passengers off before heading towards Syria?

Thankfully, I didn't have to worry about that, so after one more vehicle got in line, I pulled into the embarkation lane. I wanted to ensure our cars were loaded in the same part of the ship's vehicle hold. That way, a purported desire to access my own vehicle would give me a pretext for snooping around his.

It took a while to get each car onto the ship, and by the time I had parked mine, the driver of the 560SEL was gone. But this fact didn't affect my mission one way or the other: I was after the car, not him.

After locking up, I ascended to my assigned first-class cabin. Upon entering, I realized that "first class" doesn't have the same meaning on a Turkish ferry as on, say, a Western cruise line. My rudimentary cabin carried the distinct scent of body odour – not the mild I've-just-been-to-the-gym-for-a-quick-workout kind, but the sort that takes weeks of shower-free living to accumulate. The next morning, I realized the scent emanated from the moustachioed, beefy Turk who cleaned my room. Onur, as he introduced himself, was the nicest man, and had a huge smile, but he must never have encountered a deodorant stick in his life, the poor fellow. I kept my cabin windows open for the duration of the trip.

It was after stowing my gear and heading up to the dining room that I spotted her: a woman with the kind of body that Raymond Chandler would describe as "hard-boiled and full of sin," with long black hair arranged in cornrows and emerald-green eyes. She caught my attention not only because she was beautiful but because she seemed to be the only other Westerner on the ship. In that corner of my brain reserved for paranoid thoughts – which it was my duty as a spy to consult, and occasionally obey – something about her struck me as suspicious. In an improbable reverie, I imagined that this might be some temptress out to foil my plot.

The next day, as I was sitting at the back of the boat drinking a beer and taking some photos of the Adriatic off the boot of Italy, she approached me and introduced herself. Her name was Ute and she was twenty-two years old. She had a strong German accent, which instantly made me think of the TV show *Hogan's Heroes*.

When she asked me why I was going to Turkey, I replied cautiously, "I have some business there." As usual, my cover for the operation involved meetings arranged under the auspices of my Europe-based import-export operation.

"*Ach, zo.* I am on my way to Iraq to make photograph of Kurds."

My eyes widened, and I blurted out, "Alone?" Although Turkey's main tourists spots are reasonably safe for foreign travellers, the same isn't true of the more backward southeastern regions, where the country's Kurdish minority is concentrated. For years, many Kurds had been in a state of quasi-rebellion against Ankara's assimilationist policies. (Until 1991, the use of the Kurdish language was illegal.) During the previous decade, in fact, more than twenty thousand people had been killed in a terrorist war conducted by the Kurdistan Workers Party (PKK), then led by Abdullah Öcalan. If you didn't know what you were doing, travelling to the region in those days was a lot like going to Afghanistan, Chechnya, or Colombia today.

"Why? You want to join me?"

"No thanks," I replied quickly. "I don't think it's safe."

Her gaze lingered on me, and I felt unnerved. "Don't worry," she said. "I have some Kurdish friends who are taking me with them." Ute then explained how she'd fallen in with a clutch of activists in Germany, which has a large, politically active Kurdish population. At the time, the Kurds were desperate to get the same sort of publicity for their cause as the Palestinians had long enjoyed. This naive young documentary film-maker must have struck them as a perfect mark.

She then produced a bag and showed me her equipment. I knew enough about photography to recognize it as a serious kit. This was a safe topic for conversation, I thought. And so we sat and talked about cameras for a while, each of us snapping shots off the stern. My hope was that she'd eventually get bored and drift away, allowing me to go below deck and take a closer look at my friend's

Mercedes. Unfortunately, her flirtation persisted. The experience was more unnerving than flattering. I'm no Elephant Man, but I wasn't used to this kind of attention from an attractive woman.

My cover identity was that of a single man, so I wasn't able to shoo Ute away with a wedding ring, as most married people do when they're subject to unwanted come-ons. Eventually, I simply excused myself and got up. When she started to follow suit, I told her I needed a little nap, as I was still battling the after-effects of a hangover (this was no lie). She began to pout as I walked away, and I wondered whether it wouldn't have been better for me to pretend I didn't speak English from the get-go. Whatever she had in mind seemed likely to conflict not only with my marital vows, but the job I had to do.

Unfortunately, that job was going to be harder than I expected. Once I got down to the car deck, I discovered something the operational planners hadn't considered: there was a padlock the size of my fist on the doorway. Like me, the people at Mossad HQ had assumed that, as on most ferries, passengers had free access to their cars. For whatever reason, that wasn't the case on this boat. I felt like an idiot for not having foreseen this contingency. Over the next two days, I would have to find a way to get past that padlock.

That evening featured another odd encounter with Ute. As I passed the boat's modest bar on my way back from dinner, I saw her hanging around with a clutch of Kurdish friends, listening to tacky Dutch disco music. I declined Ute's invitation to dance but, to be polite, I hung around and spoke with her friends, who did their best to educate me about their two favourite subjects: the plight of Kurds in Turkey and the need for Western countries to accept more Kurds as political refugees.

While listening to the conversation, my curiosity was piqued by the presence of an outsider: a Turkish woman in modern Western dress who, according to Ute, had made a point of tagging along with the group since they'd boarded the ship. As Ute's friends briefed me on the plight of the Kurds, this new addition followed the dialogue with what seemed to be unnatural interest.

It was after I returned to my reeking cabin that my malodorous cabin steward stopped by my room to offer a warning. "That German girl, she is watch by secret police," he whispered with somewhat boozy breath. He spoke to me in English, but he used the Turkish name "İstihbarat" to describe the agents – a clear reference to Turkey's feared national intelligence organization Millî İstihbarat Teşkilatı (MIT). At the time, the PKK was active in Germany, so the MIT was doing its best to infiltrate Kurdish activist groups there. No doubt, this is how they stumbled on Ute's little fact-finding mission.

I asked Onur how he knew this, and he answered, "Kapitan tell me." If the information was true – and I could think of no reason for either Onur or the captain to invent such a tale – it was a worrying development. While I was neither Kurdish nor of any particular interest to the Turks, the fact that Ute had spoken with me at length made me a potential source of interest to the İstihbarat. And I did not need a set of eyes watching my movements, Turkish or otherwise.

After Onur left, I started concentrating on my primary concern: getting onto the car deck. Picking the lock wasn't an option – I had no idea how to do that sort of thing. Nor did I have access to bolt cutters, or any other heavy tools that would allow me to destroy the lock. Even if I did, using brute force wouldn't be smart. It would turn the boat into a crime scene, and thereby invite all sorts of unwanted scrutiny. I was mortified at the thought of calling HQ and telling them a simple padlock had prevented me from performing my mission. Then, fate intervened – and in the most banal form imaginable: I coughed. With that, a plan germinated in my mind for how I would get past that damned lock.

Early the next morning, I wove my way around the prostrate

Muslims at prayer in the stairwells and corridors, and sought out the ship's chief steward. He was a crisply dressed and affable man with a wide smile and, like most of the men I met on the ship, a thick black moustache.

"Excuse me, sir," I said, knocking on his office door. "I'm wondering if you can help me."

"What can I do for you, young man?" he replied in perfect English. Something about our exchange reminded me of the sort of model dialogues that appear at the beginning of English-as-a-second-language textbooks.

"I seem to have left my chest medicine in my car. If I don't take it, I could get quite ill." I tried to look contrite and desperate.

"I don't have the authority to open the car deck. Only the captain does."

"Oh, goodness. Do you think we could go see him?"

"He's very busy."

"I wouldn't bother either of you if this were not a serious matter."

"Very well. Follow me to the bridge."

The captain turned out to be a short balding man with a greying moustache and a white uniform. He looked like the responsible type – hardly the sort who would blurt out sensitive intelligence information about passengers to the custodial crew. Perhaps he'd had a few too many the night before and spoken out of class. He exchanged words with the chief steward in Turkish and then looked at me in a way that said, "So, what's your story?" I promptly repeated my tale of woe.

He spoke to the steward again, who then motioned that I should follow him out of the bridge. "You can go, but a crew member will have to accompany you," he told me as we retraced our footsteps.

"Great, thank you so much," I replied. It was false gratitude. How was I expected to attach a bomb with a Turkish sailor watching over my shoulder?

When we returned to his office, the steward summoned a crewman and gave him a key, along with a brief set of instructions in Turkish. This friendly young fellow then led me to the car deck, opened the padlock, and pulled back the big steel bulkhead door.

"I'll be right back," I said. As I spoke these words, I looked him in the eye and motioned to him to remain where he was. To my surprise and glee, he obeyed, standing smiling by the door as I wove my way in between the closely packed vehicles en route to my car.

I opened the car door and grabbed the pills sitting on the console next to the shift – yes, I had actually forgotten them there. Then, in case my crewman friend happened to have his eye on me, I made a show of dropping the bottle. I bent down to retrieve it and, while doing so, wrenched the magnetic casing containing the explosive device from the underside of my car.

I looked over toward the door to see if my fumblings were arousing any suspicion. But my guardian's attention was elsewhere. Making sure I kept the explosive charge out of his line of sight, I moved toward the 560SEL, which now sat in between me and the exit. I rechecked the licence plate number, just to be certain, and repeated my bottle-dropping ruse. I then knelt down and attached the magnetic device.

As I walked over to the door, I held up the antibiotics for the crewman to see. Motioning to my chest, I said, "I really need these! Teşekkür, teşekkür." He smiled at my thank-yous, apparently pleased to be of service.

Later, at dusk, the ship passed through the Corinth Canal with what seemed to be only a metre or so of space to spare on either side. From the banks, Greek soldiers glared, making no pains to hide their animosity for the Turkish crew, their ship, and their passengers. (Turkish ships actually had to lower the flag when sailing this canal.)

As I snapped photos of these scowling sentries, Ute sidled up and took my arm. In somewhat brusque fashion, I told her I had a dinner engagement, and walked off. I didn't want to be rude; too much had gone my way for me to blow it over a show of good manners to a flirtatious romantic. I took some food to my cabin and went to bed early.

Just after dawn the next morning, we pulled into a drizzly, foggy Izmir. The cars drove off the car deck in the reverse order that they entered. After pulling off and clearing customs, I watched my quarry do likewise. While I was waiting, I went to the nearest pay phone and reported in code that everything was a "go." It struck me then that I never really got a good look at the man whose life I might have just helped terminate. It was just as well, I suppose. For all I know, I passed him a dozen times in the ship. My ignorance ensured I never betrayed any sign of recognition.

Ute and her Kurdish friends drove off in a two-car convoy led by a dusty gold BMW 5 Series. As she passed, she smiled and waved at me. Evidently, there were no hard feelings. From her carefree manner, it seemed she had no idea she was being tailed. I only hope she didn't end up in a Turkish jail.

After dropping the car off with a local Mossad agent (alas, it was agency property), I typed out my reports in a hotel and caught a flight back to Europe, where I spent a lovely holiday with my family at Euro Disney in Paris. When I got back to work, one of my colleagues informed me that my target had detonated somewhere on a lonely stretch of highway in Kurdish bandit country near the Syrian border.

Overall, my mission at sea ranks as one of the high points in my tenure as a Mossad combatant. It was truly an adventure from start to finish and seemed to have all the plot and characters of a novel. It ran for about five weeks and was a complete success. Finally, one of my set-up operations resulted in someone actually pulling the trigger.

10 | DANGEROUS LIAISONS

A desk is a dangerous place from which to view the world.

John le Carré

Despite triumphs such as my mission in Turkey, life on the road was beginning to wear on me. Like many fathers whose jobs take them away from home for long stretches, I was beginning to wonder whether it wouldn't be better to opt for a more stable nine-to-five gig.

By now, I had put in almost seven years as a combatant. If you included my military service, my studies, and the Mossad training period, I hadn't been a full-time father and husband for a decade. I was starting to show signs of what we call in Hebrew *shchika* – emotional wear and tear from living in lonely isolation. And although my family enjoyed France and my weekend visits, they were anxious to return to their home in Israel.

I needed a change and wanted to leave Caesarea for a different job in the Mossad. My personal ennui had begun to affect my professional attitude. I was frustrated at Charles's petty manipulations and

Doron's surrender to his every whim and demand. The stress was such that I began lashing out in inappropriate ways. One telling incident occurred in Brussels, when I was boarding a crowded TGV train. A Frenchman pushed in front of me, and I became so enraged that I grabbed his wrist from behind and twisted it around over my head until he howled in pain. I knew then that I'd better make changes to my life, or I'd end up doing something that would get me into real trouble.

But I was faced with a dilemma. The usual career path for Mossad combatants returning to Israel was to become instructors for new recruits within Caesarea. This didn't appeal to me: I'd witnessed during my own training in Tel Aviv that instructors were called upon to work hours that were just as long and unpredictable as those of overseas combatants. Moreover, I felt that becoming an instructor wouldn't supply me with the real lifestyle change I needed. I wanted to throw myself into a field that was as far as possible from what I'd been doing in Europe.

There was another reason to avoid continuing my work with Caesarea: Charles.

Like me, Charles grew tired of life as a combatant. In 1996, he informed me that he was heading back to Israel to become an instructor. I knew that following his lead likely would mean we'd keep working together, and I had no appetite for a reprise of the friction and workplace irritations I'd endured over the last seven years.

As it turned out, Charles spent only a few months instructing combatants in training before taking on a role for which he was far better suited. He became a case officer in the Mossad division Tsomet, where he was responsible for recruiting "human intelligence sources" (moles and snitches) in foreign lands. Within a few years, Charles was Tsomet's golden boy – the top case officer in the Mossad, according to one of my well-informed colleagues. Thanks to their experience, former Mossad combatants typically make the best Tsomet case officers. Combatants interact with Arabs and Iranians all the time during the course of their tenure in the field and, in so doing, gain an insight into the mindset of potential human intelligence sources.

On one occasion, a few years after I had returned to Israel, Charles and I found ourselves on the same flight to Bangkok. I was on my way to meet up with some contacts in Southeast Asia, and Charles was on his way to recruit a high-level source with close links to the leadership of a nasty Middle Eastern regime. I was travelling economy class, as per the Mossad's travel protocols, but Charles was in business class. True to form, he somehow had convinced his superiors that he needed this to arrive well rested for his meeting.

It occurred to me that the travel arrangements provided a fitting metaphor for the nature of our relationship. But by this time it didn't bother me: I'd achieved what pop psychologists call "closure." I knew that, for all his professional success, Charles's overbearing, bullying manner was merely the flipside of a conflicted, insecure personality. For that reason, I wouldn't have traded places with him for all the falafel in Israel.

I would run into Charles at other times over the course of my career, and with each encounter my anger mellowed. Despite all our bickering, we'd done some important work together in the field. In fact, many people in HQ told us separately that in the early and mid-1990s we were considered the best operational team in the field. I like to think that while Charles had a hard time expressing his gratitude, he was nevertheless thankful for our pairing. I know I was. Whatever Charles's personal faults, his service to Israel was monumental. And I was always glad to know that he was on our side.

My opportunity for a new career within the Office came in 1996, a year after my trip to Turkey. This job would not only allow me to see a whole new side of the Mossad, but also give me an inside look at its much larger American cousin, the Central Intelligence Agency. The man who got me in was none other than Avi, who'd recently been transferred from head of Caesarea to the top job at Tevel, the liaison and special political operations division.*

Tevel is Hebrew for "world," and it aptly describes the division's responsibilities. Like other Western nations, Israel freely shares all but its most sensitive intelligence with allies around the globe. Tevel's job was to make sure the information flowed in a free and timely fashion. Apart from intelligence sharing, the division's most important jobs are to develop joint projects targeting terrorist groups and rogue regimes, and to provide a *karit-raka,* or "soft landing," should any of the Mossad's operatives get in trouble while on unilateral operations (also called "blue and white" operations, in reference to Israel's flag) in a friendly country.

In such cases, the objective is to extricate the agent in as discreet a manner as possible. But sometimes, despite everyone's best efforts, fate has other plans. For instance, when a Mossad operative was caught bugging a Hezbollah terrorist's apartment in Berne, Switzerland, in 1998, the Swiss intelligence service did its best to sweep the matter under the rug and released the officer. Ironically, the Israeli media blew the lid off the story and the Swiss government had no alternative but to launch a criminal investigation.

Tevel also acts as a sort of "shadow" foreign ministry by maintaining covert quasi-diplomatic relations with the governments of nations normally considered hostile to Israel, such as Indonesia and the Arab Gulf countries. It also maintains relations with stateless groups, such as the Kurds in northern Iraq.

---

* This sort of horizontal movement was common in the Mossad. The only other career steps available to division chiefs in the agency's narrow hierarchical pyramid were the top job of director general or retirement to the private sector. Avi wasn't around long at Tevel. Shortly after bringing me on, he retired after being passed over for the DG's job.

Finally, Tevel arranges training courses and seminars to allied services on subjects of Israeli expertise, such as dealing with Islamist terror. India, in particular, has benefited enormously from the counterterrorism training it has received through Tevel. This should not be surprising; from a security point of view, Kashmir resembles nothing so much as a giant West Bank.

When I began work at Tevel, I got a lucky break. Because of my English-language fluency and Canadian background, I was seen as a good fit for the North American department, a plum assignment that would allow me to work on Tevel's most critical liaison relationship – that between the Mossad and the CIA. My mandate was to maintain the bilateral intelligence exchange on counterterrorism issues with my American counterparts and to develop joint operations on terrorist targets of mutual interest. I also had to cultivate good interpersonal working relationships with my CIA and FBI colleagues as a means to ensuring that things ran smoothly.

When I showed up for work in the fall of 1996, a six-foot-six-inch giant named Guy was assigned to show me the ropes. His job was similar to mine, except he managed the Mossad's counter-proliferation liaison relationship with the CIA.

Like most of the new colleagues I was now meeting, Guy didn't know what I had been up to before joining HQ. And I liked it that way. I saw my job at Tevel as an opportunity to leave behind the petty annoyances and rivalries of my previous role and make a fresh start in a new environment.

By the time I got the job, my family already had been living in France for five years. Uprooting them to a Tel Aviv suburb did not make for an easy transition. The kids – now ages twelve and six – were leaving behind friends and entering an entirely different education system. Dahlia had a serious lifestyle change to deal with, as well: I no longer had the enhanced pay and perks that went with an overseas assignment, so she had to look for a job.

It is worth saying a word here about the economics of intelligence work. In the Mossad, as in every intelligence agency, most experienced agents prefer to work on home soil. As a result, agencies have to provide large financial and professional incentives for serving overseas. This means, for instance, that combatants are credited triple value for years worked abroad when their pension entitlement is calculated.

The flipside is that domestic desk jobs typically pay poorly, because there is an overabundance of qualified individuals willing to staff them. In the households of many of my Tel Aviv colleagues, the non-Mossad spouse was the primary breadwinner. (This was certainly true of my wife, who got a plum job in Israel's booming tech sector.)

Ex-combatants such as myself are relatively rare at Mossad HQ. Having been at the sharp end of the Mossad's operational work overseas, they are treated with deference. There are also a few formal perks – such as receiving tenure within a year, as opposed to three years for other Mossad staff. On the other hand, ex-combatants are outsiders: most are foreign born, and all are novices at navigating the bureaucracy that their colleagues have spent years mastering. Overall, I was happy to be back in Tel Aviv, but there were many times I asked myself why I'd willingly gone from being a well-paid master of my domain to a mid-level civil servant fighting the morning traffic jams.

I was now what is known as a deskman and, despite the cut in pay and different occupational dynamic, I was working in one of the plummiest jobs in the Mossad. It was both fascinating and exhausting to bring myself up to speed on the workings of this unique component of the Office. I came from an operational culture that was compartmentalized from the HQ way of working and I now had to learn everything as fast as I humanly could. I started with my new place of work. I found that the responsibilities within Tevel were divided up on a regional basis. The various departments included Far East, Western Europe "A" (northern Europe, including Germany, France, and the U.K.), Western Europe "B" (southern Europe, including Italy, Spain, and Greece), Eastern Europe, North America, Africa, Latin America (since absorbed into the North America department, which is now called The Americas), and another department that maintains covert intelligence ties with Muslim countries. Ill-informed Mossad staffers sometimes treated Tevel as if it were a glorified communications department. But, in fact, it brings in some seventy per cent of the intelligence the Mossad receives – a testament to the value of goodwill and mutual exchange in international relations.

In our department, the relationship with the CIA was managed through a number of channels in Tel Aviv, including face-to-face exchanges, group briefings, and memos replying to intelligence requests from each other's HQ. I worked opposite CIA officers from the agency's Counterterrorism Center (CTC), a body created in the 1980s to coordinate counterterrorist activities among various U.S. agencies. My perspective was unique, because I was the only Mossad officer doing liaison work with both the CIA and FBI. The experience taught me an enormous amount about why America – and, by extension, the entire Western world – was so unprepared for 9/11 and its aftermath.

Traditionally, the number two at the CTC is a senior FBI officer appointed as a gesture to demonstrate the good working relations between these two agencies. In reality, I learned, the CIA and FBI despise one another, and even actively thwart each other when they can get away with it.

Much of our work was dictated by the terror threat-*du-jour*, which meant I had a steady diet of interrupted sleep, all-nighters, and working weekends. My plan to ease into a predictable nine-to-five didn't quite work out as planned.

Like a fire station that sends a truck out every time someone pulls an alarm, we treated each intelligence alert as if it were the real thing. Keeping up with all the threats often meant sixteen-hour shifts. I did it because it was my job – but also because if I got lazy or screwed up, people might die as a result. Dahlia wasn't particularly impressed, however, and I didn't blame her. We'd come back to Israel on the expectation that I'd be home more often, but I was still spending a lot more time at the office than I was with my kids. And on top of everything else, I was studying at university in my spare time.

I'd invariably end up getting a phone call in the wee hours of the morning from the Office's communications centre, which operates 24/7, telling me that we had received information from one of our sources about an imminent attack on an Israeli and/or U.S. target somewhere in the world. Many times, the threats I was dealing with seemed real. Other times, I was quite sure they were bogus. The problem was that both the United States and Israel had a policy of putting their entire security and intelligence forces on alert just about every time a guy named Ahmed or Mohammed walked into an embassy asking for money in exchange for vague details about a massive attack supposedly in the works. With the rise of global terrorism, such frauds have become something of a cottage industry.

I'd have to drive into work and read the source report given to me by another sleep-deprived soul from the Mossad's counter-terrorism department. Together we'd assess the information and simultaneously request permission to pass the details on to my colleagues in the CIA. We always managed to get the information released because no one was prepared to withhold information to another service when their citizens were at risk.

I'd then put together a paraphrased memo, fax it over to my American colleague on the secure link, and wait for their million questions, which I couldn't answer because all we knew was what was in the memo. The device we used for encrypted communications was known as the STU, which is a special telephone and fax device that, with the push of a button, switches to a secure mode that ensures any eavesdropper will hear nothing but digitized gibberish. (A secondary, somewhat comical effect is that the decrypted voices come across on the other end as if they were emitted by chipmunks with a speech impediment.) In modern STU systems, a unique encryption code is generated electronically every time a secure call is made. But our 1998-era apparatus used a clunkier protocol, whereby the same code was used for a month, and then changed manually (by me, as it happens) when we received the new code from the Agency.

I mention the STU not just because it's an interesting piece of technology, but because it exemplifies the way the Mossad and the CIA work together. The equipment, which belongs to the CIA, is kept at Mossad HQ in a locked, soundproof room, specially constructed by our science and technology division. The phone itself is sealed by the CIA with special holographic stickers to prevent our opening it. This odd arrangement serves as a metaphor for the relationship between the two intelligence services: intimate and co-operative – to a point. The CIA, having been penetrated by Soviet moles, has some serious trust issues when it comes to outsiders.

The other main liaison channel was through our station in Washington. Our officers would meet with their CIA counterparts at Langley, Virginia, and perform the same function as the CIA station representatives did in Tel Aviv. Maintaining an office in Washington was important, as it allowed us to have a presence close to America's primary power circles. But it also caused a turf war with the Mossad's Tel Aviv station, since both offices wanted the relationship with the

Americans managed on their end. The winner of such battles was often decided, indirectly, by the Americans. If the CIA's Tel Aviv chief of station was a powerful appointee, as Stan Moskowitz was under Bill Clinton, then our Washington office pulled the short straw.

Aside from Uri (our volcanic department head), his deputy, Guy, and Lucinda, an English girl who had served eleven years in Caesarea before joining Tevel, there were three other members of our department. We all shared Uri's secretary, and we had access to a departmental translator for translating documents from Hebrew into English. That was the extent of our manpower, which explained why our department was by far the hardest working in the division.

Uri was your classic powder-keg type. Every issue was handled as if it were a major crisis. He had never served on the operational side of the fence but had instead risen through the ranks in the liaison division. He had previously done a stint in Washington as number two of a three-person Mossad station and had a good feel for the Americans. His favourite expression was "This is a carnival of insanity!" which was so weird that it always made me laugh.

He had his critics within the department, but Uri was highly intelligent, and led by example as one of the hardest working individuals I'd ever met. He also was forced to work under immense pressures. Both the Mossad director general and the division head had him at their beck and call whenever they needed information the United States might find valuable. Because of the enormous importance of the CIA–Mossad relationship to U.S–Israel relations in general, he was even faced with urgent requests passed down directly from the prime minister's office. Finally, he also had to contend with Stan Moskowitz, a self-important Beltway climber who drove around Tel Aviv in the back seat of a white Mercedes sedan. There was no love lost between the two men. And the mere mention of Moskowitz's name usually was followed by some malediction uttered by Uri.

Moskowitz was a Jew from the Bronx. But odd though it may seem, Israelis do not cheer when a Jewish person is appointed to a top job like chief of station Tel Aviv. There's always a feeling that the Jewish appointee might need to overcompensate to dispel any doubts about his or her loyalty to the United States. We'd seen it many times: being a badass to the Israelis was presented as evidence of being a fair broker.

The number two at the CIA station was a very personable and hard-working case officer named Mike who did all the real administration tasks. I liked Mike, an athletic, fifty-something former marine officer who'd become a successful case officer in Africa (and elsewhere) in the Agency's clandestine service. He looked about thirty-five years old, and I often told him that his portrait was aging in someone's attic. The moment I met him at Mossad HQ in 1996, I could tell he was from the operational side of the fence, and he knew the same of me. We both regarded our respective HQs' bureaucracy and power plays with the eyeball-rolling disdain that all field men share.

There was also Pete, an old boy from Oklahoma who had served with the CIA during the Vietnam era. He was full of down-home sayings like "It's colder than a well digger's ass." When he got together with Roscoe, the station's admin officer, they sounded like characters from a *Hee Haw* sketch.

When I started off at Tevel, I was sharing an office with Guy. But soon after I started, he moved upstairs a floor to take over the nuclear weapons branch of the counter-proliferation department, and was replaced in the North America department by Danny, a newly minted twenty-something graduate of the Mossad's case officer course. He'd come to Israel from the United States with his family in the mid-1980s, and had also spent some of his adult years in east Asia.

During the few slow days at the office, Danny and I had a lot of laughs at the expense of our colleagues. He was a good mimic, and his riffs would often set the two of us off on impromptu sketch comedy. "Pete and Roscoe" skits were always our favourites, as in:

Me: *"Pete, this is Roscoe, I got a dog over here foamin' at the mouth, can you come over and shoot it?"*

Danny: *"Hey, good buddy, I'd love to, but I got me some black ops in Laos that need my attention."*

Me: *"Sheeeat! Don't you know that our little war with the VC is over and Charlie done kicked our asses?"*

Every year on the Fourth of July, our CIA colleagues would invite members of Tevel's North America department to the U.S. ambassador's party at his seaside residence on the sandy cliffs of Herzliya, north of Tel Aviv. In keeping with the crudest anti-American stereotypes, the ambassador's staff would set up food stands sponsored by such worldwide culinary legends as Burger King, McDonald's and Dunkin' Donuts. Danny and I loved the stuff. One year, he and I brought garbage bags and filled them up with this valuable loot. The Marine guards laughed at us, but when I got home I was a hero with my kids, for whom the Fourth of July was synonymous with an all-you-can-eat feast of Whoppers and chocolate donuts. (They normally ate a healthy Mediterranean diet, so we didn't mind indulging them once a year.)

A few months after I joined the team, Uri decided I would also take on liaison duties with the newly opened FBI station in Tel Aviv (which was formally described as the office of the FBI's legal attaché, or "Legat" for short). Legat was manned by two FBI agents named Paul and Wayne. Like an inordinate number of FBI agents, Paul was a Mormon, and hailed from sin-filled Las Vegas. He was tall, distant, and patrician. His wife suffered from health problems, but she was a lovely and engaging woman who had mothered half a dozen sons. This was to be Paul's last posting before retirement.

His deputy, Wayne, was a Jew from Chicago, a Ph.D. who considered himself an expert on Persian and Arabic culture. He was short, bespectacled, and somewhat timid – what Yiddish-speakers would call a *nebbish*. Neither he nor Paul gave me any reason to doubt their professional competence, but in an organization like the FBI individual skills don't count for much: both men had been ground down by their agency's bureaucratic bungling and petty turf wars.

This *Odd Couple* pair were often undermined by their own HQ, which seemed to take a sadistic pleasure in keeping foreign FBI offices in the dark on key files. In many cases, key information about FBI activities in Israel would come to me through my colleagues in Washington before it would come to Wayne and Paul. Wayne, in particular, was humiliated by this treatment, and vented his anger to me with extraordinary candour. One time, he called me in such a froth that Paul had to physically wrestle the phone away from him. I felt bad for both of them. Whatever petty slights I'd endured in the Mossad, it was nothing compared to what these men had to go through. Even more bizarre was the fact that FBI HQ sometimes failed to communicate at all with its Legats and field offices. Often the Mossad officer in Washington would meet with his FBI counterpart and receive updates and memos about joint operations, meetings, and visits to take place in Israel and Washington as part of the bilateral relationship between the services. After such a meeting, he would cable me a report detailing the various topics discussed. But the FBI never bothered to tell their own Legats anything, which meant it would fall to *me* to update them about things they should have heard through their own FBI channels – including basic information like what their HQ was planning and who would be visiting from stateside. On more than one occasion, I found myself playing amateur psychologist to Legat staff members who would complain bitterly about this state of affairs.

If anything, I thought I was being given *too much* authority. In particular, I argued with Uri that the relationship with the FBI really belonged to the Israel Security Agency, our domestic security service. The ISA had been lobbying hard to have a direct relationship with the FBI independent of the Mossad, and I was sympathetic. Although the Mossad is supposed to handle all liaison with foreign intelligence services, the FBI is essentially a glorified law enforcement agency. At the time, moreover, there already was an ISA officer in Washington who was part of the Mossad's D.C. station. And by all accounts, he was managing the liaison relationship between his shop and the FBI quite well.

I also pointed out that the Mossad is a foreign intelligence service that on occasion operates in breach of other nations' sovereignty. The strait-laced Joe Friday types at the FBI were paranoid that the Mossad was trying to spy on the U.S., and putting the two agencies in liaison contact was not exactly a match made in heaven. Rogues and Boy Scouts do not mix.

Eventually, my view prevailed; the FBI file did pass over to the ISA. The only caveat was that the ISA update the Mossad on their joint goings-on. It was a fair and logical arrangement, a triumph of common sense over bureaucratic inertia and turf squabbles.

Before that happened however, the Mossad and the FBI had one last hurrah together, an operation centred around a Hezbollah agent operating in the U.S.

His code name: "Ramez."

11 | RAMEZ

It needs but one foe to breed a war, and those who have not swords can still die upon them.

J.R.R. Tolkien

Two decades before American soldiers encountered improvised explosive devices in Iraq, Hezbollah was perfecting them in southern Lebanon. Israel tried everything to detect the explosives – sniffer dogs, increased road patrols, chemical detection equipment, thermal vision cameras, drone aircraft outfitted with high-tech imaging systems, but nothing worked with much success. Having fought in Lebanon as a combat engineer, I had seen Hezbollah's handiwork up close.

The main problem is that IEDs are difficult to detect once they're covered with dirt and rock. The explosives can be detonated by remote control using an infrared beam, much like the kind emitted by television remote controls. But the explosive device itself is electro-magnetically passive: it does not send out any telltale radio-wave signal or heat signature. Couple that with sophisticated camouflage disguising the dug-up IED pit – in some cases, featuring synthetic rocks and vegetation worthy of a film set – and detection is almost impossible. For all its technological prowess, Israel never learned how to defeat the IED scourge. During the July 2006 fighting between the two sides in southern Lebanon, Hezbollah demonstrated that even Israel's most powerful tank, the Merkava, can be destroyed with such devices.

The man most responsible for developing this deadly weapon was Hassan Hilu Laqis, a shadowy explosives expert who operates as Hezbollah's chief procurement officer. Laqis did more than any other individual to precipitate Israel's withdrawal from Lebanon in May 2000 – the only time in the Jewish state's history that an Arab force had pushed Israel off a contested piece of real estate. The campaign is now remembered as one of the most frustrating chapters in Israel's military history. Prior to that, the IDF mostly had fought the conventional military armies of neighbouring Arab countries, but IEDs took the battle to a new level.

Although my main job at Tevel involved liaison work with the CIA and FBI, I remained engaged in Israel's efforts to confront Hezbollah's bomb makers through my participation in an Israeli intelligence community interservice forum on terrorist explosives and weaponry. The body included representatives from the police demolitions laboratory, the ISA's science and technology division, the Mossad, and a major named Gadi from the IDF's special explosive ordinance disposal (EOD) unit, which was known by its acronym, Yachsap.

In some cases, my explosives expertise overlapped with my liaison duties. In 1997, for instance, shortly after my transfer to Tevel, the CIA station in Tel Aviv brought a specialist over from Langley named Roger to help us in our efforts to dispose of TATP we'd seized from the Palestinians. TATP, or triacetone triperoxide, is a highly volatile and powerful compound that is relatively easy to produce from ace-tone (paint thinners), hydrogen peroxide (antiseptic or bleach), and dilute sulphuric acid (drain cleaner) – ingredients readily obtainable from hardware stores and pharmacies. Known by terrorists as *Mother of Satan* (due to its lethality and instability), TATP can be set off by a spark or a bump, with devastating results. Five years later, when I heard that al-Qaeda shoe bomber Richard Reid was trying to light a chunk of plastic explosives with a triacetone triperoxide detonator on board an airplane, I was horrified to think how close those passengers had come to death.

Roger wasn't a spook like Pete and myself. He came across more as an outdoorsy, professorial type, the sort of young palaeontologist I imagine you'd find hovering around a dinosaur dig in Montana. From the way he talked about explosives and bombs, it was obvious he had a real interest in the subject. During his visit, I offered to show him and some of the CIA's Tel Aviv personnel, including Roger and Pete, the EOD's bomb museum at the Sirkin army base.

Few countries can lay claim to Israel's level of expertise on the subject of explosives: the Jewish state has been attacked by just about every combustible substance known to man. Roger examined the unit's "museum of contemporary explosives" as if he were a kid in a candy store. Pete was fascinated too, but for a different reason: the old-school devices reminded him of the ones he'd seen in Vietnam during his stint there with the Agency.

Gadi gave them a talk about the types of explosives the IDF was encountering in the disputed territories and in Lebanon. He intimated that some of the better Palestinian "engineers" had learned their craft at the feet of Hezbollah's specialists and their Iranian Revolutionary Guards Corps supervisors. Gadi also went into detail about how his unit trains and operates. Yachsap is constantly defusing IEDs planted by Arab terror groups. The soldiers who perform this work are professionals who undergo an intensive training course in addition to their special forces regimen. It is dangerous work, and these men have suffered their share of casualties.

Roger was struck by the level of sophistication of the Hezbollah explosives featured, as well as by the props used to camouflage them. I clearly remember him lifting what looked exactly like an ordinary rock. His hand jerked up suddenly, as he was unprepared for the object's feathery lightness. He gasped as he realized that the "rock" was actually made of Styrofoam. In this regard, Hezbollah has turned murderous terrorism into an art form.

In addition to the IEDs, we had also been contending with Hezbollah's entrance into the suicide bombing market previously monopolized by Hamas and Palestinian Islamic Jihad terrorist cells.

The first incidence occurred in the spring of 1996 and involved Mohammed Hussein Miqdad, a Lebanese-born member of Hezbollah who was taught the fine art of explosives by IRGC operatives working out of the Iranian embassy in Beirut. Apparently Mr. Miqdad, who entered Israel on a forged British passport under the name of Andrew Newman (I often remarked to my colleagues that it should have been Alfred E. Newman) hadn't paid attention in class, because as he was packing a one-kilogram explosive device into a Sony radio, it went off prematurely in his Jerusalem hotel room. Thanks to Israel's expertise in dealing with trauma cases, Miqdad survived his ordeal, except he was now minus both legs, his eyes, and one of his hands. I watched him interviewed by the ISA on a tape from his long sojourn in the hospital. He was unrepentant, so I had very little sympathy for his work-site accident. In fact, when I showed the tape to Andy, the Tel Aviv CIA station's main counterterrorism coordinator, I gave him a list of points to add to his report, including: Miqdad has apparently lost his touch; You have to hand it to him, at least he tried; He doesn't have a leg to stand on; He can't quite put his finger on what went wrong, etc. I made up about twenty of them. It was puerile gallows humour, but it rubbed off on you after seeing the scattered body parts. Later, Andy informed me that some Hezbollah analyst back in Langley hung my list up on his office wall.

The second attempt (that we knew of) was in May 1997. A source in Europe informed us that a German national named Steven Smyrek had been recruited by Hezbollah and was going to take a little trip to Israel. I was all over it, and as we only had a few days before his departure, promptly put a surveillance team on him with the co-operation of the German Bundesamtes für Verfassungsschutz (BfV), their domestic security service. It was a big operation and involved myself, my CIA counterparts, the Mossad's counterterrorism department, the Mossad liaison officer working the German counterterrorism desk, and half of the ISA's Arab Affairs Division. The plan was to have the Germans follow Smyrek to his El Al flight from Frankfurt and then seat him on the plane next to two ISA aviation security specialists who would in turn hand him off to the surveillance team of the ISA's operations division. I strongly advocated that we not arrest him until we had clearly identified who he was going to meet with and what he was going to do. But the ISA got cold feet and informed us just before his arrival that they were going to have the Israel National Police arrest him upon touchdown at Ben Gurion Airport (the ISA, like MI5 and CSIS, have no powers of arrest and must rely on law enforcement to do the dirty work).

I was quite pissed off and let everyone know it. "This is our first chance to see what these fuckers are up to!" I told Menachem from the ISA's counterterrorism department. "We can't take the risk," he replied glumly. "What if he blows up a bus or something bigger and kills a bunch of people?" The ISA was mandated with defending Israel's home soil, but by not seeing what Smyrek did once on the ground, we were putting off the inevitable. The ISA was concerned that if their surveillance team lost him, and a lot of people died in a terrorist attack, then it would be on their heads.

As planned, Smyrek was arrested at the airport. He sat in prison until 2004, when he was released in a prisoner swap with Hezbollah. Smyrek worried the hell out of me because he represented something new: a white, European Westerner who could easily fly under the counterterrorism radar. His stepfather had even been an officer in the British army serving in Germany.

Miqdad and Smyrek were Iran and Hezbollah's clear attempts to bring terrorist attacks to Israeli soil, but there may be more in the offing. When I presented Miqdad to Andy, I pointed out that during his interrogation, Miqdad said that he was one of seven Lebanese Shiites trained at an IRGC facility near Janta, in the Bekaa Valley. All the suicide bombing moles were chosen for their foreign-language skills and outward appearance, enabling them to pass as Western tourists. When I concluded my briefing, I looked at Andy squarely and said, "None of Miqdad's classmates have yet been accounted for. They're still out there."

It was during this period that a new colleague named Sheila arrived on the counterterrorism desk in Tevel's North America department. She came from the Mossad's counterterrorism department and formerly had been both a Hezbollah analyst and naval intelligence specialist. She was bright, charismatic, and a devoted mother of twin boys. As a bonus, she came with a Mossad pedigree: her father had become a legend in the Mossad during the post-Munich era for tracking down and eliminating the terrorists responsible for the 1972 Olympic Games massacre.

We were having a staff meeting in Uri's office one day when Sheila announced unexpectedly, "Don't you think the Americans would like to know they have a Hezbollah agent wandering around in between their legs?"

She had been investigating a certain lieutenant of Laqis named Fawzi Mustapha Assi. "Ramez," as Assi was code-named, operated out of the large Arab-American community in Dearborn, Michigan. His day job, Sheila told us, was working as an engineer at the Ford Motor Company's famous River Rouge plant, which Henry Ford had established in 1915 just west of Detroit. Off-hours, however, he spent his time procuring the export-restricted technology Hezbollah needed to create IEDs and other weapons. Because of the technical nature of Ramez's work at Ford, his day job provided the necessary cover to perform his illicit procurement duties.

Aside from his Hezbollah affiliation, Ramez was by all accounts an unremarkable Lebanese immigrant to the United States. He had arrived some twenty years earlier at the age of eighteen, then married and divorced, leaving three children in the custody of their mother. Like all good sleeper agents, Ramez gave the outward appearance of living an ordinary workaday life.

Sheila hauled out a sheaf of transcripts from intercepted telephone calls between Ramez and Laqis that she'd plucked out of the SIGINT chatter – intelligence gleaned from intercepted communication transmissions.* Because of the nature of the intercept, we only got Laqis's side of the conversation. But that was damning enough. The Hezbollah honcho was running down a list of goodies Ramez was supposed to buy and send back to Lebanon – including thermal

---

* SIGINT is typically seen as more valuable than HUMINT– intelligence conveyed directly from human sources – because people frequently lie. Moreover, disclosing SIGINT is sensitive because it implicitly entails disclosing your technical information-gathering capabilities, and the identity of those you're targeting. This explains why there is such an enormous taboo in the intelligence community about disclosing secret information without the permission of those who originally procured it. This applies not only between nations, but *within* spy agencies as well. I could no more take a piece of intelligence from another unit in the Mossad and pass it on to a third unit without permission than I could take a piece of CIA intelligence and pass it on to the British SIS. Breaking what is known in the trade as the "third-party rule" condemns you to the silent treatment evermore.

imaging equipment, night-vision goggles, electronic components, Kevlar bullet-proof vests, and global positioning satellite modules. The total value, we calculated, was about three hundred thousand dollars (US) – more money than your typical Ford engineer has in his chequing account.

Sheila and I went upstairs to the Hezbollah branch of the Mossad's counterterrorism department for a consult and stopped by Etti's office on the way. An institution in the Mossad, Etti then sat as the branch head for terrorist attack alerts and acted as a clearing house for counterterrorism-related intelligence and its dissemination to foreign services. Though only in her early fifties, she was already a certified spinster – part of that middle-aged female cohort in the Mossad that is married to their jobs. I ended up working closely with Etti until the end of my career and grew immensely fond of her.

We hovered at the entrance to her office, where she was puffing away on one of her forbidden cigarettes (Mossad HQ has a strict but unenforced no-smoking policy) and talking on a red secure phone with someone in military intelligence. She signed off by saying, "If your dick were half as impressive as your intellect, you'd be a girl."

"Army putzes," she muttered as she waved us in. "What do you toads want? Look at you both – you should breed."

I filled her in on what we knew about Ramez. The story intrigued her – but only a little.

"Those fucking *Amerikakim* [her charming way of compounding the Hebrew word for shit with 'American'] will probably lose him the first chance they get. What a bunch of useless schlemiels." Etti was incredibly profane in Hebrew, English, and Yiddish.

"They can all go to hell," she added, then absent-mindedly went back to her computer and began typing at what seemed like a thousand words per minute. I thought to myself: "How could *anyone* not love this woman?"

We then met with Nissim, a dark-featured Arabic-speaking Hezbollah specialist who was working the Iran desk with a small cadre of other analysts. He agreed to let us have access to the complete dossier of communications between Hezbollah's Lebanese commanders and Ramez, knowing full well that we would then share some of the contents with the FBI. It was a significant moment: To my knowledge, this was to be the first ever joint FBI–Mossad operation in history.

While working for Tevel, I always took a smug satisfaction in surprising my U.S. colleagues with stunning revelations about an enemy operative working clandestinely in their own backyard. The combination of gratitude, respect, and humility that my counterparts exhibited on those occasions was one of the things that made the job worthwhile.

In this case, our plan was to avoid running the operation through our hopelessly out-of-the-loop FBI contacts at the Tel Aviv Legat, and instead work through Sarah, a Mossad liaison officer working in the Washington station. Before going to her, Sheila and I met with Paul and Wayne to ensure that the Legat had a heads-up on what we were doing. I had anticipated that their noses would be out of joint, but they actually appeared relieved to remain on the sidelines. As it turned out, they had more than enough files on the go to keep themselves busy. Plus, a secretary had screwed up their computer system so badly that a technician had to be flown in from D.C. to fix it. And to top things off, Bill Clinton's people were starting to act like peacemaking busybodies during this period, which meant the FBI had to deal with various Palestinian factions and warlords on nonintelligence-related matters.

Without further ado, we sent Sarah a package of material to take to FBI HQ, along with our recommendations on how best to proceed. We emphasized that the Mossad should retain as much control as possible, even though the operation was going to take place on U.S. territory. It was an ambitious request, but since we were the ones bringing the Americans the intelligence, we figured they owed us one.

A short time later, Sarah told us that her FBI contacts were stunned by our intelligence and eager to take up the chase. Within another day or two, they'd procured FISA warrants that allowed them to eavesdrop on Ramez's phone calls. FISA stands for *Foreign Intelligence Surveillance Act*, a 1978 law that sets out the procedures the FBI and other government agencies must (theoretically) follow before spying on the movements and communications of individuals suspected of being agents of a "foreign power." FISA was a fairly obscure statute until December 2005, when the *New York Times* broke the story that the Bush administration was ignoring FISA, and had given the National Security Agency (NSA) carte blanche to spy on domestic phone calls.

Many of the Bush administration's critics have argued that the NSA's so-called Terrorist Surveillance Program is not only illegal (a U.S. District judge ruled it unconstitutional in August 2006), but unnecessary as well – since it's always been fairly easy for law enforcement agencies to get FISA authorization for surveillance. I can't comment on that as a general principle, but I definitely was amazed at how fast the FBI got its FISA mandate against Ramez. I later learned that the newly appointed chief of the international terrorism section at the FBI's National Security Division, a man named Dale Watson, was enthusiastic about the operation, and had given instructions that we were to have at our disposal all the resources necessary to bring Ramez and his procurement operation down.

Ramez, we all discovered from the ensuing surveillance, was one busy boy. He was travelling all over the United States, methodically seeking to locate and purchase military equipment for Hezbollah. We listened to his calls for almost a year, generating almost thirteen hundred transcripts, which the FBI and Mossad shared.

In our reading of the translated intercepts we received, we kept hoping that Ramez would tip us off to other Hezbollah operatives and networks in the United States, but it became clear he was operating as a "singleton," or lone operative. Being a former combatant myself, I could relate to his compartmentalized modus operandi (if not his murderous ideology). Unlike some of the amateurish operations that have been busted in Western nations since 9/11, Hezbollah is not a ragtag group of fanatics. Thanks to all the help they get from their sponsors in Tehran, they are adept at foreign intelligence and counterintelligence operations.

As the months rolled on, Ramez slowly ticked off the items on Laqis's list. He took his time and proceeded carefully; none of his purchases, taken in isolation, would have alerted anyone of his intentions. But Laqis wasn't impressed. He would call Ramez occasionally and berate him for the slow pace. He regularly played the guilt-trip card, reminding him how Hezbollah terrorists were falling prey to Israeli soldiers while Ramez dilly-dallied in the United States.

By late spring 1998, with Ramez's shopping list almost complete, Sarah called my office and told me that the FBI was about to make an arrest. But there was a catch: the Bureau wanted one of us to testify against Ramez in court. This was a problem. The Mossad is a covert intelligence-gathering operation. Our agency would be compromised if we were forced to disclose sensitive details about our methods (including many I am omitting in this book) under cross-examination in open court. This was exactly the sort of conflict that inevitably materialized when you paired up scofflaw spies with buttoned-down G-men.

"No way are we going to put either one of you on the witness stand," Uri told Sheila and me.

I played devil's advocate. "What if this is our only chance to bring him down? Maybe I could do it in camera or by way of a written affidavit?"

"No way," Uri replied. "The DG won't go for it and it isn't going to happen. Besides, they've got mountains of evidence. What do they need you for?"

We went back to Sarah and she took the matter up with FBI HQ. A few hours later, she called us back. "Watson is coming out to see you guys," she said. "And he seems kind of pissed."

I met Dale Watson, along with Paul and Wayne, at a seafood restaurant on the beach in north Tel Aviv. This was essentially a get-to-know-you gathering in anticipation of a substantive meeting the following day at Mossad HQ. Watson was an amiable fellow with a southern drawl, not very tall, with blue eyes and neatly combed brown hair. While he commanded respect, the man was far from overbearing.

Watson was intrigued by my Western appearance and lack of Israeli accent, and took a particular interest in my background. I answered his questions as vaguely as I could, but he probably guessed I was from the operational side of the business. We drank lots of wine and kept the discussion away from Ramez. He appreciated the hospitality and invited me to give him a call if I ever visited D.C.

The next morning I received a call from Andy at the Tel Aviv CIA station. Andy was an easygoing Californian, complete with goatee and laid back Haight-Ashbury attitude. Like Kerouac, this flower-power type didn't fit the spy stereotype. But he was competent and professional all the same. He told me that one of their officers would be sitting in on the meeting with the FBI.

"What for?" I asked, sensing some kind of CIA–FBI turf battle was in the works.

"Hezbollah is a foreign terrorist organization and therefore falls within our mandate, so we have to be in on it."

"Does the Bureau know you're going to be there?" I asked. "Because if they don't, you'd better tell them now." I felt like a dinner party host trying to preempt an embarrassing catfight between two guests.

"Yeah, they know. And they ain't happy about it. But don't worry. We're just in observation mode."

Sure enough, Mike from the CIA Tel Aviv station presented himself at the meeting. He was deferential and didn't say a word, but he sure took a lot of notes. The FBI folks ignored him as if he wasn't there. I marvelled at how cold and adversarial their relationship was. It was particularly ironic in this case, as Watson had served the previous year as deputy head of the CIA's Counterterrorism Center.

When we got down to business, Watson surprised everyone by announcing he didn't need our testimony. The FBI, he told us, was going to launch a sting operation in concert with U.S. Customs. It appeared that many of the articles were export-restricted to Lebanon under customs rules, a fact that would facilitate a criminal proceeding under a 1996 law that outlaws material support to terrorist organizations such as Hezbollah. Watson told us that Ramez could face up to life in prison and a $750,000 fine if convicted.

"That works for us," I said. In fact, it seemed like such a win-win that I wondered why he'd bothered to fly ten hours to give us the news.

After the meeting, I took Watson over to meet Admiral Ami Ayalon, the head of the Israel Security Agency, at their HQ near Tel Aviv University. It was a courtesy meeting, and we met in a boardroom that adjoined Ayalon's office.

Although I'd never met the man before, I knew the Ayalon legend. As a member (and, subsequently, commander) of Israel's elite naval commando unit, Flotilla 13, he'd been decorated numerous times for bravery. He had been put in the ISA job after the assassination of Yitzhak Rabin in 1995, to revitalize the demoralized service, and by all reports, he'd succeeded in turning things around. Now fifty-three years old, he had the gruff but friendly demeanour of a native-born Israeli, and the terse speaking manner of a military veteran. Everyone regarded him as a man's man. The ISA's rank and file adored him.

Despite being on the short side, Ayalon was an intimidating presence. He was bald and well muscled. A single glance told you he was tough as old nails. One of my office mates told me he would see Ayalon swim several kilometres in the Tel Aviv University pool and then do hundreds of push-ups and sit-ups in the dirt and mud outside the building – even on rainy days – as if he were back in boot camp. That's old-school tough.

When I introduced myself, he practically crushed my hand and looked me up and down. I could tell what he was thinking: here's another wimpy, foreign-born Mossad aristocrat.

Watson and the admiral briefly discussed issues related to co-operation between their two services. I politely waited until the meeting concluded, then I returned Watson to his hotel, where we exchanged parting pleasantries. The next time I would see him would be on CNN in 2002, testifying before the Senate Select Committee on Intelligence and the Permanent Select Committee on Intelligence about the events that led to 9/11.

A few weeks later, Ramez began trying to ship out some of the goodies he'd purchased from the Detroit airport. His first shipment included seven pairs of night-vision goggles, one infrared heat detection device, and two global positioning satellite modules. The FBI arranged for U.S. Customs to conduct a "random" search of his packages and – lo and behold – they were full of export-restricted items. In an act of calculated leniency, Customs seized the items and let

Ramez go with a fine. He immediately called Laqis, who told him to sit tight.

But Ramez, sensing (correctly) that the gig was up, began to panic. One night, he tried to get rid of all the items he'd purchased for Hezbollah by putting them into a dumpster near his home in Dearborn. Fortunately, he was still under surveillance, and the FBI was able to seize the discarded goods – which included more night-vision devices, thermal imaging scopes, and literature on Israeli Cabinet members with details of their home addresses. This gave the FBI all they'd need for a conviction.

FBI agents arrested Ramez without incident at his house. From that moment on, it became a criminal proceeding and the Mossad was cut out of the loop. But Sarah learned that more incriminating items had been discovered hidden in his house, and at his Ford office. Evidence seized by the FBI also indicated that he'd already managed to ship Kevlar bullet-proof vests and various other items to Laqis before we got a hold of him. No doubt, some of those very items were used by the Hezbollah troops Israel fought against in 2006.

Ramez was to become the first person in American legal history to be indicted using the "material support" provisions of the 1996 anti-terrorist law, and we were all looking forward to the successful prosecution of this case after such a long build-up.

At this point, however, the story goes south. Ramez was charged and brought before U.S. Magistrate Virginia Morgan, who, despite the pleas of all concerned, granted Ramez bail – he put his parents' house up as a hundred-thousand-dollar bond – with the condition that he wear an electronic tether. Once released, Ramez promptly cut the tether, grabbed his brother's passport, crossed into Canada, and fled to Lebanon.

After September 11, 2001, this sort of thing would never be allowed to happen, of course. But back in 1998 few Americans took the threat of terrorism seriously – despite the fact that Hezbollah had been tied to numerous terrorist attacks against American targets, including the 1996 Khobar Towers attack in Saudi Arabia, which left nineteen American servicemen dead. The judge's reckless action was as perfect an example as I'd ever encountered of the pre-9/11 mindset.

When I heard the news, I was dumbstruck, and I fumed around the office for days. We just watched a year's worth of work get poured down the drain. What really bugged me was the tantalizing prospect of what we could have gotten out of Ramez. He had a jittery personality, and probably would have provided a wealth of intelligence about Hezbollah's procurement methods and Laqis in return for leniency.

For Hezbollah, Ramez's capture was but a minor setback. In recent years, the group has received an estimated US$120-million in aid from Iran, as well as a roughly equal amount through overseas donations from sympathetic Shiite expatriates. The group used this cash to acquire a wide range of valuable military hardware – as its deadly attacks against Israel in 2006 demonstrated.

Moreover, Hezbollah is still active in the United States, Canada, and other Western nations, and in Southeast Asia. If push comes to shove between the United States and Iran over the Islamic Republic's nuclear program, one of the ways Iran can be expected to attack the U.S. is through Hezbollah's network of North American and worldwide cells.

In fact, in 2000 in North Carolina, the FBI arrested eighteen men connected to a Hezbollah smuggling ring that had transferred some eight million dollars back to Laqis to assist in the financing of Hezbollah's operations. The main ringleader was a man named Mohammad Dbouk, a senior operative based in Canada, who had been in direct contact with Laqis and had helped manage many of Hezbollah's procurement operations across North America. Had Ramez been faced with the prospect of spending the rest of his life behind bars in a federal penitentiary, he might have led the FBI to that network a few years earlier. Instead, a single naive judge managed to screw everything up. Not for the first or last time, Etti had been right.

Six years later, long after I'd left the Mossad, another odd twist came. In 2004, Ramez suddenly returned to the United States on a flight from Beirut. Why did he come back? I can only speculate. He probably missed his estranged family, who were still in Michigan. I also doubt that he'd received a particularly warm reception in Lebanon, seeing as how he'd screwed up his mission and attracted the FBI's scrutiny to Hezbollah's procurement network. He was a blown operative, and of no use to anyone. Even his parents probably weren't too happy with him, seeing as how they lost their home when he jumped bail.

I understand that Fawzi Mustapha Assi, aka Ramez, is currently a resident of the federal correctional institution in Milan, Michigan, a low-security facility. Given the general mood on terrorism in the U.S., I'm guessing that he'll be there for a long time.

Maybe I'll drop by for a visit?

12 | THE MASHAAL AFFAIR

Before Israel dies, it must be humiliated and degraded. Allah willing, before they die, they will experience humiliation and degradation every day. America will be of no avail to them. Their generals will be of no avail to them. Allah willing, we will make them lose their eyesight, we will make them lose their brains.

Khaled Mashaal

Even before the wake-up call of September 11, the United States received multiple warnings about the scale of the threat from militant Islam. In the wake of these tragedies in Africa, Saudi Arabia, and Lebanon, a small but growing stream of forward-thinking American security officials came to the Mossad looking to educate themselves about Middle Eastern terrorist groups.

Of the many meetings I had with CIA and FBI agents during this period, the one that took place on September 25, 1997, stands out in my memory. The CIA's Counterterrorism Center had sent a three-man delegation to discuss Hezbollah, including the possibility of the CIA and Mossad conducting joint operations against the group's leaders. We saw it as a golden opportunity to involve the United States more actively against a foe that we sometimes felt we were fighting single-handedly.

Of the three visiting Americans, the one I remember best is Harry, then the CIA's principal Hezbollah analyst. The day was hot and humid, and Harry must have been the only person in Israel wearing a tie. He reminded me of a smooth salesman, complete with ready smile, toothpaste-commercial teeth, stylish suit, and shiny cufflinks. He presented quite a contrast with his Israeli hosts, clad in the usual Mediterranean uniform of open-collar shirts and too much chest hair. Even with the air conditioning running full blast, the rest of us were sweating, yet Harry seemed cool as a cucumber.

We met in the area of HQ that, for some reason, we all called the *midrasha,* or "seminary." Along with the liaison meeting rooms, it housed a commercial-style kitchen, plush suites for visiting dignitaries requiring a discreet place to stay, a conference centre, and training classrooms.

Harry was joined by his grey-haired, avuncular boss, David, and a shy tag-along who never said or did anything that recorded itself in my memory. From the Mossad's counterterrorism department, we brought along Nissim and Lior, both Hezbollah analysts. We also had with us the head of the Mossad's counterterrorism department, Yuval. I was there in my capacity as liaison officer along with Mike, the deputy from the CIA's Tel Aviv station. (Mike's senior colleagues had shown up for the opening pleasantries but, as was usually the case, they vanished once we got down to details.)

Lior presented the delegation with aerial photos outlining the locations of Hezbollah functionaries, along with intelligence data about their activities. None of our proposals went beyond electronic eavesdropping or human intelligence recruitment operations. Certainly, assassination plots were out of the question: in the pre-9/11 days, the CIA was a skittish, risk-averse organization, a far cry from the agency that led the invasion into Afghanistan in late 2001, and that used a drone-mounted Hellfire missile to blow up a car full of jihadists in the Yemeni desert a year later.

Seen in retrospect, that skittishness likely cost many lives. If the United States and its allies had taken the Hezbollah threat seriously in those early days, the Shiite terrorist group might never have built up the weaponry it used to such deadly effect during the Israeli–Hezbollah war of 2006. Nor would Hezbollah have been able to lend their expertise to al-Qaeda in the run-up to the Kenya, Tanzania, and New York attacks. On the other hand, I suppose it's human nature to ignore a threat until it matures: even Israel under Ariel Sharon largely turned its back on Hezbollah for the six years following its evacuation of Lebanon in 2000.

After a long round of discussions, we broke for a catered lunch, and I went down to my office to see if any time-sensitive messages had come in. I was sitting at my desk by myself; Danny was off at the dining room with some of his case officer buddies – no doubt regaling them with stories of Israel Security Agency chief Ami Ayalon doing calisthenics in thirty-five-degree heat. It was hot, and I had just manoeuvred myself close to the air conditioning outflow duct when Sheila walked into my office with a grave expression on her face.

"Nobody knows this yet," she said, "but two Mossad combatants from the Kidon division have fallen into Jordanian hands in Amman."

Since leaving my combatant job with Caesarea, I'd fallen out of the loop. But Sheila had close contacts in the branch, given her father's former position in Caesarea. As in any organization, blood connections carried a lot of weight.

"I heard they were taking out a senior Hamas leader and the mission went awry. Two were captured and four are holed up in the Israeli embassy."

It was stunning news, and I had trouble believing it for two reasons. The first was that – as an empirical matter – combatants just *don't* get caught. The other was that I'd never heard of Caesarea's Kidon unit being deployed in an Arab country before. Their sphere of operations is everywhere outside of "target countries" that pose a threat to Israel.

"You can't tell anyone because we're not supposed to know," she added. "Even in Caesarea, only a few people know about it."

I gave her my vow of silence – who would I tell anyway? All I could think to say was, "What a colossal fuck-up."

As I walked back to the liaison meeting rooms, my head was reeling at the implications. If her news was true, this was virtually unprecedented: the last time a Caesarea combatant fell into enemy hands was when the legendary Eli Cohen was captured by the Syrians and publicly executed on May 18, 1965, more than three decades earlier. Cohen had managed to ingratiate himself with Syria's military and government officials, and sent intelligence to Israel via secret radio transmissions, encoded written correspondence, and debriefings by his controllers in Europe and Israel. In one famous episode, he even convinced Syrian generals to permit him access to their army's main fortifications in the Golan Heights, which would soon pass into Israeli hands. Feigning sympathy for the Syrian soldiers, he had offered to plant trees near their barracks so they could have some shade – trees that were then used as targeting markers by the Israelis. He was ultimately caught by Soviet counterintelligence experts who triangulated the frequency of his radio communications. After his execution, he became a legend in Israel. While I worked at Tevel, the lobby of Mossad HQ featured an exhibit in his honour, displaying some of his surviving equipment and personal effects.

I put myself in my colleagues' shoes. Like every combatant, I'd worried often about the prospect of capture throughout my career. The world is unkind to captured spies. There are no Geneva Conventions governing their treatment, nor even any gentlemanly codes of conduct. In places such as Iran and Syria, a captured Mossad agent could expect to be hanged – after any useful information had been extracted from him through torture and inhumane confinement.*

In this case, however, my fears were somewhat mitigated by the fact that the captors were Jordanian. Israel and Jordan fought bitter wars against each other in 1948 and 1967. Jordan had also played host to Palestinian terrorists who murdered many Israelis in the PLO's early years. But, over time, a mutual understanding emerged between the two countries – something resembling respect, if not affection. King Hussein, who would rule until his death in 1999, was an honourable man who'd forged a strong relationship with many Israeli leaders and diplomats. He had a particularly warm relationship with Ephraim Halevy, who'd retired as deputy director general of the Mossad after negotiating the Jordan–Israel peace treaty in 1994.

Needless to say, I was somewhat distracted by Sheila's bombshell. I found it hard to concentrate on the afternoon meetings with our American visitors; I kept looking at Uri, my department head, but he betrayed no knowledge of the day's events. I felt sorry for him,

---

* Arabs suspected of spying informally for Israeli intelligence also receive brutal treatment. Countless Palestinians have been summarily executed in the West Bank and Gaza after leading the Israeli army to terror cells. And when Lebanese citizens suspected of being Israeli informants were shot by Hezbollah in July 2006, the news was seen as so unremarkable that the media barely reported it.

because he was about to walk into a bunch of stormy liaison meetings with the Americans, who would no doubt be furious.

Whatever the Americans' reaction, I knew Uri would do everything in his power to bring Washington on board in resolving the crisis. In this kind of case, U.S. help could mean the difference between getting our team back safe, and having them spend years in an Arab prison.

Uri and Harry were friendly from Uri's stint at the Mossad station in D.C., and they agreed to meet in downtown Tel Aviv for drinks and dinner after our meeting broke up. We were all invited, and I said I'd be there – knowing full well there would be no dinner. Uri mentioned offhandedly that he'd been summoned to the office of Danny Yatom, Mossad's director general. Once that meeting was over, I knew, neither Uri nor anyone else would be in the mood for a night out.

Danny Yatom had been parachuted into the DG's office after the 1996 retirement of Shabtai Shavit. I liked and respected Shavit, as did most of his subordinates. He'd worked as a HUMINT case officer and head of Caesarea, and understood how an intelligence service operates. He'd also been schooled in the modern, Harvard MBA-style of business administration and management, and tried to instil in the Mossad a measure of corporate efficiency.

Yatom, by contrast, came to the Mossad as an army man. As part of his distinguished career, he'd fought with some of Israel's most elite military units, including the legendary Sayeret Matkal (or General Staff Reconnaissance Unit). One of the unit's responsibilities is hostage rescue. During one famous 1972 mission, Operation Isotope, Yatom and his fellow soldiers (including unit commander Ehud Barak and Benjamin Netanyahu, two future prime ministers) disguised themselves as airline mechanics and successfully stormed a Sabena Airlines jet that had been hijacked by Palestinian terrorists.

The problem was that Yatom, a major general, never traded in his rank badges, and still seemed to think he was in charge of a military unit. His stern gaze, cropped short hair, and military gait were easy to pick out in the Mossad's corridors. And his uncompromising, top-down Prussian management style often seemed out of place in an intelligence agency, where subtlety is a prized quality and colleagues can't be rigidly categorized and valued according to the number of stripes on their shoulders.

I can imagine how Yatom exploded when he heard the news that two of his agents had been caught like common crooks. In any event, after Uri met with Yatom, our department convened in Uri's office and he broke the news that I already knew. I locked eyes with Sheila, but otherwise didn't betray the fact that I had advance knowledge.

The screw-up, we learned in that meeting, was part of a botched assassination attempt that had been approved by Prime Minister Benjamin Netanyahu. Two combatants from the Kidon unit had organized an ambush of Hamas's Jordanian branch chief, Khaled Mashaal, at the entrance to the terrorist group's Amman offices. When Mashaal showed up, they seized him, and sprayed his ear with a lethal time-release chemical while four other team members remained in close surveillance of the building.

Noting that Mashaal's chauffeur and bodyguard had spotted the fracas and were about to give chase, two of the combatants in the support team tried to create a diversion by staging a public shouting match. They then jumped into their rental car and took off. The bodyguard commandeered a passing car in hot pursuit.

Inexplicably, the combatants remained ignorant of the fact they were being followed – a total amateur-hour botch-up. And when the pair eventually parked the vehicle, they were arrested by plain-clothes policemen, who later discovered they were carrying bogus

Canadian passports. Meanwhile, the remaining four combatants (including the two who'd actually assaulted Mashaal) escaped to the Israeli embassy, where they remained holed up.

Before he headed up for another meeting with the DG to get further instructions about involving the Americans, Uri asked me to summon Stan Moskowitz and Mike from the CIA station to a meeting later that evening. The story hadn't been broken by the media yet, and I had to hurry.

Mike was at his desk when I phoned, and he agreed to come by with Moskowitz. But when he showed up an hour later, Mike arrived alone. Moskowitz, he said, had other business to attend to. From experience, I suspected this meant he was drinking tea with Yasser Arafat, or on the golf course. But in retrospect, I think it's possible Moskowitz was trying to tell me something.

Before Uri broke the big news, I started off by telling Mike who Khaled Mashaal was. Uri and I figured that after I'd described some of the terrorist attacks the guy had organized – including some that had killed U.S. citizens – he wouldn't be so surprised that we'd tried to kill him.

I told Mike that Mashaal was the chief of Hamas's political wing, which was then based in Amman. But that same office, I added, controlled and financed the Izz al-Din al-Qassam brigades, the organization's armed (i.e., terrorist) wing.* After reeling off a list of some of Hamas's many crimes, I hit him with the big one: "Mike, Mashaal was behind the Mahane Yehuda market attack in Jerusalem."

I knew Mike would know exactly the incident I was talking about. The blast had taken place just two months previous, killing

---

* The brigades are named after a Syrian sheikh, Izz al-Din al-Qassam, an Islamist who helped organize revolts against the French in 1921, and against the British in 1935. To this day, he is venerated by Palestinians as the embodiment of grassroots violent resistance. The Qassam rockets fired from Gaza are also named after him.

sixteen people and injuring 169 others. A team of FBI officers was in Israel at the time, and I'd personally taken them to the site soon after the bombing. Their visit to that awful scene was the talk of the FBI Legat for some time.

"I remember," Mike said.

I continued. "On September 4, he authorized a suicide attack on the Ben Yehuda pedestrian mall in Jerusalem, in which five people were killed. American citizens were injured and killed in both attacks. One of them was a fourteen-year-old girl visiting Israel from Los Angeles." The American government was sensitive about the welfare of its citizens abroad, and I hoped that these highlights from my short briefing would make their way up the food chain when Mike reported our request for political aid to his superiors.

I then let Uri take over, and he succinctly explained what had happened in Jordan. True to Mossad form, Uri stuck to the generalities of the mission and did not go into any operational details. Uri then requested the Agency's assistance through their good contacts with the Jordanian security intelligence service and its head, Samih Battikhi.

Mike looked shocked, and he took a while to respond. As for me, I was feeling slightly ridiculous. A few hours earlier, we'd all been in a room together, and my team had been trying to enlist the Americans in high-risk operations against Hezbollah. Now we were admitting to Mike that we'd completely screwed up a mission against Hamas, a far less professional terrorist outfit.

Mike said he'd pass the request along, but that he really didn't know how they'd react at Langley. The meeting broke up, and I rode with Mike to the front gate. His parting words to me were, "I hope you get your team back." I know he meant it. Mike was that kind of guy.

In the end, after negotiations in which the Mossad was not involved (we were not exactly flavour of the month in Jordan) took place over a period of weeks, the two captured Kidon team members eventually arrived safe and sound back in Israel. In exchange, an Israeli physician had to fly to Amman to deliver a life-saving antidote to Mashaal. We also had to free Sheikh Ahmed Ismail Yassin, Hamas's paraplegic "spiritual leader," who'd been imprisoned for life by Israel in 1989 for ordering the execution of two Israeli soldiers. (Yassin should have stayed in Jordan. In 2004, after Israel reached the end of its tolerance for his "spiritual" activities – which typically involved young Palestinians exploding themselves amid Israeli crowds – he was killed by an Israeli missile as his handlers were wheeling him to morning prayers in Gaza City.)

The incident was a huge embarrassment for the Netanyahu government, which had authorized the mission. And many in the Mossad claimed that the assassination attempt had been "forced" upon the agency by politicians. I was skeptical of these excuses because I knew the Mossad was strong enough to stand up for itself and reject a mission its leaders believed was too risky.

Moreover, Caesarea was fully capable of a simple job like this one. In my view, the screw-up lay not with the decision to kill Mashaal, but with the plan for doing so. I remember discussing this with Charles shortly after the affair, and we both agreed that it made no sense to perform the operation with Kidon, whose combatants had no experience operating in Arab countries. We speculated that the unit was used only because it was the favourite of Caesarea's deputy head, who happened to be a former Kidon unit commander. He'd long argued that Kidon could be used in hostile countries, despite its combatants' lack of deep-cover skills.

Netanyahu's government had to do the grovelling without American help: the CIA didn't give us any assistance. Ultimately, Ephraim Halevy saved the day by flying to Jordan and calling in a favour from his friend King Hussein. It was a master stroke by

Halevy, and it was no surprise that he took over as Mossad director general when Yatom finally resigned in February of 1998.

With the combatants safely back in Israel, a three-man state commission was mandated to investigate what became known as the "Mashaal Affair." Many of my colleagues were called to testify, and some volunteered to put in their two cents' worth. The mission became a spy-world byword for amateurish bungling.

At the time, Tevel managed a productive two-way intelligence flow with the Jordanian intelligence service, and my colleagues who were responsible for this relationship were particularly angry at seeing all their hard work and earned trust go up in smoke. Our department also had to contend with the Canadians for "borrowing" their passports. (For the record, Canada was not aware of the operation and had no supporting role. The job was strictly "blue and white." In fact, assassination missions like this one are so compartmentalized that even the Mossad's other operational divisions were unaware of it until it blew up.) Interestingly, however, the Canadian Security and Intelligence Service was sympathetic, and it was business as usual with them at Tevel despite the diplomatic flap. During a liaison exchange by our counterterrorism officers to Canada soon after the Mashaal affair broke, many CSIS members mentioned that their only regret in the whole matter was that we didn't succeed.

As for Khaled Mashaal, he survived his brush with the long arm of Israeli justice. In 2004, he was appointed the "world leader" of Hamas and took to hiding out in Damascus, where he now issues fiery manifestos against Israel and does his level best to undermine moderate Palestinian elements. Many analysts believe he ordered the kidnapping of an Israeli soldier in June 2006, specifically to sabotage the efforts of some of his Hamas political colleagues who were inching toward reconciliation with Israel.

Whenever I see his name in the news, I think back to September 1997 and remember what might have been – if only two Mossad combatants operating in Amman had taken the time to look in their rear-view mirror. I suggest Mashaal keep an eye out. One way or another, the Mossad will complete its mission.

13 | THE OSLO SHELL GAME

I may not have been the greatest president, but I've had the most fun for eight years.

Bill Clinton

The most enduring image arising from Bill Clinton's failed effort to bring peace to the Middle East was the former president's three-way handshake on the White House lawn with Yasser Arafat and Yitzhak Rabin. Behind the scenes, however, it wasn't Clinton who led the peacemaking effort, but a mild-mannered, middle-aged American diplomat named Dennis Ross. As part of my liaison work with the Mossad in the 1990s, I met Ross on various occasions, and found him to be intelligent and thoughtful. A little dull and long-winded perhaps – his unreadable and exhaustive 2004 opus, *The Missing Peace*, covered such details as what kind of cable television packages diplomats had in their guest rooms at Camp David – but overall a nice guy.

At the time, much was made of the fact that Ross is Jewish. But by my observation, he was impeccably even-handed. If the peace envoy had any flaw, it was that he was too gullible when it came to swallowing Yasser Arafat's cynical promises. As I will demonstrate, neither Ross nor Clinton was willing to acknowledge the truth about the inveterate terrorist, even when Israel's intelligence establishment presented them with the plainest evidence imaginable.

By 1998, Palestinian terrorism had become a common feature of the post-Oslo Accords landscape. These attacks were conducted with a nod and a wink from Arafat. But Ross, along with the rest of the West's diplomatic corps, insisted they were the handiwork of marginal radicals – and that the best way to thwart them was to prop up Arafat as a "moderate" alternative.

For the cameras, Ross put on a brave front. But when I met him in person, he usually looked tired and frustrated. In private conversation, he conceded that Arafat was maddening to deal with. Most of us at the Mossad saw Ross as a well-meaning diplomat with a near-impossible mandate.

It's no secret that Clinton's determination to bring peace to the Middle East was not motivated only by geopolitical goodwill; it was also a bid to burnish his presidential legacy and win the Nobel Peace Prize. And so he used every available tool at his disposal to accomplish the goal – including the CIA. The Agency's station in Tel Aviv was staffed with thirty-plus officers, far more than were needed for standard intelligence functions. At Tevel, it was common knowledge that the majority of these agents were doing quasi-political liaison work with the myriad warlords and Arafat lieutenants who were the real power behind the ostensibly democratic Palestinian Authority.

As a naive West would finally find out when Arafat launched his all-out terrorist war against Israel in 2000, Clinton's no-questions-asked approach to Palestinian nation building was misguided. One of the most deadly consequences was that the techniques the CIA taught the PA security apparatus – covert operations and counter-terrorism, in particular – served to professionalize an organization that would soon be openly at war with Israel.

In order to make a success of Oslo before the end of Clinton's second term in 2001, Ross and the other Americans I dealt with turned a blind eye to the growing evidence that Arafat had no intention of pursuing a peaceful two-state solution. But Israeli leaders were more concerned with protecting Israel than winning international awards. And eventually, there came a time when we had to start showing the Americans the facts they didn't want to see.

One of these instances came in the spring of 1998, when I got a call from the head of the ISA's Arab affairs division, Silvan. He told me the ISA had something that Stan Moskowitz, the CIA's chief of station, needed to see.

I headed out to the ISA office to see what Silvan had in mind. When I arrived, he was with the ISA's counterterrorism chief, Menachem. They had with them a small file box, from which they produced a set of Arabic documents issued by the Palestinian Authority.

"We brought some visual aids," said Menachem, a dark, bespectacled fellow who'd spent years at the sharp end of the ISA's campaign against Hamas and Islamic Jihad. "This is evidence linking Arafat and one of his security chiefs with shooting attacks against Israeli civilians."

After a few minutes of Menachem's show-and-tell, I knew that what I was hearing was a bombshell. In 1998, the world – and even many Israelis – still saw Arafat as an erstwhile killer who'd made a genuine, if imperfect, conversion to peaceable statesman. Just four years earlier, he and Yitzhak Rabin had shared the Nobel Peace Prize. Yes, everyone knew Arafat was playing a double game politically, saying one thing in English and another in Arabic in order to appease militant Palestinian factions. But no one then suspected that Arafat was reverting to full-bore terrorism, orchestrating killings of Jewish civilians from his government offices in Ramallah.

Later, we came back to Mossad HQ, and I set the pair up in a conference room equipped with a video projector. Soon thereafter, Moskowitz's white Mercedes pulled up. I came outside and greeted him, then gave an Arabic greeting of "Ahalan wa Sahalan" to Ezra, his Circassian driver. The security guards opened the gates and bomb barrier, and Moskowitz's limo glided into the compound.

Moskowitz was clearly irritated to have been taken away from whatever he'd been doing at his stylish apartment in Jaffa, but he maintained the outward forms of diplomacy; the presence of Silvan, a division head, meant this was no run-of-the-mill briefing. I got Ezra a drink as he waited in the car, and took Moskowitz into the meeting room.

The chief of station took his seat, and I sat next to him while Menachem turned on the overhead projector. He began the presentation by asking Moskowitz if he'd ever heard of Ghazi Jabali.

"He's the police chief in Gaza," Moskowitz responded in a bored voice.

This was true. But everyone in the room knew that the term *police* had a different meaning in the Palestinian Authority than in Israel or the United States. As in the West, police in the PA settled neighbourhood disputes and caught petty criminals (when they felt like it). But they also constituted a well-armed paramilitary force that Arafat could deploy as his personal enforcers. Jabali himself was a notoriously corrupt Fatah apparatchik. Until this point, however, we had little reason to believe he was directly involved in anything worse than standard shakedown operations.

Menachem put up an organizational chart detailing the PA's security hierarchy and how Jabali fit into it. He knew that Moskowitz was as familiar with the PA's personnel structure as we were. But for the sake of what was to follow, Menachem needed to establish the fact that Jabali was an Arafat appointee and a senior member of his security infrastructure.

Then Menachem sat down and Silvan took over. Moskowitz sensed it was time for the punchline, and he started to stir. Silvan's English wasn't good, and I suspected he was nervous about dealing with the Americans. But he spoke slowly, and his words were clear. He started by listing off a series of recent shootings against Israeli civilian motorists, many of them women and children. These were the days when mass suicide bombings weren't everyday events in the Middle East, as they are now. Such ambushes by Hamas and Islamic Jihad gunmen were still seen as significant terrorist attacks. The point of the Palestinian security apparatus – funded, armed, and supported by the United States and the European Union – had been to prevent exactly this sort of lawlessness. Every act of violence offered proof that the Palestinians weren't up to the job.

In fact, as my ISA colleagues demonstrated that day, the truth was much worse. Not only was Arafat doing little to stop terrorism, he was one of its sponsors.

Following his catalogue of recent terror attacks, Silvan turned on a VCR and began playing a movie. On the video screen was a Palestinian police officer who'd served under Jabali. He was sitting up in a hospital bed, eating a sandwich and answering questions that were being asked off-screen by an ISA case officer. Like everyone in the Arab affairs division at the ISA, Menachem spoke Arabic fluently. He provided simultaneous translation for Moskowitz's benefit as the video played.

According to his informal hospital bed confession, the injured Palestinian was one of three police officers who'd recently been shot in a gun battle with an IDF special forces unit operating on the Israeli side of the green line. (*Green line* refers to the armistice line established following Israel's War of Independence. It separates the West Bank and Gaza from Israel's pre-1967 territorial holdings.) The other two Palestinians had been killed in the battle, and this one was singing like a bird. By his own account, the wounded police officer was being treated well. The interviewer clearly had established a good rapport with the man, and the discussion was almost collegial in tone. To prove these weren't actors, Menachem opened his file and produced the Arab's Palestinian Authority ID, along with various photocopied Arabic-language identity papers.

During the recorded interview, which went on for about twenty minutes, the police officer admitted he and his colleagues were members of Ghazi Jabali's police force, and that they had been dispatched on missions to strike at Israeli civilian targets. The officer described again and again how Jabali ordered the attacks, and that he was taking orders from "Abu Ammar" –Yasser Arafat's nom de guerre.

For the first time since I'd met him, Moskowitz lost his cocky air and looked sincerely stunned. He said little, but everyone in the room could tell that he understood the importance of what he'd seen. Oslo and everything that followed had been predicated on the idea that Arafat was a sincere peace partner. Here on the screen was evidence suggesting everyone had been duped. And Moskowitz knew it fell to him to break the bad news to Ross and Clinton.

As for Menachem and Silvan, far from appearing triumphant, they looked nearly as deflated as Moskowitz. Critics are forever accusing Israel of using terrorism as a pretext to undermine the peace process. But the ISA's leadership is actually quite sympathetic to the concept of territorial compromise – if for no other reason than that it would make its job easier. Indeed, ISA case officers understand the Palestinian worldview better than any other non-Arab intelligence entity on earth. They live with Arab Israeli families for a year before they are put in the field, an experience that tends to give them some empathy. Some of the biggest peaceniks I've met in Israel were officers who'd served in the ISA.

When the meeting had ended, I accompanied Moskowitz to his car and made the short drive with him to the gate. He said very little. I got the feeling he was dreading his next report to Washington.

In the end, however, the Clinton administration decided to ignore the intelligence and stick to its game plan. I guess they hoped Ross would somehow find a way to convince Arafat to abandon his double game. As for Ghazi Jabali, he became a sort of pariah among the other Palestinian warlords, who were no doubt seeking to distance themselves from this outed terrorist.

The rest of the story is by now well known. For the next two years, Arafat continued supporting terrorism against Israel, and the United States kept pretending to ignore it. Then, in September 2000, following the failure at Camp David, Arafat rolled the dice with one final all-out offensive against Israel – a relentless campaign of butchery that culminated with Israel's invasion of the West Bank in 2002.

By this time, no one doubted Arafat's role in directing the terror. Documents seized by the Israelis during their 2002 invasion proved as much, as did Arafat's own calls for a "million martyrs" to descend on Jerusalem. By the time of his death in 2004, his career had come full circle – from terrorist to feted diplomat back to his true calling as terrorist.

I met Dennis Ross for the last time in Australia in 2001. By then, I was back in the field, and operating under a different Mossad pseudonym. The encounter took place at a social function to which we both happened to be invited. The well-intentioned host insisted on dragging me over to "meet" the famous Dennis Ross, who was holding court with a scrum of admiring listeners. Clinton was out of office, and

Ross had left government. The former envoy was now at liberty to speak candidly about Arafat, which was just what he was doing. Thankfully, he didn't remember me. Or, more probably, he knew exactly who I was but had the good grace not to betray it. Otherwise, my cover would have been blown sky-high in mixed company. That alone was reason enough for me to like and respect the guy.

Ross's theme that night was that Arafat had refused to deal at Camp David because he was incapable of accepting any final deal that definitively closed the door on any of the Palestinians' long-held maximalist demands. The conceit that Israel would one day grant the "right of return" to millions of descendants of 1948-era Palestinian refugees, fantastic as it may be, was particularly precious to Arafat. And so the only agreements he could bring himself to sign were those which, like Oslo, relegated the most explosive issues to future negotiations. After listening politely for a while, I asked Ross what Arafat really wanted.

"A one-state solution," he responded flatly. "Not independent, adjacent Israeli and Palestinian states, but a single Arab state encompassing all of historic Palestine."

However gullible Ross might once have been, it was clear the scales had fallen from his eyes. He hadn't achieved peace, but he'd at least succeeded in learning the truth.

14 | A MEGA SCANDAL

When people use the word "failure," failure means no focus,
no attention, no discipline, and those were not present in
what we or the FBI did here or around the world.

George Tenet

Jonathan Pollard, the American convicted of espionage in 1986 while working for the U.S. Navy Field Operational Intelligence Office, was not, as most people continue to believe, a Mossad-recruited spy. If he were, the U.S. government wouldn't have cottoned on to him so easily. The Mossad wouldn't touch such a poorly conceived and run operation like the Pollard case with a ten-foot pole. Rather, he was controlled by Lakam, an obscure and since disbanded office of Israeli intelligence run out of the prime minister's office.

The Pollard case was certainly a black eye for Israel. But in the country's defence, I should note that it's actually quite common for allies to spy on one another. (In 1995, to cite just one example, France deported five CIA officers who'd been caught with their hands in the cookie jar. The CIA lamely tried to spin the incident as a diversion orchestrated by the French to deflect attention from a scandal involving former prime minister Édouard Balladur, whose re-election was looking doubtful. Talk about lame excuses.) Moreover, the only reason Israel resorted to using Pollard was that Washington was at that time withholding crucial intelligence from Israel, even as we were sending valuable information back in the other direction.

In any case, the harsh treatment Pollard received – a life sentence with a recommendation against parole – was more a reflection of American embarrassment than any damage wrought by his espionage activities. The U.S. government wanted to make an example of Pollard, one that would discourage more serious acts of espionage by other allies. That's the only way to explain his receiving a prison sentence and gag order worse than those meted out to some convicted terrorists and Soviet-era communist moles.

The nature of the information Pollard gave to Israel remains secret. But some journalists have speculated that he handed over the names of CIA sources in Russia, which were in turn delivered to the KGB in return for the release of Russian Jews. To anyone who actually knows the ins and outs of international espionage, this theory is ridiculous. An analyst of Pollard's rank and station wouldn't be trusted with the code names of the CIA's Soviet-resident sources, let alone their true identities. Such information is rigidly compartmentalized within the CIA, and is rarely shared with military intelligence. (The CIA's dislike for the FBI is mild compared with its hostility toward the Pentagon.)

The relationship between the Mossad and the CIA has become strong in recent decades, and Israel now receives far more through its liaison channels than it ever could through a well-placed operative. But ever since the Pollard scandal broke, a vocal segment of the U.S. intelligence community remains convinced that Pollard was just one of many Israeli moles. This paranoia was only fuelled in

1990, when Canadian-born author Victor Ostrovsky, in his book *By Way of Deception,* purported to describe a top-secret Mossad department known as "Al" that is tasked with spying on the United States.

There was a Mossad department called Al – which means "above" in Hebrew. But it didn't spy on the United States, and being a mission-specific unit, it was shut down in 1998. Nevertheless, such tales as Ostrovsky's are widely believed. According to the fantasies entertained by Israel's critics, the Mossad is a sinister, ubiquitous force, its tentacles extending everywhere. As a result, perfectly innocent remarks or coincidences involving Mossad agents are seen by the Americans as evidence of Israeli scheming.

I recall one instance in 1997 when Stan Moskowitz summoned a group of Mossad officers into a CIA conference room and confronted us with photographs purportedly depicting an Israeli surveillance team spying on CIA operations at the U.S. embassy in Abidjan, Ivory Coast. With a condescending air of *j'accuse,* he reeled off the operatives' names, passport numbers, and hotels.

But when Uri and I did a little investigating that afternoon, we found out the surveillance team was actually targeting a local Hezbollah operative who'd been identified as a possible recruit. (Hezbollah has a long history of setting up shop in third world countries. Currently, Southeast Asia is the group's preferred location, but at the time it was sub-Saharan Africa.) Through some weird happenstance, the Mossad team had unwittingly stumbled across an unrelated CIA operation. The Americans immediately assumed they were the targets.*

The Ivory Coast affair was never publicized, so the only people who dwelled on it were members of the U.S. intelligence community.

---

* Conflicts between allied intelligence services such as the CIA and Mossad are rare, but they do happen. In the late 1990s, for instance, when it became clear that Iran was on a campaign to arm itself with unconventional weapons, its scientists became targets for

Unfortunately, the same wasn't true of the so-called Mega Affair, a similarly silly nonscandal that made news around the world thanks to a May 7, 1997 *Washington Post* story written by journalists Nora Boustany and Brian Duffy.

The scandal centred on a single taped remark made to a senior Israeli intelligence officer in Washington by a superior in Tel Aviv: "This is not something we can use Mega for." The tantalizing speculation underpinning the *Post* story was that "Mega" was some super-secret Israeli mole who'd burrowed deep into the heart of the U.S. national security establishment. A front-page story in the *Washington Post*, the Mega scandal became headline news around the United States and was subsequently picked up by much of the world press. The interest in the story was nestled in the fact that it was being portrayed as a major rift between Israel and the United States – which are regarded as uneasy allies at the best of times. In fact, there was no Mega mole. The whole brouhaha was based on a misinterpreted communication, coupled with the improper use of a Mossad cryptonym on an open telephone line.

The Mega scandal broke during my time at Tevel, and I was involved in many meetings where we discussed the best way to prove to the Americans that the NSA and the *Washington Post* had made a mountain out of a molehill. The easiest approach would have been simply to pick up the phone and dish the facts to someone senior at Langley. But for a variety of reasons, that wasn't the way these things were usually handled by the Mossad. For one thing, such a dialogue would require divulging Israeli tradecraft secrets to the Americans, who might or might not keep the information to

---

* HUMINT recruitment by the counter-proliferation departments of every Western intelligence service. There were so few targets, and so many eager to recruit them, that "deconfliction protocols" had to be established between services in order to ensure that a potential target for recruitment wouldn't end up fielding calls from half a dozen different spies.

themselves. Secondly, by the damned-if-you-do-damned-if-you-don't logic of Israel's critics, the mere fact that the Mossad was defensive about accusations of espionage provided further proof of guilt. In such situations, the Mossad's higher-ups tended to revert to the instinct that made them good spies earlier in their careers: they kept their mouths shut.

But shortly after the Mega scandal broke, the Mossad was handed a golden opportunity to debunk the matter in a discreet and definitive manner: a high-profile meeting on home turf with CIA Director George Tenet. And as things turned out, I was to have a role in the proceedings.

The Mossad uses cryptonyms for most of the figures in its orbit. (Mine remained "Ridley," as it had been since my first day of training back in 1989.) Some of these secret nicknames were merely silly, but Tenet, who was known to all of us as "Greaseball," was less fortunate. The term wasn't meant as an insult to the CIA director. It was simply that he seemed to fit the part of stereotypical Mafia don, complete with big cigar and sycophantic entourage.

As part of my work at Tevel, I often had to help play social host to visiting intelligence officials. The bigger the fish, the more elaborate the protocols. And Tenet was just about as large as they came. His visit to Israel in 1997 was his first as CIA director, and while his subsequent trips became almost routine, they were nowhere near in scope and importance as this initial foray into the region. He came with an army of assistants. I was always shocked by the sheer size of visiting American VIP delegations. By contrast, when Tenet's Israeli counterpart, the Mossad director general, travelled abroad, he took a single assistant with him, usually a communications specialist with a special laptop computer to handle his encrypted correspondence, and that's it. No security detail. No motorcade. No Air Force C-141

Starlifter outfitted with VIP appointments. The DG's only perk was that he flew business class.

My first meeting was with John, Tenet's security-detail commander, who arrived in Israel weeks before the CIA director. He was a fit young guy in his late twenties, carefully groomed, with short hair. The two of us hit it off immediately and became fast friends. (I gave him some Israeli wine from the Golan as a parting gift. In return, he gave me a CIA pen and a kind note instructing me to "aim the pen in the direction of my window for better reception.") We worked out the security details. During Tenet's visit, he and his team, including some thirty-five armed personnel, would ride in six armoured Chevy Suburbans from the U.S. embassy fleet. Escorting Tenet's core team would be two Mossad vehicles, fully loaded navy-blue turbo-charged Volkswagen Passat sedans, complete with chauffeurs and Mossad security officers armed with 9mm Uzis and GLOCK 19C pistols. I'd be in the first Passat, travelling a few minutes ahead of the pack. My Tevel colleague Danny would drive in the second vehicle, which would lead the motorcade, along with Mike from the CIA's Tel Aviv station.

Danny and I would be issued what we jokingly called "get-out-of-jail-free cards" – special passes that tell police we are on official business and that they should help us in any way we requested. We would also get magnetic police strobe lights to put on the roofs of our cars should we need to break a traffic rule or two. You'd think the Israel National Police would be among the first informed that Tenet was coming to town, but aside from the head of INP intelligence, they were completely in the dark. Telling the police was almost certain to produce a media leak.

From the tarmac at Ben Gurion Airport, the motorcade would travel to the Tel Aviv Sheraton, where Tenet would spend the night. In the morning, he would travel to Jerusalem for a meeting with

Netanyahu; then on to the Israel Defense Forces HQ for a meeting with the head of military intelligence and the IDF chief of staff; from there to the Israel Security Agency HQ for a meeting with Admiral Ami Ayalon; and finally back to the Mossad for meetings with the DG, Ephraim Halevy.

The next day, Tenet and his entourage would be on their own as they headed into bandit country to meet with Yasser Arafat and his various warlords. I knew Tenet's people were dreading that part of the trip because, as in present-day Iraq, everyone and his mother was running around with an AK-47 and a grudge against the United States.

When the big C-141 Starlifter landed at Ben Gurion, and taxied to the special area designated for VIP flights, Uri, Lucinda, Sheila, Danny, and I all approached the aircraft as part of the reception line. Stan Moskowitz and Mike were there, along with about a dozen members of the CIA station. Once the plane door opened, the on-board security detail fanned out and Tenet's entourage disembarked.

When Tenet got to me and Danny, he complimented us on our English with a smile and a wink. His charisma was immediately apparent. As I watched Tenet charm every Israeli he met over the next few days, I would come to understand why – notwithstanding his organization's failures surrounding 9/11 and the Iraq war – Tenet was so popular with the White House and the folks at Langley.

John, Pete, and I jumped into the lead Passat, and I gave Yigal, our driver, the signal to make for the Sheraton. As the car roared off, I reached up and placed the strobe on the roof. Sure enough, we immediately hit a traffic jam on the No. 1 Jerusalem–Tel Aviv highway. Yigal managed to avoid the gridlock by riding on the shoulder – until some idiot ahead of us tried the same trick without looking in his rear-view mirror first. We were doing about 130 kilometres an hour when Yigal hit the brakes, almost rear-ending the jackass.

The next day, security was especially tight at the PM's office: Yitzhak Rabin had been assassinated just two years earlier, and the place was swarming with buff, heavily armed people from the ISA's protective security division.

In the few minutes before Tenet's motorcade appeared at the PMO, I noticed a white Peugeot 605 sedan pull into the secure parking area. It was one of the Mossad DG's cars, and I recognized his driver, Golan, as he stepped out to open the back door. Ephraim Halevy emerged and stood waiting for Tenet. Rather than leave him standing idly, I walked over and shook his hand. I liked Halevy, and was gratified by this rare opportunity to spend some one-on-one time with him.

Halevy was British born, a nephew of Sir Isaiah Berlin, the renowned political philosopher and historian. Many considered him remote and donnish, but I could understand his sense of social detachment: he was a foreign-born Jew. Being an Israeli-born sabra is still a badge of honour. (In my case, even after living in Israel for many years, and serving in both its military and intelligence services, I was often jokingly called Kanadi, or Canadian, by my colleagues. They meant no harm, but the appellation served as a constant reminder that I, like everyone else, was marked by my birth.)

Halevy reminded me of George Smiley – John le Carré's fictional spymaster, as famously brought to life on screen by the late Alec Guinness – perhaps more than anyone else I encountered in my career. Like Smiley, he was bookish and reserved, while at the same time passionate about his cause – Israel, the Jewish people, and their continued survival. As a young child, he endured the Nazi Blitz in Britain, a formative experience that allowed him to appreciate the same brand of murderous hatred when it manifested itself in Middle Eastern garb following his emigration to Israel in 1948.

Despite his fame and power, Halevy was humble. I recall one day being passed a personal letter from his secretariat on the top floor of

Mossad HQ, which I was supposed to hand deliver to the liaison officer in London. I was permitted to read the note, and saw that it was a personal missive from Halevy to British playwright Tom Stoppard (author of the screenplay for *Shakespeare in Love*, among other famous works), whom Halevy had never met.

Stoppard is also Jewish, and he endured a similarly tumultuous childhood during the Second World War. In his note, Halevy reached out to Stoppard by lamenting all the common travails they'd endured in their younger years. It was a poignant letter that seemed entirely motivated by empathy rather than by any desire on Halevy's part to ingratiate himself with a famous personality. It says something about Halevy's humility that he started the letter out by explaining his job position as director general of the Israeli Secret Intelligence Service. This was during a period when the Mossad DG's name appeared regularly in every major newspaper in the world. I'm sure Tom Stoppard would have known who Ephraim Halevy was.

At the prime minister's office, I exchanged a few pleasantries with Halevy, and he inquired how the visit was proceeding. I told him that it was going off without a hitch, and barring any unforeseen incidents, was likely to remain as such. He nodded and I escorted him into the entrance of the building and then continued my vigil outside to wait for Tenet's arrival.

Once the motorcade arrived, Tenet had a cordial meeting with Netanyahu and a clutch of diplomats – Danny, Uri, and I included. There was much general discussion of the ongoing peace process, and the PM duly praised the CIA's efforts. It was mostly bromides about the need to co-operate and promote democratic principles in the world, but there was also some substantive discussion, and Netanyahu didn't hide his disdain for Arafat. Tenet was savvy enough not to make any remarks signalling his commitment one way or the other. I don't know if he was buying into Clinton's peace plan, but he wasn't about to let on in a room full of Israelis looking for signs of dissent.

Next, we took off for the IDF's headquarters, where I flashed my military ID card at the front gate. The document was supposed to allow me access to any military installation in the country. Unfortunately, the guard didn't recognize it and called his superior, at which point I had to go through the same discussion with a very serious young lieutenant. (This is why diplomatic motorcades generally have an advance car ten minutes ahead – so the VIP himself doesn't have to sit there waiting through such shenanigans.) I could have ordered the man to do what I wanted in a matter of seconds merely by pulling rank as a Mossad officer, but Mossad rules forbade doing this. All I was permitted to tell the lieutenant and his boss was that I was a special assistant in the "prime minister's office." (The vagueness of this job description made it useful in a wide variety of situations. In fact, even as late as 2003, long after my departure from the Mossad, I would describe myself in this way in the credit line of articles that I published in Western newspapers.)

After Tenet's visit to IDF HQ, the motorcade sped off to the last meeting at Mossad HQ, where we all took the elevator from the main entrance atrium to the DG's suite on the top floor. The director of the Central Intelligence Agency is the only foreign intelligence official in the world who is received in this way; all others, regardless of rank, must meet in the Mossad's liaison meeting rooms.

This was the meeting I was waiting for. I knew it was a golden opportunity for Halevy to tell Tenet what my colleagues and I already knew – that the Mega Affair was merely a misunderstanding arising from a single misinterpreted comment on a bugged phone line. The tone of the meeting was friendly – jovial, even. After a routine discussion of the many issues in which the two services have a shared interest, Halevy surprised everyone there – including me – by passing on a prime, top-secret intelligence resource, one that would supply the CIA with a steady stream of data for years. While I cannot divulge details, I can report that Tenet was impressed.

Unlike Tenet's meeting with the PM, this one did not deal much with the implementation of the Oslo Accords. Halevy merely warned Tenet about Arafat's duplicity, and affirmed the fact that the Mossad, as an apolitical government agency, could not be involved in peace-making. Despite the heavy subject matter of their discussions, there was an obvious warmth and chemistry between the two men, and it was gratifying to see them discussing matters on such good terms. While there is a lot of distrust between the two agencies, there is also a converse, friendlier side to the relationship, which proves that the CIA and the Mossad could accomplish just about anything together if they set aside their mutual suspicion. Some of the incredibly successful joint operations the two agencies have performed are monuments to their respective strengths.

Throughout it all, not a word was said about Mega. Whether this was because the Mossad had provided the CIA with the appropriate explanations through back channels (which I doubt), or because Halevy believed it was too hot a topic to be brought up in mixed company, I have no idea. But I remember being disappointed that he did not take the opportunity of this august meeting to definitively put the Mega scandal to rest.

Afterwards, we took the motorcade to the Sheraton and delivered Tenet to his security personnel, who were responsible for the next day's trip to Ramallah. For me, the only remaining event was a fancy dress-up dinner the next day at Mossad HQ – a good chance to hit the gin after what I considered to be a job well done.

As I mingled amidst the assembled CIA and Mossad big wheels, my cellphone buzzed. It was a call from the front desk informing me of the arrival of Tenet's wife, Stephanie Glakas-Tenet, and the couple's adolescent son, John Michael, in their armoured Chevy Suburban after a round of sightseeing.

I raced down to the gate, strained to open the Suburban's heavy bullet-proof door, jumped in, and introduced myself to Ms. Glakas-Tenet, an unusually lovely and poised woman. We sat in the Suburban's big leather seats and made small talk as the heavy vehicle rumbled up to the *midrasha*'s entrance, where the bored-looking security men waved us through.

Sensing the hour of chivalry upon me, I leapt dexterously out of the vehicle, turned graciously toward Ms. Glakas-Tenet, and offered her my hand, which she gripped at the wrist. As I completed this gesture, I spun toward the building, announcing with some grandeur that I would be only too pleased to escort her to her waiting husband.

But even as the words came out, I felt the heat emanating from an oversized cigar, its glowing business end not a foot from my face. It was Tenet, of course. Unbeknownst to me, he'd decided to meet his wife curbside, and apparently had been standing there throughout my brief Sir Walter Raleigh routine, studying my turn on the red carpet in bemused fashion.

Rescuing what dignity I could, I took a step backward and presented the Tenets to one another. The entourage around him tittered as I made my way toward the bar, where I soothed my wounds with a stiff gin and tonic.

And so, the Mega scandal was never officially debunked, nor even mentioned, during the course of our liaison relationship. For all I know, the counterintelligence paranoiacs in D.C. are still looking for an Israeli mole who doesn't exist.

The boring truth is that Mega had nothing to do with a Mossad secret agent buried deep in the heart of U.S. national security. It's half of the Mossad cryptonym for the CIA's Israel branch liaison at their

HQ in Langley. Just as Tenet was known as "Greaseball," this particular CIA officer – with whom the tiny Mossad station in Washington met almost daily – was known as "Megazord," a whimsical nickname derived from a character on the sci-fi children's television program *Power Rangers*. A Mossad officer had picked the cryptonym off the computer because his kid happened to like the show.

The Washington Mossad station in question was a two-person outfit consisting of Yoram, a U.K.-educated Mossad veteran, and Irit, a thirty-something intelligence analyst. Irit's liaison posting in D.C. was her first stint overseas, and it was her inexperience that led to the whole scandal.

Here is what happened:

Israel's ambassador in Washington, then Eliahu Ben-Elissar, called Irit at her embassy office and requested a copy of a letter written by former secretary of state Warren Christopher to Yasser Arafat concerning the 1997 Hebron Agreement between the Palestinian Authority and Israel.

Not knowing how to handle a request of this sort, Irit called Yoram, her superior, on a normal land-line telephone to his home in Chevy Chase. She passed on the ambassador's request and asked if they should take it to "Mega," which would have been an entirely appropriate and above-board thing to do.

Yoram, apparently irritated by his own ambassador's request, told her flatly, "No, this is not something we can use Mega for." The comment was heard by a National Security Agency snooper, who passed it up the chain. And along the line, someone apparently thought it was juicy enough to leak to the *Washington Post*. The story that touched off the scandal was based on a verbatim rendering of the leaked NSA intercept. This in itself served as evidence to us in the Mossad that someone with a political agenda hostile to the Mossad–CIA relationship stood behind the leak. NSA transcripts are classified top secret and their dissemination is very controlled. (I wasn't surprised years later when I read that newspaper columnist Robert D. Novak outed Valerie Plame, a covert CIA officer, in retaliation for public criticisms made by her husband about the Bush administration's case for invading Iraq.) If there was any scandal at all, it was that the NSA had bugged the Israeli embassy and the residences of its staff, which suggests that, in the late 1990s, the U.S. intelligence community was spending a lot of its precious time and resources chasing allies instead of terrorists. In any case, the NSA should have known that Israel didn't need them or some super-secret mole to find out about Christopher's letter to Arafat. There were plenty of Palestinians ready to tell us that. Netanyahu knew the contents of the letter within two weeks of its being sent to Arafat.

Despite the manner in which his words were misinterpreted, Yoram was right to deny his underling's request. The Mossad does not pester the CIA liaison with queries that are unrelated to intelligence matters. Certainly, during my tenure as a liaison officer, I never called up my CIA or FBI counterparts to ask for copies of diplomatic correspondence or the like.

And that's really all there was to it – except for one little six-degrees-of-separation detail: "Mega," as we all knew in Tevel's North America department, was none other than Harry, the same smooth CIA Hezbollah analyst who was visiting us in Tel Aviv for talks when two of our combatants were captured in Jordan.

To my knowledge, this true version of the Mega scandal has not been publicly revealed prior to the publication of this book. The real irony is that if Irit had simply said "Harry" instead of "Mega," the whole brouhaha would have been avoided. I don't know why Irit used a cryptonym on an open line anyway and can only put it down to her inexperience.

The morning after Tenet's visit to the PA, Danny and I stood on the tarmac at Ben Gurion Airport next to the stairs of Tenet's U.S. Air Force C-141 Starlifter as the CIA director approached to say his farewells. He shook our hands, and his parting words to us were "I wish I could have spent more time with you guys."

"Me, too," I said. But what I really wanted to say was, "Say hi to Harry for me!"

15 | JUST CALL ME MR. BOB

Every morning in Africa, a gazelle wakes up. It knows it must outrun the fastest lion or it will be killed. Every morning in Africa, a lion wakes up. It knows it must run faster than the slowest gazelle, or it will starve. It doesn't matter whether you are a lion or a gazelle: when the sun comes up, you'd better be running.

African proverb

My first face-to-face encounter with the entity the world now knows as al-Qaeda began on Friday, August 7, 1998, the day the group detonated truck bombs outside U.S. embassies in Nairobi, Kenya, and Dar es Salaam, Tanzania, killing 291 innocents, including twelve U.S. citizens (among them the unreported death of a CIA resident officer of the Agency's Nairobi station), and injuring over 4,500 African bystanders. On August 7, I was at home in Israel, enjoying a rare day off, but soon after the blasts my pager went off. It was an urgent request to call the Mossad's 24/7 communications centre.

I checked in by phone, then raced to HQ in my tiny Renault, and ran up the two flights of stairs to the counterterrorism department.

There, I found Etti, now an analyst in the World Jihad branch (known informally as the "department of awful Ahmeds"), and a few others studying the cable traffic from our liaison station in Nairobi. I noticed Etti had a cigarette going; a tough old hand like Etti could get away breaking the no-smoking rule under these circumstances. She greeted me with her usual flurry of casual obscenities and handed me a stack of reports that brought me up to speed.

I sat at my desk and took a deep breath. As the point man in the Mossad's counterterrorism liaison relationship with the CIA and FBI, I knew my phone was about to start ringing off the hook. The first call came from Mike at the CIA station in Tel Aviv. After commiserating over the bombings in general terms, he hung up and called me back on the secure telephone unit. Mike's voice warbled through the line as he went through a series of questions. Did we know anything about the attacks? Had we received any prior warnings? Could the Mossad help find the perpetrators?

I answered no to the first two questions and a definite yes to the third.

In the summer of 1998, the Mossad and CIA were exchanging daily memos on a number of liaison issues: unconventional weapons proliferation; Islamic terrorism; and the activities of rogue states such as Syria, Iran, North Korea, and Iraq – to name a few. Sometimes, the memos were exchanged during face-to-face meetings held in the liaison division's conference rooms. At other times, they were exchanged at the Mossad's front gate in plain manila envelopes. Mike usually called to find out if any U.S. citizens had been killed or injured in the latest terrorist attack on Israeli soil by Hamas or Islamic Jihad (almost two hundred thousand American citizens live in Israel). Now he was calling me because his country had been attacked directly. The evolution in our relationship was grim confirmation of something I'd instinctively realized years before: Israel's battle would eventually become the world's.

Mike and I agreed to set aside other matters and work single-mindedly on the African file. Over the next seventy-two hours, I leaned hard on the Mossad's counterterrorism department, calling on Etti and her colleagues repeatedly for any tidbit of information the Americans might find useful. Etti dismissed me as a *nudnik*, a Yiddish term that translates roughly to "boring pest." But I wanted to show the CIA that the Mossad was eager to help America in its time of need.

It wasn't hard to figure out who had committed the embassy bombings. On February 23 of that same year, Osama bin Laden and his deputy, Ayman al-Zawahiri (the head of Egyptian Islamic Jihad, which was soon to be subsumed into al-Qaeda), issued a fatwa telling followers that "to kill Americans and their allies, civilians, and military is an individual duty of every Muslim who is able." A few months later, bin Laden told ABC News that al-Qaeda intended to launch attacks on U.S. targets around the world. Shortly thereafter, in July, U.S. and local authorities succeeded in foiling a planned attack by al-Jihad al-Islami (also known as Egyptian Islamic Jihad) on the U.S. embassy in Tirana, Albania. (Those terrorists were promptly extradited to Egypt, where they were likely interrogated and executed after a speedy, meaningless trial.)

A few days after the embassy attacks, I found myself in a room with Uri, the liaison department head; Etai, head of the counter-terrorism department's World Jihad branch; and Etti. We were watching video footage from Nairobi taken shortly after the bombing by a team of Israel Security Agency counterterrorism experts and a contract civilian structural engineer. It was horrific to watch; ruined and dismembered bodies were strewn everywhere and many of them were charred and smoking. Some of the people were clearly still alive and had been spared bleeding to death only because their wounds were instantaneously cauterized by the flash of the explosion. Many people were trapped under the rubble, and those that had the strength to do so were screaming. To have been there must have been to witness hell on earth.

None of us were virgins when it came to this kind of thing. In our professional capacities, we'd all seen the results of suicide bombings before. But this one was particularly awful. The Kenyans were clearly unprepared to deal with such a scenario, and mass confusion ruled. Even hours after the blast, when the footage was taken, wounded victims were still staggering about. No doubt, dozens died for lack of timely medical care.

Sadly, Israel is experienced like no other nation on earth in dealing with such post-attack emergency-management scenarios. In Tel Aviv and Jerusalem, the wounded typically are cared for within minutes. And it's not uncommon for commercial venues that have been attacked to be up and running within days, as if nothing had happened. The speed reflects the proficiency of our first responders and forensics teams. But such haste also carries a political message to the terrorists: "Yes, you hurt us, but life goes on." Personally, I think the bravest people in the world are the shop and café owners who open their doors again after having suffered a terrorist attack. That takes more guts and determination than strapping on an explosive belt and blowing up innocent men, women, and children.

I watched the video with a mix of revulsion and anger. There was a personal connection for me: by coincidence, I had been in Kenya only the previous year with my Dad. He had invited me to go on safari, and it was one of the best times we'd ever shared together. I loved the place, warts and all.

During that trip, we lived under canvas with no electricity, gas, or refrigeration for three weeks – as Hemingway had during his own trip to Africa. (Forgive the lofty comparison, but the man is a personal hero.) My father would arise at dawn each morning and inquire as to whether I had been eaten by some predator in the night. When I'd reply that I was still in one piece, he'd sound disappointed. We affected British colonial administrator accents (easier for my father, who had resided in the U.K. for almost two decades). I called him "Carruthers" and he called me "Simpkins" for the duration of the safari (and for some time afterward). The Africans thought us mad.

What I remembered most fondly were the indigenous people. We had Masai and Samburu tribesmen accompany us and guard our camp at night. They were magnificent fellows with their red robes, sandals, and spears. Their customs fascinated me, and I often day-dreamed about joining their tribal ranks and leaving the worries of the Middle East to a past life.

My father observed me with bemusement as I hung around their campfire, asking them how to say this or that – lion, cheetah, ele-phant, hello, goodbye – whatever I could soak up in their local dialect or Swahili. They probably thought me a pest, but they were kind enough to answer my questions. We went to one of their vil-lages, and it was all mud huts, flies, and dusty cattle. I remember marvelling at how unchanged this way of life had remained for thou-sands of years. Before we left Africa, my father, who passed away in 2004, gave me a phrase booklet that explained Swahili grammar and diction. The Masai gave me a walking stick made from an African olive tree. I still treasure both.

Terrorism is indefensible. But targeting such a poor country, where the only apparent crime was hosting a U.S. embassy, is espe-cially senseless. It was yet another sign to me that Islamic terror really had little to do with a supposed battle against Western impe-rialists, as its practitioners insisted. Rather, it was a pseudo-religious death cult animated by a xenophobic and nihilistic ideology.

The one image from the ISA video that haunted me most was the smoking, torn-up remains of an elderly man being pulled from the wreckage of a collapsed building. The poor man was dressed in what looked like his best (and probably only) brown suit. All I could think about were the many kind smiles that men like him had given me during my recent visit. I turned to Uri, Etti, and Etai, and said, "Ma ha'ish hazeh assa lehem" (What did that guy ever do to them?). No one answered me. I left the room. I'd seen enough.

Over the next few weeks, more evidence came in. There was no longer any doubt about al-Qaeda's involvement.

The African embassy file brought me into prolonged contact with the both the CIA and FBI. As America's federal law enforcement agency, the FBI operates primarily within the United States. But since breaches of U.S. laws often take place overseas, many of its agents are deployed abroad. The CIA regarded this situation with disdain. Even in my presence, Agency officers would casually deride the FBI as "the bastards across the river."

Since Legat was new in Tel Aviv and strapped for cash, they couldn't implement a secure communication system with the Mossad. A simple solution would have been for the CIA station in Tel Aviv to let the FBI officers use their equipment. But of course they didn't – the result being that I couldn't communicate with the FBI unless it was through face-to-face meetings.

As a result of this juvenile behaviour, much American manpower was wasted on both sides. As part of the Oslo peace effort, for instance, the CIA and the FBI were both courting various Palestinian factions – each oblivious to the other's efforts. In a meeting with the two groups, I commented that before the CIA and FBI created peace between Israelis and Palestinians, they should try it out on each other.

On another occasion, at a joint conference on counter-terrorism issues, I witnessed an exchange in which an FBI officer made a nasty crack about the CIA, only to hear a CIA officer respond, "At least we never had a transvestite for a director" (a reference to the secret habits of legendary FBI director J. Edgar Hoover). Such juvenile barbs couldn't be serious, I thought. Yet no one on either side was laughing. In fact, some CIA officers even complained that the FBI was putting surveillance on them. Whether this was true or not, I couldn't say. But the fact that the CIA would even suspect as much was astounding. Of course, the rift between the two agencies is no laughing matter. In fact, better interagency communication might well have led to the detection and thwarting of the 9/11 conspiracy.

As is now well known, the CIA tracked two of the 9/11 hijackers – Khalid Almidhar and Nawaf Alhazmi – to a 2000 terrorist summit in Kuala Lumpur, Malaysia, where they met 9/11 organizer Ramzi bin al-Shibh and other über-jihadists. After that meeting, the CIA learned, the pair went on to Los Angeles. But the Agency didn't share this information with the FBI, the Immigration and Naturalization Service, or the State Department.

As a direct result, the names of the two men were never added to the terrorist watch list accessed by border agents. Even in June 2001, when the CIA finally came to the FBI for help in tracking down Almidhar and Alhazmi, the Agency pointedly refused to divulge critical information about the pair. According to a senior FBI official interviewed by a reporter for the PBS program *Frontline*, that meeting, held just three months before the World Trade Center attacks, ended in a shouting match.

Even within the FBI itself, there were problems. For all its other flaws, the CIA has a streamlined reporting system similar to that of the Mossad, ensuring a steady flow of information back to Langley,

Virginia. The FBI is different. From what I observed, the Bureau's New York field office operates like a separate FBI, and goes its own way independent of what HQ dictates.

I saw further evidence of CIA–FBI screw-ups first-hand. Once, I received a memo from the CIA requesting information about Sami al-Arian, Palestinian Islamic Jihad's Florida-based chief of U.S. operations. Six weeks down the line, I received the same request, using different wording, from the FBI. When I asked a member of the CIA's Tel Aviv station, "Do you not share?" he replied with a terse "No." Being neither a servant of the U.S. government nor a member of either organization, I couldn't do anything about the situation. All I could do was feel embarrassment for both outfits for behaving so childishly in front of the Israeli intelligence community.

To an Israeli's eyes, it was an odd way to defend U.S. national security. From the moment I joined Mossad HQ, it was clear that Israel's intelligence community functions as one, and freely shares intelligence on any number of issues, terrorism in particular. Disagreements occurred – I saw plenty in my time – but they never affect things at the operational level. In fact, many Mossad and ISA officers are great pals outside of their professional lives.

If interagency co-operation within the United States was a joke, you can imagine how co-operation with other nations was conducted. As I learned the hard way, the stereotype of the CIA as an all-knowing, all-controlling, cloak-and-dagger outfit is the furthest thing from reality. In truth, it more closely resembles a bloated corporate bureaucracy, weighed down by deadwood, scared of change, and suspicious of outsiders. During my tenure as liaison officer, the CIA did not consistently co-operate with Israel on the terrorism file, even when it was clear the two nations had the same interests at stake.

One reason was that the U.S. intelligence community – which, in 1998, had a disclosed annual budget of US$27 billion – had difficulty taking the Mossad seriously. Our entire North America department consisted of about six people, one of whom worked with the Canadian Security Intelligence Service. That left five of us to deal with the CIA and FBI. To put that number in perspective, the CIA station operating out of the U.S. embassy in Tel Aviv *alone* employs about thirty personnel. Meanwhile, the Mossad station in Washington consisted of two very overworked officers.

But the more important reason the Americans didn't share information with us, in my opinion, was that they were afraid of what we'd do with it – that if they gave us, say, the whereabouts of a senior Hezbollah commander, we'd go bump him off and they would be implicated. In pre-9/11 days, the CIA was constrained by Executive Order 12333, which prohibits any U.S. government from carrying out assassination operations both directly and through second or third parties. At the upper reaches, the CIA was in fact a very conservative organization due to the intense oversight of all its activities, and more than a little gun-shy since the heyday of their operations in Vietnam and Latin America. They adopted an organizational culture that preferred words to actions in all but the most extreme situations.

In this sense, there was (and probably still is) a rift between the Agency's leadership and its field agents, many of whom share the same proactive, gung-ho spirit as their Mossad counterparts. But often politics would thwart their best efforts. When George Tenet, the CIA's director, became a key intermediary in the Israeli–Palestinian conflict – as he did by order of the Clinton Administration shortly after the Oslo Accords were signed – it was obvious that the intelligence agency had lost its way. The CIA was never intended to be an arm of the State Department.

Despite the lack of reciprocity, Tel Aviv continuously fed Washington information.* I wasn't bitter about the largely one-way nature of this information flow, I was simply looking to catch the bad guys through any means possible.

The Israeli contribution to the African bombing investigation began with a single careless phone call – a conversation between an officer of the Iranian Ministry of Intelligence and Security (MOIS) and a pair of Egyptian al-Jihad al-Islami leaders who were hanging about in Baku, Azerbaijan. The two parties were arranging a meeting. They didn't know that the Mossad was listening in on their call.

It was Thursday – six days after the embassy bombings – and the MOIS–al-Jihad meeting they discussed was scheduled for the coming week. We didn't have much time to react. But I felt that, with more information, the Mossad might be able to act on this intelligence. I met with Etai and requested that we put intensive SIGINT coverage on their telephone communications. The move paid off. During subsequent phone calls, the targets revealed that they'd organized the African attacks. They also disclosed the exact time of their upcoming meeting, and the place as well: the lobby of the very Baku hotel where all of them were staying. Finally, they let on that one of the al-Jihad members in attendance would be none other than a very big fish named Ihab Saqr, a Zawahiri lieutenant who'd masterminded the 1995 bombing of the Egyptian embassy in Islamabad

---

* In at least one recent case, it was the Americans who reportedly misused Israeli-provided intelligence. In October 2005, Israel passed on to Washington the contents of a letter written by al-Qaeda second in command Ayman al-Zawahiri to Abu Musab al-Zarqawi, the terrorist group's leader in Iraq. The letter was not to be made public. But John Negroponte, the U.S. director of national intelligence, subsequently published it on his office website, and President George W. Bush mentioned it during a radio address. According to Israeli intelligence sources, who were reportedly furious over the episode, these indiscretions may have compromised their intelligence-gathering network in Iraq.

under the auspices of another bloodthirsty Egyptian terrorist group, al-Gama'at al-Islamiyya.*

Furthermore, we learned that a certain Ahmed Salama Mabrouk was hiding out in Azerbaijan, and would join the meeting. Mabrouk was a ranking member of al-Qaeda who'd been sentenced to life in prison for his role in the 1981 assassination of Egyptian president Anwar Sadat. After serving just seven years, he'd returned to his terrorist roots, living on the run in Afghanistan, Pakistan, Sudan, Albania, and finally, Azerbaijan.

I began drafting a memo for the CIA, in the hope that they could act on our intelligence. But first I had to get clearance to share the information. Whatever the risks, I thought it was important that the Americans know about the meeting in Baku. And so I invested whatever professional capital I had in securing permission to give the Agency the memo. After some intra-Mossad horse-trading – including various promises to bring home expensive boxes of Belgian chocolates on my next trip overseas – I gained the needed permission.

I typed the translation from Hebrew to English myself because the translator had left for the weekend – as I have said, the Mossad runs a shoestring operation – and then proceeded to call Andy, the Counterterrorism Center representative at the CIA's Tel Aviv station. When I called Andy on the secure link, he responded in his semi-stoned way. "I have something that may be of interest to you," I announced.

"Cool," he replied.

---

* Al-Gama'at al-Islamiyya was also responsible for the murder of fifty-eight tourists in Luxor, Egypt, in November 1997, an attack so vicious that it prompted the Egyptian government to implement a major crackdown on homegrown terrorists. The strength of that crackdown is ultimately what motivated Zawahiri and other Egyptian terrorists to take their jihad beyond the Arab world.

After I sent the fax, I waited to hear some kind of excited reaction.

"Thanks," Andy said dully. "I'll pass it on."

"Andy, do you know who these guys *are*?" I asked.

"No," he said, with a foggy honesty that I had to admire.

I gave him thumbnail biographies of Saqr and Mabrouk. Then I suggested he not only pass the information on to the CTC at Langley, but also call the Agency's station in Baku and try to get their officers to have the "locals" raid the meeting. I reminded Andy that we were on a tight timetable and that he might want to convey a sense of urgency.

"I'll call them right away and get back to you later," he promised.

Washington was seven hours behind, and it was getting late in the day. But I stuck around, hoping Andy would be able to get hold of someone in a position of authority.

He did call me back and reported that the station in Baku consisted of two officers – one who was ill and one who was away on vacation, but on his way back to Baku. He gently suggested that the Agency regarded the landlocked former Soviet republic as something of a backwater (which I'd already guessed), and that the staffers there weren't exactly A-list. Before hanging up, we set a meeting for the next day at our offices. Then I updated Etai and went home for the night.

On Friday, Andy called me early in the morning. He told me the CIA really wanted to pick Saqr up. He also said the CTC boys were quite impressed by our ability to generate SIGINT in a hole as obscure as Azerbaijan, which gave Etai and me a nice ego boost.

To the Agency's credit, they were willing to divert resources to accomplish the operation without the usual six months of lobbying, bureaucracy, congressional hearings, and heavens knows what else that typically preceded CIA operations in the pre-9/11 world. This was good news.

I called Uri, my department head, and he told me he'd already discussed the matter with Itzik, the division chief. "Itzik wants you to go to Azerbaijan and make sure we are kept in the loop," Uri told me. "These are big fish and we want fishing rights. This is our operation as much as theirs," he added. "Don't ask them. Just tell them that you'll be there."

I knew one of the reasons Itzik wanted me to go was that, being a native English speaker, I could pass myself off as one of the Americans and not let on that Israel was running the show from behind the scenes.* Though I felt myself coming down with a bug of some kind, this order was coming from the top. I told Uri I'd go.

When Andy arrived at the Mossad's front gate on Friday afternoon, I escorted him to a meeting room in the main HQ building. When we got there, Etai was waiting, along with coffee and an assortment of pastries. (The Mossad is renowned for its hospitality to other services. The liaison division, in particular, has a small catering department that is famous for its cheesecake. The officers in the Mossad station in Washington complain that such hospitality is rarely reciprocated – especially at the FBI, where they are lucky to get a can of Coke from the vending machine.)

During the meeting, I emphasized that it was important to make sure the Azerbaijan security services didn't know who the targeted individuals were. "It's nothing personal, we just have to protect our sources, and Azerbaijan is not yet out of its diapers intelligence-wise," I told the others. I then dropped my little bomb on Andy:

---

* For a variety of reasons, I never let on to the Americans that I was Canadian-born. To keep them guessing, I often would use expressions commonly used by South Africans and Brits. (I'd call the trunk of the car "the boot" and refer to street lights as "robots," for instance.) Once, at a meeting with a high-level delegation that had arrived from the United States to discuss Hezbollah, I sat with a copy of a small dictionary that "translated" expressions from American to British English.

"I have been instructed to travel to Azerbaijan as part of the operation. You can handle the Azeris, but we want to make sure that everything goes down as planned."

The only proviso, I added, was that we would like to have access to all the intelligence extracted from Saqr and his friends. We especially wanted them to grill the MOIS officer. I'd never come face to face with an Iranian intelligence officer, and I was eager to hear what he'd cough up after being worked over by the locals.

Andy clearly wasn't happy about the prospect of Israeli supervision. But he remained polite and told me he'd let the people at Langley know about the change in plans.

Etai then made an audiovisual presentation to brief Andy about the upcoming terror conclave in Baku. Andy told us he did not foresee any problems: the Agency station had good contacts with the Azeri locals, and they'd pretty much do as told.

Andy called me later that day, and told me Langley would be sending a team from "somewhere in Europe" (which turned out to be Germany) to Baku the next day. I was already booked for my flight and would arrive on the Tuesday – notwithstanding my increasingly nasty flu.

Some may wonder why al-Qaeda would have anything to do with an obscure locale like Azerbaijan. But terrorists intentionally seek out weak states where the lack of public order makes it easy to evade or co-opt local authorities. Afghanistan, Sudan, Lebanon, the tribal areas of Pakistan: they all follow this pattern. Azerbaijan presented al-Qaeda with another advantage as well: it provided a staging area for infiltration into nearby Chechnya, a jihad hotspot since the early 1990s.

Baku was sunny when I arrived. The city is surprisingly picturesque, and the people are generally friendly to Westerners. If I had

had more time, I would have spent a few days taking in the city's famous architecture – a vivid mix of medieval forms and eclectic nineteenth-century European influences. But instead I had to rush to a meeting with Jason, the head of the import CIA team that was coordinating efforts with the Azerbaijan locals.

This was not one of the local B-raters Andy had warned me about. Jason was a tall fellow in his fifties with greying temples and hazel eyes. He looked lean and somewhat patrician, a type that I understand to be in favour in the Ivy League ranks of the CIA. He had a nice smile, and projected an air of competence.

My flu had gotten even worse during the flight, and Jason could tell I was woozy. When I reassured him that I'd be fine, we drank tea in a neutral hotel lobby. Quickly moving to the subject of cover, we agreed that I would be cast as part of the U.S. delegation as far as the Azeris were concerned. My name would be Bob – boring but stereotypically American, and easy to remember in my somnambulant state.

Despite our agreement to co-operate, we still maintained a guarded posture with each other. Jason didn't want me to be too familiar with the CIA's methods, and I wasn't about to elucidate our ways for him either. We both agreed on one thing, however: the arrest should be as low-key as possible. "The locals know the suspects are Islamic extremists but are thinking more in terms of Chechnya," Jason said. "They'll pick them up and hold them, and then we'll have our crack at them, but it's their jurisdiction."

We exchanged cellphone numbers and I returned to my hotel, where I put a call through to HQ and gave them what details I could over the phone. (I could have gone over to the Israeli Embassy on Izmir Street and sent a secure cable, but I didn't want to arouse any-one's suspicions.) I took some Acamol – Israel's answer to Tylenol – and promptly got into bed.

I was fast asleep, shivering through my fever, when the masterminds of the Africa bombings were arrested. When the call informing me of their arrest came through to my room, I was totally disoriented. Jason asked me to meet him again at the same hotel lobby. Without changing clothes or bothering to do anything about my haggard appearance, I ran downstairs and tumbled into a beat-up taxi.

When I arrived, Jason saw that I was a wreck, but I brushed off his concerns and asked for a recap. He said that Ihab Saqr, Ahmed Salama Mabrouk, and another al-Jihad activist named Essam Marzouk were in custody after being apprehended in a lightning-fast raid on their hotel by the Azeri security forces. (Our SIGINT later picked up a few calls from al-Jihad activists and a very pissed-off Ayman al-Zawahiri, who wondered where in the hell his men had disappeared to. The Azeri arrest team had bagged them so quickly that none were able to alert their masters.) They offered no resistance and, given my understanding of the Azeri methods, to put up any kind of fight would have resulted in a lot of physical pain for the al-Qaeda terrorists.

Apparently, the MOIS officer never showed up or, having been stood up, ran back to Tehran. Who the Iranian was and what happened to him remains a mystery to this day. None of us ever figured out why he was a no-show.

In a strange twist of fate, it turned out that Essam Marzouk recently had been part of an al-Qaeda cell based in Vancouver, Canada – less than two hours from my hometown. Marzouk had been a radical from a young age. When he was nineteen, he left Egypt and made his way to the Wild West terrorist frontier of the Pakistan–Afghanistan border, where he fell in with al-Qaeda. In 1993, he fled to Vancouver with a suitcase full of fake ID, and duped Canadian authorities into giving him permanent residence status with a view to full citizenship. But in 1998, he returned to Afghanistan to serve bin Laden and Zawahiri.

They promptly dispatched him to Baku, where he'd been coordinating terrorist operations ever since – including the embassy bombings in Nairobi and Tanzania.

Jason took me to the Baku security services' holding cells and interrogation centre located in a building not far from my hotel. It was a dank affair and a crumbling relic from the Soviet days. There I was introduced to a fellow named Ayaz, who referred to me as "Mr. Bob." Ayaz was clearly in charge – and he projected it unapologetically, as only a third world alpha male can. He was squat with gold teeth and a black moustache that would make Saddam Hussein and his onetime entourage envious. He smiled as we were introduced, and I experienced a waft of garlic breath that could strip paint. He looked very pleased with the day's developments. As Ayaz took us to the cells, he barked commands to his underlings in a language that sounded like something between Russian and Farsi to my ear.

I needed to have a look so that I could confirm their arrest for the benefit of Mossad HQ. Sure enough, there they were – each sitting in his little holding cell – as a direct result of my intelligence gathering and some pretty fast manoeuvring by the Mossad's counterterrorism department. Because of our initiative, three of the highest-ranking masterminds behind the murder of Kenyans and Americans were locked away in an Azeri jail. They looked dazed and roughed up, but I didn't have any sympathy for them. In my flu-induced delirium, I was thinking about the poor old African man pulled from the Nairobi bombing in his Sunday best. Like a drunkard, I blurted out "You are fucking pricks."

I must have seemed a fool, as Jason looked embarrassed for me. We don't get personal in this business, because it's pointless to take the world on your shoulders – you'll only end up drinking too much or sucking on the end of a pistol. Jack told me to go get some rest. There was to be no questioning for now and the three were to remain on ice for the time being. I returned to my hotel feeling a real sense of accomplishment and knowing that I would make some terrorism analysts very happy once the questioning began. I was imagining the wealth of leads and insights this would open up into the shadowy and murky world of al-Qaeda terrorist operations for all of us waging the battle against them.

At this point, the tale goes weird. Things didn't go quite as we'd planned.

Before I left Baku, Jason and I had another powwow, and I brought up the question of keeping the three amigos on ice for a while longer, because I knew the Mossad's counterterrorism department, and possibly the ISA, would want to send some interrogators to Baku to question them. Jason said that would be fine, and we agreed to let our respective HQs work out the details.

And then . . . that was it. Nobody from the Mossad, myself included, ever saw the trio again.

I later found out, through Arab media reports, that the three men had been handed over to Egyptian authorities and prosecuted as terrorists. In other words, they'd become early victims of the process now commonly known as "extraordinary rendition." Since 9/11, the CIA has reportedly dealt with hundreds of terror suspects in this manner – essentially creating their own mini-airline for purposes of getting jihadists out of Western jurisdictions and into the hands of countries like Egypt, where men in the mould of Ayaz know how to make people talk.

I'm not a strong proponent of renditions – not because I'm a human rights purist, but because they lead to the sort of scandals that recently have plagued the CIA. Hawks typically sneer at the idea that terrorism can be treated as a criminal justice problem, and in many cases, they're right. But there really was no reason these three terrorists couldn't have been tried in a U.S. Federal court. If

Zacarias Moussaoui could stand trial for his peripheral role in the 9/11 attacks, why couldn't this trio be treated in the same way?*

In an interview with the London-based *Al Hayat* newspaper, Ahmed Salama Mabrouk said his group had drafted a plan for "carrying out 100 attacks against U.S. and Israeli targets and public figures in different parts of the world." These plans, Mabrouk claimed, were frustrated when the CIA arrested him and seized a computer disk containing details of the attacks.

When I was in Azerbaijan, I never heard anything about a computer disk. But I have little doubt that Mabrouk and Saqr were guilty, ditto Marzouk. In late 2001 and early 2002, U.S. forces sifting through the materials left by al-Qaeda terrorists in Afghanistan safe houses came across business cards for a certain Canadian company called 4-U Enterprises. Marzouk was one of the company's directors.

The Egyptians sentenced Mabrouk to life in prison. At the time, he was number three in the al-Qaeda hierarchy, and probably ranks as the most significant al-Qaeda leader ever taken alive – at least until 9/11 mastermind Khaled Shaikh Mohammed, al-Qaeda's chief of operations, was captured in 2003. Marzouk got fifteen years – so I guess I won't be running into him at my local Starbucks. As for Saqr, his fate is unknown. Personally, I hope he was hanged.

We never received a word about the fate of these men from the Agency – we had to read it in the media and subsequent communications intercepts. Andy was apologetic, but it was clear he wouldn't tell us anything. He'd apparently received instructions from his superiors at Langley to shrug a lot and remain quiet behind his Ray-Bans when queried.

---

* What makes America's approach odder is the fact that U.S. prosecutors launched criminal prosecutions against other embassy bombing conspirators. In October 2001, four of those men – Mohamed Rashed Daoud al-Owhali, Mohammed Odeh, Wadih el Hage, and Khalfan Khamis Mohamed – were sentenced to life in prison without parole.

Though I was disappointed we'd never had the chance to inter-rogate the trio, I was told by Itzik to leave the matter alone. Etai got the same instructions before he flew to Washington a few months later for bilateral talks on al-Qaeda activities. Both of us were award-ed a director general's commendation for the operation. But the Americans never gave us so much as a thank-you for handing them three al-Qaeda heavyweights.

16 | OUT OF ZIMBABWE

For to be free is not merely to cast off one's chains, but to live
in a way that respects and enhances the freedom of others.

Nelson Mandela

The disappointing conclusion of the Baku operation coupled with two years of sleepless nights and interagency office politics were enough to convince me that I'd had enough of my liaison job. My desk job at Tevel definitely had its perks and even a few glamorous moments, but a promotion to running counterterrorism operations in Southeast Asia and Africa seemed better suited to my abilities. It was the kind of job I had been looking for after the white-collar environment that was making me restless and fidgety. Truth be told, I missed the excitement of life undercover.

Although going back into the field would mean spending less time with my family in Israel, Dahlia and the kids knew it was something I needed to do in order to avoid falling into the sort of ennui-driven rut I'd found myself in two years previous. And so, in December of 1998, I finally put in for a transfer.

The new unit I'd joined, Bitsur, was mandated with recruiting locally based assets (helpers that are either recruited or inherited by predecessors to provide intelligence, background information, and logistical support, conducting covert operations, and helping out other overstretched operational divisions. One of its primary missions was helping Jews in countries where they faced persecution. Shortly after the Mossad was founded in 1951, in fact, it was Bitsur that helped secretly exfiltrate some of Israel's first immigrants from North Africa, Syria, Lebanon, Iraq, Iran, Yemen, and even Ethiopia. I was proud of my new division's lineage: because the very purpose of Israel's creation was to provide a home for endangered Jews, I wistfully regarded Bitsur as the Mossad's soul.

One factor that helped my working conditions with Bitsur was that an irritant from my 1990s-era combatant days, Charles, wasn't in the picture. Nor was any partner, for that matter. Because Mossad manpower was so scarce, backwaters in places like Africa were all but ignored, and I was required to operate solo. From 1998 to 2001, I was the Mossad's *only* agent in all of subequatorial Africa except for liaison stations in Nairobi and Pretoria.

My new boss, Michel, was originally from France. At the time I joined Bitsur, he'd just taken over as head of the unit following a posting in Europe. Michel was in his early fifties, a clinical psychologist by training and a pretty decent guy (although, truth be told, I never really wanted to spend much time with him because he was such a heavy smoker). Like many Mossad officers, he looked the farthest thing from a Hollywood spy. Michel was short and bald, and taken with wearing the kind of vest favoured by sports fisherman. "I love zee pockets," he would say. "Zey are, 'ow you say, ideal for zis kind of work." (This is no cheesy Pepé Le Pew stereotype. Michel actually *did* talk like this.)

The unit Michel had inherited in 1998 was rundown and regarded as something of a joke by the Mossad's other operational divisions. But in just two years, he turned it around by recruiting choice manpower from other parts of the Mossad. (Michel was on pretty close terms with Director General Ephraim Halevy, and this helped get him the support he needed when other division heads complained about his poaching. To Halevy's credit, he understood the importance of helping out fellow Jews in trouble – even if, like him, they weren't Israeli-born sabras.) It wasn't long before circumstances in Africa renewed Bitsur's traditional role as rescuers of threatened Diaspora communities.

Perhaps no country epitomizes the lost potential of sub-Saharan Africa more perfectly than Zimbabwe. Here is a nation of thirteen million people that, by rights, should be one of the economic tigers of the developing world. Its soil is among the most fertile on the continent and, until recently, its farms the most productive – in large part thanks to the corps of experienced white farmers who stuck around after the country shed colonialism in 1980.

But all this ended in 2000 when long-time ruler Robert Mugabe, feeling the heat from a democratic opposition campaign led by Morgan Tsvangirai, launched a series of pogroms against the country's tiny white population, who he claimed were supporting his political opponents. Armies of thugs loyal to Mugabe's ZANU-PF movement occupied the choicest white-owned farms, which were carved up and doled out to the president's gangster cronies. Most of the farmers relocated to neighbouring African countries. Their land, which once produced bumper crops of corn, wheat, cotton, coffee, sugar cane, and peanuts for export, now yields only weeds.

But Mugabe's crude tactics had the desired effect: he managed to hold off Tsvangirai and his Movement for Democratic Change (MDC) party. In the process, Zimbabwe's democracy was transformed into a dictatorship, with the government shutting down independent media outlets and effectively criminalizing political dissent. The country's economy has also been decimated. A nation once called Africa's breadbasket is now reliant on foreign handouts to feed much of its AIDS-ravaged population.

It was in the midst of this sad transformation that I arrived at Harare's new, garishly furnished airport in the spring of 2000. Unlike the other foreigners on my plane, I didn't come for a safari or a chance to gaze on Victoria Falls. I was there on a mission to help Zimbabwean Jews threatened by the Mugabe regime flee the country. It was my third visit to the country in as many months. My previous trips consisted mostly of reconnaissance. But now it was time for action.

In preparation for my Zimbabwe trip, I'd been working closely with my assets in the region. My "man in Harare," a former member of a now defunct Rhodesian special forces regiment named Larry, was particularly useful.

It was Larry who picked me up when my plane landed. Larry was an energetic egghead who was well connected through joint commercial ventures to a number of senior people in Mugabe's regime. Though not Jewish himself, it was he who originally tipped us off that a number of Jews were on Mugabe's to-do list. Through his dealings with Cabinet members and their staff, he'd heard rumblings about "special treatment" for certain well-known Jews. What exactly was meant by "special treatment" is hard to say. But given Mugabe's track record, Larry knew the safe bet was on detainment, torture, or worse. And so he thoughtfully handed the information over to one of my primary assets in South Africa, who then passed the information on to me.

Anti-Semitism is not a mainstream form of prejudice in African society; most hotheads are more interested in getting one black tribe riled up against another. But Mugabe saw himself as a great anti-colonial revolutionary and actively sought alliances with others who shared his conceit. These included both Muammar al-Gaddafi and Yasser Arafat, who helped school Mugabe in the basics of Jew hatred. The Palestinian Authority's representative in Zimbabwe, an odious specimen known as Ali Halimeh, was particularly active in this regard. He was a regular on Zimbabwean television, where he held forth with the sort of anti-Semitic incitement and propaganda you usually get only in the Arab media.

As Larry and I drove to the hotel, I spotted groups of soldiers everywhere. At gas stations, the queues were a kilometre long.

"There's no petrol, no foreign currency reserves, and violence is running rampant," Larry said, summarizing the situation. "Meanwhile, a good portion of the ZNA [Zimbabwean army] is off diamond mining in the Congo."

I stared out the Jeep's window at the people sitting patiently in their cars. If this scene had been taking place in North America, the crowds would have descended into fistfights and screaming matches. But Africans are cursed with patience. They'll patiently wait out every problem imaginable – war, famine, plague, and whatever the local strongmen throw at them. My experience in Africa is one of the reasons I have little regard for the "poverty equals terrorism" theory, according to which suicide bombers are driven to explode themselves because of the poverty and repression they experience in their societies. If squalor and tyranny inspire self-immolation, then sub-Saharan Africa would be one big fireball.

When I arrived at my hotel, the lobby was full of young men giving a close eye to everyone who came and went. I did my best to avoid their glare. Before I'd left for Zimbabwe, I had received a cable from the Israeli embassy in Harare telling me that Mugabe had been warned of a "Zionist agent" aiding the MDC with arms and instruction in political subversion techniques. Thankfully, the name mentioned in the cable didn't correspond to the alias I'd adopted for the mission, but it made me nervous nonetheless. Outing a fictitious "Zionist" plot – complete with a real-life Israeli seized in a local hotel – was just the sort of demagogic stunt that Mugabe loved.

Later on, Larry and I drove to a restaurant to discuss our forthcoming meeting with local Jews who were on Mugabe's radar screen. After our meal, one of Larry's drivers – a short, laconic Shona tribesman named Nelson – picked me up. We drove toward the border with neighbouring Mozambique, where I wanted to check out one of our possible exfiltration routes.

After about forty minutes of driving on the Harare–Mutare Highway, we ran into a roadblock manned by two members of the Zimbabwe National Army. These were a common sight. In his paranoia, Mugabe was certain that a coup was imminent, and that the MDC was moving weapons around the country in preparation. But this was the first time we'd been stopped.

One of the soldiers, a tall man with appalling teeth, an AK-47, and a jauntily angled dun-coloured hat, approached the vehicle and asked where we were headed. Nelson started to answer but, spotting me in the passenger seat, the soldier interrupted and insisted that I roll down my window. Coming around to my side, he asked in perfect English, "What is your business today?"

"We're heading to Mutare," I answered without hesitation. My prepared response was, I thought, entirely credible. Mutare is a lush tourist destination located three hours from Harare, high in the eastern highlands on the border of Mozambique. The mountain streams are teeming with fresh mountain trout. Recalling some ancient advice given to me a lifetime ago by my instructor Oren, I wished I'd brought a fishing rod for cover purposes.

Then, to my total shock, the soldier put the barrel of his Kalashnikov up against my forehead. He pushed hard and my head started to tilt back. Things slowed down. I heard a strong, high-pitched whine from the nearby insects, accompanied by the thudding bass line of my own heart.

The episode was surreal. Yet this didn't prevent a spasm of fear from convulsing me. This wasn't Europe or Israel. Shooting a nosy foreigner in such circumstances would be no big deal for one of Mugabe's thugs.

After a few seconds, without a word of explanation, he withdrew his weapon and my head sprang back toward him like one of those bobble-headed sports figures you see stuck on people's dashboards. "Give me your papers," he ordered. I immediately handed him a photocopy of my passport (the original being back in my hotel safe). He inspected it briefly, then handed it back and said something in a local dialect to Nelson, who hopped out and opened the trunk. It was empty and we were free to go – back to Harare.

As we drove in silence, I inspected my forehead in the mirror. There, smack in the middle, was a perfect red circle – the imprint of this young thug's weapon in my skin. During the whole of my tenure in the Mossad, this was the only time I'd had a weapon pointed directly at me. Not to put too fine a point on it, the experience scared the absolute crap out of me.

Nelson dropped me off at my hotel. Before we parted, he looked at me and said with touching sincerity, "Sorry, boss." I gave him some cash and thanked him for standing up for me at the roadblock.

Had I been on my own, I might well have ended up lying in some ditch with jackals and vultures dining on my innards.

The next day, Larry picked me up, and we drove to see the local Jewish community leader. Morris lived in an affluent Harare suburb with his wife and two dogs, a black Labrador and a Jack Russell. All whites in Zimbabwe have dogs, and for unexplained reasons, one always seems to be a Jack Russell. I don't know why because they can be more demanding than a small child.

As I went to pet the Lab, the Jack Russell jumped at me and almost bit my nose off, the second assault on my face in as many days. While the Labrador and I exchanged mutual looks of commiseration, Morris's wife called me a "poor dear" for the mark still on my forehead and promptly asked Larry to prepare me a cup of tea. I was grateful for the hospitality, especially when Morris slipped two fingers of very good Lagavulin single malt whisky into the cup.

Before Mugabe expelled most of them in recent years, Zimbabwe's whites lived in a time warp. Morris's house, an unintentional retro tribute to 1960s British decorating, was typical. It was a living, breathing anachronism of a time when Zimbabwe was Rhodesia, Ian Smith was in charge, and the country had close ties to Mother England. With the striped wallpaper, lace curtains, and Georgian-style furniture, I could have been in the drawing room of any middle-class family in Finchley. I found the decor strangely familiar, even comforting.

Five other targeted members of the Jewish community were at Morris's home. One of the men, a single father of three girls whose wife had recently died of cancer, had already been picked up and tortured by the security services. Only through Larry's intervention had he been released.

As we sat in the living room, I told them the plan. I now knew the route through Mozambique was a no-go, which meant the best option was west into Botswana, where I knew the border was fairly porous. Moreover, the trip west would allow us to pick up a few Jews from Bulawayo, Zimbabwe's second-largest city. No one in the room took any joy in planning to leave a country they'd called home for decades. But we all knew it was better than Mugabe's electro-shock alternative.

The next morning, I departed for Bulawayo in a rickety old plane that I shared with all manner of colourful locals – some openly brandishing the sort of knives and spears that would have post-9/11 airport security officials reaching for their walkie-talkies. At Bulawayo Airport, the wife of one of my escapees picked me up. It was a long drive, and I was humbled by her extravagant use of precious gasoline. She was a matronly and tight-lipped woman, and seemed to have mixed feelings about my presence. Like everyone else I met, she loved Zimbabwe, and she probably half-resented my plan to uproot her.

Bulawayo is the hub of the province of Matabeleland, which comprises the whole of western Zimbabwe from the South African border in the south to Victoria Falls in the north. It's a sleepy town of wide tree-lined streets, surrounded by beautiful parks, a legacy of its founder, Cecil Rhodes. The jacaranda trees were in full bloom. The roads are wide because Rhodes insisted trains of oxen and their burden should be able to perform a U-turn if necessary.

We drove to the cramped doctor's office that belonged to my driver's husband, a jovial, portly man who had been practising medicine for most of his life. The patients crowding his waiting room were of all colours. (Despite his service to the black community, Mugabe's men didn't like the doctor because, aside from being Jewish, he'd been treating senior opposition leaders in the region.) He informed me that the other local escapees were on their way and put me in a tiny examination room to wait. I busied myself fiddling with the quaint medical instruments, which wouldn't have been out of place in Rhodes's time. It was oddly comforting to be in the examining room. I felt relieved to be out of Harare and in the relative safety of Bulwayo. I had been routinely checking for surveillance since my departure out of the capital and was quite certain that I was not being watched.

When the others arrived, the doctor abruptly told us he was staying put. "I'm sorry," he said in an apologetic tone, "I shan't be coming with you. I've too much to do here and, well, you can see that I'm needed here." He had that look of resolve in his eyes that said he wasn't about to change his mind. I'd seen the look at varying points over my career and knew better than to argue. Besides, I'd been in his waiting room and seen the crowds of people requiring his attention.

"If you change your mind, you know how to reach me, day or night" was all I could think to say. A country where a third of the population is HIV-positive needs its medical men. The doctor's place was taken by Cyril, a tall, string bean of a man with a thin military moustache and an ascot. I resisted the urge to stand up and salute when he entered the room. He was a veteran of the Second World War and organized the final details of our little exodus with military precision. The next day, it was agreed, we'd begin the long drive to Botswana after the arrival of Morris's group, which would be driving in from Harare.

After we discussed the escape plan, one of the escapees took me to his house for lunch. As we pulled up to the gate, he leaned on his horn. We sat in silence for a while, and I began to wonder what we were waiting for. Then I saw his housekeeper, a large black woman who was wiping her hands with a dishtowel, scurry from the house to open the gate for her boss. In Africa, old habits die hard.

After lunch, I asked to visit the local Jewish school, which was still theoretically Jewish but had no more Jewish students: the Jewish community in Zimbabwe is old and the young have all left. In their place,

African children sang nursery rhymes in Hebrew, and I applauded their performance.

I visited the Jewish old folks' home as well, to make sure everyone there was safe. One old man called me into his room. He had giant hearing aids on both ears and enormous eyeglasses. He proudly showed me a certificate from Queen Elizabeth in commemoration of his one hundredth birthday. Sixty-one years his junior, I congratulated him. He was lucid and spry, and I took note of his other framed certificates and medals for service in both world wars. Some people you just never forget.

For our journey, I was assigned an African driver named George. We had a convoy of well-appointed long-wheelbase Land Cruisers with extra jerry cans of fuel. They were bought with money from the American Jewish Joint Distribution Committee (or "Joint" for short). The Joint's mission is to serve the needs of Jews throughout the world, particularly where their lives are threatened through political or natural upheavals. Zimbabwe certainly fit the bill, though in this situation, they didn't know that a Mossad officer was running the show.

I retired to my hotel and tried to contact my headquarters. Using a global system for mobile phone communications, I informed my desk officer in a barely audible, static-ridden voice that we were a "go," and that I would call her once we reached our destination. It was a short, businesslike call due to the insecure method of communication. Any time you make a call in Zimbabwe, you risk having Mugabe's men listening in.

The next day, we met at the prearranged rendezvous point and started off for the border. A few kilometres from the scrubby desert of Botswana, we cut away toward an unofficial crossing, which turned out to be abandoned. We entered Botswana without incident under a clear sky, and made for the road to Selebi-Phikwe. From there, the escapees made their own way to South Africa, which has become something of a haven for Zimbabwean Jews in recent years. Everyone was relieved to be out of Zimbabwe, including me. Yet given the incident I'd endured at the roadblock, this uneventful ending seemed vaguely anticlimactic. There is always a feeling of slight depression when things are over. I was just tired and anxious to go home. In retrospect, I know that the roadblock incident had contributed greatly to my professional mental fatigue but I was in denial about it.

George and I promptly drove back to Bulawayo. I called my headquarters and let them know that all had gone well. Without delay, I then went to the airport, drank lots of Zambezi Lager, and caught the first flight out.

A number of months later, I was surprised to be awarded a commendation in front of my division by the Mossad's deputy director general, Ilan Mizrachi, in large part for the job I'd done in Zimbabwe. The fact that reports from our embassy in Harare indicated repeatedly that Mugabe's security people were looking for an "Israeli agent" and I kept making repeated visits to the country to complete my mission must have impressed my superiors. This was the first commendation I'd received as an individual while working for the Mossad.*

Seven years have passed, but my memories of Zimbabwe's self-destruction are still fresh. I am amazed that Mugabe hasn't yet been turfed out. Anyone who has read news reports from the country knows just how thoroughly he's ruined Zimbabwe. Even as I write these words in August 2006, a Christian NGO reports that seven hundred thousand people are now homeless thanks to Mugabe's recent campaign to drive politically restless urban dwellers into the

---

* I'd received a unit citation in 1998 in Tevel along with my North America department colleagues. And I also shared a commendation with Etai, my friend from the Mossad's counterterrorism department, for nailing the three stooges in Baku, described in Chapter 15.

outback by razing the country's poorest slums. Through his so-called "land reform" policies, Mugabe seized white-owned lands and redistributed them to black Zimbabweans, prompting an exodus of the country's white entrepreneurs, farmers, and doctors. Though those whites were unfashionable in their views and habits, they were the backbone of·the nation's economy. Mugabe threw them out for no other reason than bold-faced demagoguery.

I don't know what's become of the escapees, but one day I plan to return to the region and find out. And when I do, I sincerely hope Mugabe and his hangers-on have gone the way of fellow dictators Saddam Hussein of Iraq and Nicolae Ceaușescu of Romania.

17 | ODD JOBS

Do not dig a hole for somebody else; you yourself will fall into it.

Russian proverb

During my time as Bitsur's man in Africa, I was what's known in the Mossad as a "jumper." This meant I lived in Israel much of the time, travelling to my target region as needed. Jumpers are rarities: most Mossad agents who work overseas stay overseas, and either work out of the local Israeli embassy or live undercover.

The downside of my new job was that I seemed to spend half my time on an airplane. And no, I didn't get to fly business class, nor was I permitted to keep the millions of frequent flyer points I would have racked up. But the arrangement did allow me to see my family often. My kids were growing up fast, especially my older son, who at fourteen was exhibiting all the normal symptoms of being a teenager. He taught himself the guitar and was playing everything from Jimi Hendrix to Metallica. (I wondered where this talent originated, given that his father is tone deaf.) His eight-year-old younger brother, meanwhile, had taken up horseback riding and martial arts – and still competes in both to this day.

When I was in Israel, I did my best to make the odd school play and neighbourhood social function. For the most part, however, my social life revolved around my Mossad colleagues, with whom I could speak candidly. When the weekend came, I invariably ended up with my work buddies and their families, talking shop around the barbecue with beer in hand.

Being a jumper also meant I spent a fair bit of time at Mossad HQ in Tel Aviv, which gave me the opportunity to meet agents from other departments and learn about their projects. Sometimes, I would even get a chance to lend a helping hand.

Such was the case in 1999, when I fell in with two analysts, Tomer and Eran, working with the Mossad's counter-proliferation department. They had become apprised of a scheme by a former Soviet general to sell Syria the technology needed to place chemical warheads on Scud-C missiles. The irony was that these were the same Scud-C missiles that Charles and I were supposed to have blown up in 1991. Yitzhak Shamir's refusal to sink the *Al-Yarmouk* had come back to bite Israel in the ass.

The two analysts identified the Russian as Lieutenant General Anatoly Kuntsevich, a former Soviet officer who'd commanded the Russian defence ministry's research and testing institute, and had since earned a reputation in intelligence circles for peddling Soviet-vintage chemical technology. Astonishingly, this same Kuntsevich had been a consultant on chemical disarmament to the United Nations in 1988. In the mid-1990s, we were told, Syria received some eight hundred kilograms of raw material for the production of VX gas through a shady commercial venture facilitated by General Kuntsevich, even as he was working under Boris Yeltsin as commander of the Russian Military Academy for Chemical Warfare. Now, it seemed, Kuntsevich was going to sell the Syrians the means to drop that VX on Tel Aviv.

Tomer and Eran told me they wanted me to help scuttle the Scud deal in the negotiation phase. I said that I was interested, but I'd have to clear things with Michel first. I'd been in the Mossad long enough to know that the one thing guaranteed to make a department head go ballistic is the unauthorized commandeering of underlings.

Seeing as I happened to be between assignments at the time, Michel didn't have a good excuse to say no. Although he started off by telling me, "Tu me casses les couilles" (you drive a hard bargain), he understood that helping out other departments made for smart office politics. Or, as he put it: "If you air successful, zis will enhance our stachoor, non?"

Helping out the counter-proliferation department was a particularly astute move in those days. In the pre-9/11 era, the Mossad's counterterrorism department was a poor cousin to its counter-proliferation counterpart (which happened to be located just down the same corridor). Terrorism, while a significant problem, was not then cast as a strategic threat: a bus bomb, however horrific, did not threaten Israel's existence to the same extent as an incoming Scud-C with a WMD warhead. (It was only years later that the West came to realize that if you get enough Muslim extremists with enough bombs strapped to them, they can terrorize a nation as thoroughly as a fleet of missiles.)

Tomer gave me all the relevant intelligence that the counter-proliferation department had on the Kuntsevich–Syria relationship, and then left Ayal and me to come up with a plan.

What we settled on was this: I would fly to Europe and set myself up as a freelance investigative journalist targeting Kuntsevich. In this guise, I would pester his government and the West's various counter-proliferation watchdog groups, spreading the incriminating intelligence Tomer had provided to me during the course of my "interviews." The point of the exercise was to focus so much unwanted attention on Kuntsevich that either he or one of his bosses in Moscow would kibosh the transaction. And for a variety of reasons – including protecting the Mossad's intelligence sources – it all had to be done without leaving Israeli fingerprints.

I chose a foreign identity with appropriate fake documents, and put together a convincing front as a journalist working with a free-lance documentary production company. I printed business cards and opened an office services address in Zurich. I then flew to Europe and started working the telephone.

An important part of the plan was to ensure that I didn't sound as if I was out to get Kuntsevich, but that I was merely an impartial documentary filmmaker looking to verify the truth of allegations that I'd heard from others. The advantage of this cover story was that I never had to reveal the origin of the classified intelligence I'd been provided by Tomer. Whenever asked how I knew what I knew, my prepared response was that I couldn't say: I was sworn to protect my sources.

Once I got someone on the phone who spoke English, my spiel went like this: "Hello, my name is Alex Turnbull of Turncoat Productions. We're making a television documentary for sale to the major networks about the illicit trade in Soviet weaponry since the fall of the Berlin Wall."

After some more general patter in this vein, I'd get to the important part: "Our sources have learned that General Kuntsevich, a former Red Army general, is selling chemical weapon delivery systems to the Syrian government. More specifically, he is alleged to be selling warheads that will be modified to carry Sarin, VX, and other chemical agents on Scud-C missiles. Are you aware of this sale and could you please give us additional information about General Kuntsevich's activities?" I used the general's name often so they'd remember it. I also left them the telephone number, fax number, and e-mail address that I'd set up in Zurich.

Many of the people I spoke to in the Russian defence establishment came across as honest folk who were genuinely appalled at Kuntsevich and the other former Soviet military officers who were now doing back-alley business with third world dictators and rogue regimes. A few others – presumably those who were themselves implicated by Kuntsevich's transactions – could barely suppress their panic. One official connected to President Vladimir Putin's office became extremely agitated, especially after I told him that I'd already spoken to the Organization for Security and Co-operation in Europe, and the nonproliferation officials at the EU's Common Foreign and Security Policy offices. When I pressed him, he claimed that Putin's government would do what it needed to in order to put Kuntsevich out of business.

I'll never know how much of this was talk. I was a (fake) journalist after all, so no doubt most or all of these people were just trying to spin me. But I do think that I got a few balls rolling. In any case, after I'd spoken to everyone I could think of over the course of five days, I returned to Israel and wrote up my reports.

Whether I impeded the Kuntsevich–Syria commercial relationship is impossible to say. If I had to guess, I'd say my efforts had little effect. In any case, whether through Kuntsevich or not, the Syrians did eventually manage to build Scud-Cs equipped with chemical warheads. (In 2004, the Mossad's DG, Meir Dagan, announced in an address to the North Atlantic Treaty Organization council that Syria had adapted Sarin and VX nerve agents to Scud warheads and aerial bombs.) When you're dealing with a rogue state such as Syria that has absolutely dedicated itself to procuring weapons of mass destruction, it really is only a matter of time. This is why counter-proliferation missions are so frustrating: you're just trying to delay the inevitable.

General Kuntsevich died on April 3, 2002. The details of his demise are sketchy, but according to one uncorroborated report, he died on a plane departing from Syria, where he'd just delivered stolen precursors for Novichok, a Russian-made agent several times more deadly than conventional nerve gases.

As things turned out, the Kuntsevich affair wasn't my last foray into the field of counter-proliferation. Shortly after returning from my "journalism" assignment in Europe, the CP department came knocking again with a similar request.

This time, the villain was an Indian missile scientist whom I'll call Mr. Gupta, from the Research Center Imarat near Hyderabad. Imarat is the site of a secret military base where India conducts all its missile research, development, and testing in the fields of convention-al and nonconventional weapons. Gupta, my colleagues had learned, was trying to sell the technology behind India's Prithvi short-range ballistic missile to Libya. The Prithvi (Sanskrit for "earth") is not par-ticularly sophisticated by Western standards. But its ability to carry nonconventional warheads (including nukes) meant Israel was eager to keep it out of Muammar al-Gaddafi's arsenal.

The good news here was that India was (and remains) an Israeli ally. Moreover, New Delhi kept a tighter rein on its military scientists than Moscow did. And so we were fairly confident that when the Indian government found out what Gupta was doing, they'd shut him down in short order.

At the time the counter-proliferation department called me about the project, I happened to be travelling on other business in Asia, with an itinerary that would take me through Hong Kong and

Mumbai. My plan was to reprise my role as globe-trotting journalist. I'd do my preliminary phone calls from Hong Kong, and then follow those up with more calls from inside India. I was an obvious choice for the job; not only was I in the area, I'd done a similar operation against General Kuntsevich and could conduct myself under foreign cover with relative ease. One thing about the Mossad, the number of missions versus the number of operational employees that can carry them out is disproportionately on the side of the number of missions.

Since I was on Israeli diplomatic documents during this trip, I didn't bother with a front company. To protect my identity, I instead used the low-tech method of simply placing all my calls from public telephones in hotel lobbies. As I'd discovered during my training in Tel Aviv, hotel lobbies are to spies what ports are to fisherman. As long as you're dressed smartly, order a drink occasionally, and exhibit the look of someone doing legitimate business, the world will leave you alone.

There was just one freak complication: this was in the middle of the 1999 Kosovo war, and NATO planes had just bombed the Chinese embassy in Belgrade thanks to faulty CIA intelligence and an inexperienced target-spotting team. Gangs of stick-wielding youths, whipped into a fervour by official Chinese government propaganda, were roaming the streets of Hong Kong looking for anyone who bore a resemblance to an American. With my North American accent and demeanour, I certainly fit the bill.

I holed up in the Peninsula Hotel and started to make calls. Adopting my journalist alter ego, I started with the Indian Defence Ministry and worked my way up to the Ministry of External Affairs and the Ministry of Law and Justice until I finished off with the prime minister's office. Apparently, my schtick was quite convincing: I managed to speak directly to the Indian PM's press secretary, and was almost granted an interview with the PM himself.

Once I was satisfied that I'd hit all the necessary departments, I put down the receiver and thought about getting some fresh air. By this time, it was late evening in Hong Kong. Surely the mob had called it a day, I thought. And so I set out in search of one of those Hong Kong watering holes where English-speaking expats endlessly reminisce about the days of British rule.

I trudged my way through Kowloon on foot. After a few blocks, I turned a corner and saw a clutch of goons chanting their slogans into the night air. The placards were in Chinese, so I couldn't understand them. But when they pointed at me and bellowed, I got the gist. I turned around and started to jog in the other direction. When the crowd followed, my jog became a dead sprint.

Fortunately, I'm pretty quick on my feet – I ran track and played short forward on my high school basketball team. My pursuers followed me back to the Peninsula but, even in their hot-headed state, didn't dare enter a fancy hotel for the purposes of bludgeoning one of the guests. As they turned back, I stood in the lobby drenched with sweat and panting as if I'd just run a steeplechase.

The next afternoon, I caught my flight to Mumbai, a city so crowded it makes Hong Kong look like Little House on the Prairie. From a hotel, I made follow-up calls to the same officials I'd spoken to from Hong Kong. In each case, I inquired whether there'd been any follow-up about Mr. Gupta and his missiles.

Sadly, there wasn't much to report. The Indians seemed interested in the issue, but not so much that they would short-circuit their famously convoluted bureaucracy. I did have the assurance of a senior counsel at the Ministry of Law and Justice that Mr. Gupta would be investigated, but that was as far as I got. I called my desk officer back at HQ and had her relay an interim report to Eran and Tomer. I was ready to come home.

Of the two missions, I think I was more successful with the hapless Mr. Gupta. Once I was back in Israel, I managed to get the Indian press involved, and they duly ran some editorials about the need to monitor India's military exports – more out of fear that they'd end up in Pakistan than anything else. We also shared some of the details with the CIA's Nonproliferation Center, which in turn used the intelligence to pressure their own contacts in the Indian government. In fact, the CIA stated in its 2002 unclassified *Report to Congress on the Acquisition of Technology Relating to Weapons of Mass Destruction and Advanced Conventional Munitions* that "India was among the countries supplying assistance to Libya's ballistic missile program." After being tarred with the same brush used on Gupta, the Indian government likely took a closer look at its missile scientists and the goings-on near Hyderabad.

In any case, this one has a happy ending: Gaddafi never did get his missiles. Score one for the good guys.

18 | A PRE-EMPTIVE STRIKE

If heaven's for clean people then it must be vacant.

Matthew Good

Not long after my globe-trotting efforts to help put out the Mossad's counter-proliferation department's brush fires, I found myself back roaming my patch in Africa and Southeast Asia. We had recently discovered evidence that the Iranians were using locally based Hezbollah agents to collect operational intelligence on Israeli and Western targets in Singapore and Thailand for terrorist attacks. For a supposed Lebanese resistance movement, Hezbollah is very active in Southeast Asia; its agents had infiltrated the region in the 1980s, setting up shop in Thailand, Singapore, the Philippines, Malaysia, Indonesia, Taiwan, Korea, and even in Lakemba, a suburb of Sydney, Australia. Hezbollah was known to be procuring weapons and dual-use technology, and recruiting locals to carry out terrorist attacks in Israel and Australia – in some cases, going so far as to marry into local Muslim families.

The group tried to blow up the Israeli embassy in Bangkok, Thailand, in the spring of 1994, using the same truck-bombing modus operandi that achieved such devastating results against the U.S. embassy in Beirut in 1983. (The Thai attack failed when the truck carrying the explosives got into a traffic accident.) The next year, a Hezbollah source in Manila helped the Mossad unearth a plot to attack the U.S. and Israeli embassies, as well as Singapore's tiny Jewish community. Through information from the Manila source, I was able to determine that the Chesed-El Synagogue was one of their primary targets. Singapore has a Jewish population of about three hundred people and virtually no history of anti-Semitism. The discovery that Iran would stoop so low as to blow up a ninety-year-old synagogue, presumably with praying men, women, and children inside, helped to ignite a cascading anger in me that began with a spark and picked up momentum with each passing week. Iran, and in particular its intelligence services, were really beginning to piss me off.

In an unrelated operation, Hezbollah didn't restrict itself to going after the Jews. Its agents also carried out a casing operation on Singapore's coastline and harbour as part of a plot to sink visiting U.S. naval vessels. As with all things connected to Hezbollah, region-al security services didn't have to dig deep to find links to Hezbollah's benefactors in Iran.

Iran hasn't always been Israel's sworn foe. Under the Shah, the country was an Israeli ally and oil supplier. The two nations shared intelligence, and Israel helped train Iran's armed forces. That rela-tionship ended with the Shah's ouster in 1979, and Iran's subsequent transformation into a Shiite Islamist dictatorship. The country's new ruler, Ayatollah Ruhollah Khomeini, called for the "eradication" of the Jewish state, and gave Yasser Arafat's men the keys to Israel's mis-sion in Tehran.

Twenty-six years later, Iran's ongoing efforts to develop nuclear missiles represent the most serious strategic threat on Israel's horizon. In December 2001, former Iranian president Hashemi Rafsanjani hinted ominously at the motives behind his country's atomic research program. "The use of a nuclear bomb in Israel will leave nothing on the ground," he declared, according to Iranian news accounts. Any Israeli reprisal, on the other hand, would "only damage the world of Islam."

In the meantime, Tehran supports Palestinian terrorism, and attacks Israel through its own terrorist proxies, most notably Hezbollah. Hezbollah is controlled primarily through Tehran's elite Iranian Revolutionary Guards Corps, and the nation's leading intelligence service, the Iranian Ministry of Intelligence and Security. The IRGC also acts as Iran's chief ideological enforcer, executing dissidents and torturing political opponents, at home and abroad. Since 1979, the Revolutionary Guards have become embedded in the nation's power structure. Numerous IRGC thugs have gone on to Cabinet positions, including the country's current Holocaust-denying president, Mahmoud Ahmadinejad.

Iran's influence extends indirectly to al-Qaeda and its affiliated regional terror networks as well. Analysts typically place great emphasis on the fact that Hezbollah is a Shiite group, while al-Qaeda subscribes to the puritanical, Saudi-based Sunni creed known as Wahabism. But the truth is that Islamist terrorists of whatever denomination tend to co-operate at the working level, and leave the religious arguments for the imams. Hamas, Palestinian Islamic Jihad, Hezbollah, al-Qaeda – they all have some degree of contact. In Gaza, for instance, Hezbollah has trained local Sunni terrorists in the methods used to destroy Israeli tanks with massive, shape-charged explosives buried under roads. In the early 1990s, Osama bin Laden himself met Hezbollah's terrorist mastermind, Imad Mughniyeh. All this explains why the Mossad continued to focus so many of its assets on Iran and its shadowy minions.

In my case, however, there was something else at play – a visceral contempt for Tehran's mullahs that felt a lot like a personal vendetta. Even now, when I think of Iran's despots, I think of Israeli Air Force Lieutenant Colonel Ron Arad.

In 1986, Arad was flying over Lebanon when a malfunctioning bomb damaged his F-4 Phantom. He bailed out near the town of Sidon, and was captured by Amal, an Iranian-backed Shiite militia. In the last photo released by the group, he is seen sporting a heavy beard and wearing a T-shirt incongruously emblazoned with the words "Victoria to Maui Sailing Race."

At the time, Arad was a twenty-eight-year-old newlywed with a baby daughter and was studying engineering at the prestigious Technion Institute of Technology near Haifa. Israel negotiated with Amal for his release, but talks broke off after Arad was transferred to the control of Hezbollah and their Iranian overlords. The Iranians know what happened to Arad, but they've told Israel nothing. Instead, Tehran's agents sent his family a fake videotape, which showed a man with heavy Persian features lumbering around a park in an intentionally distant and unfocused blur. The senders claimed the man was Arad, but it was obviously just a crude ploy to torment the family.

Arad's capture, and the horrors that likely followed, reflect the worst nightmare of every Israeli combatant and intelligence officer. And so even though I have never met Arad, it's hard not to feel a personal connection to him. His treatment says a lot about what Iran has become under Islamist rule. The mullahs and their proxies don't follow the Geneva Conventions, or any of the other rules of civilized engagement. In late 2003, Israel agreed to free over *four hundred* Arab prisoners in exchange for a single kidnapped Israeli businessman held by Hezbollah and the remains of three Israeli soldiers. The lopsided arithmetic reflects the relative value the two sides assign to human life.

I relate all this as background to the mission described in this chapter, lest readers judge me harshly. Tehran's agents have done many unspeakable things in the last quarter-century, and when I was presented with the opportunity to help even the score – even a tiny bit – I couldn't help but sign on.

In the late 1990s, the Mossad was tipped off that Iranian agents were visiting South Africa to purchase advanced weapons systems from Denel Ltd., a government-owned manufacturer that produces artillery, guided missiles, unmanned aerial vehicles, and a variety of other sophisticated equipment.

Despite its own reputation as a rogue state, Iran enjoyed friendly relations with South Africa. The African National Congress came to power in 1994 as a mix of pragmatic politicians and hardcore anti-Western revolutionaries. Many were, and remain, perfectly happy to overlook Iran's status as a brutal dictatorship. As for Tehran, it saw South Africa as a place to shop for both conventional arms and nuclear technology while remaining under the West's radar. South African President Frederik Willem de Klerk's 1993 announcement that South Africa had secretly developed a small nuclear arsenal and then junked it was no doubt especially tantalizing.

As a case officer on Bitsur's African desk, my task was to send Iran's agents packing by whatever means necessary. I was after two IRGC agents who had been given the job of procuring weapons and technology for the regime and who had the temerity to run around on my turf. My plan wasn't complicated: pick up the Iranians, put the fear of Allah into them, and send them home with the clear message that they were unwelcome on South African soil.

I'd gotten the idea from an operation I'd witnessed during my tenure as the Mossad's counterterrorism liaison officer to the CIA. "Operation Shockwave" was conceived by Cofer Black, until recently the State Department coordinator for counterterrorism and chief of a CIA task force responsible for disrupting Iranian intelligence operations on a worldwide basis. On one occasion, Black flew out to Tel Aviv and presented his strategy for doing so.

The CIA, Black told us, had laboriously prepared a database containing the names and addresses of all known MOIS and IRGC officers, who would then get a visit from a local CIA team, typically accompanied by well-armed, refrigerator-sized security personnel. The CIA team would tell their quarry that they could either defect to the West, or their names and biographical details would be broadcast to all and sundry, including the host country's intelligence service. In third world nations that didn't share South Africa's affectionate attitude toward Tehran, this could mean summary imprisonment, torture, or death.

A few MOIS and IRGC officers turned and became CIA sources. Many others returned to Iran never to be heard of again, overseas anyway. Among the rest, the CIA had at least planted the seeds of doubt and fear. The Iranians were scrambling for a good long while trying to figure out who'd been exposed, who'd defected, who was doubled, and who never reported their CIA encounters but should have. Paranoia spreads like the plague in intelligence circles. Black's plan infected Iran, and good.

Operation Shockwave had its critics among the Mossad because it was a one-off gambit that would be difficult to repeat. But I liked it because it was proactive. I learned later that it was especially effective in Bosnia, where the Iranians were working overtime to export their brutal brand of theocracy to the newly autonomous Muslim enclave established following the 1995 Dayton Accords. If Hezbollah is a nonentity in Bosnia today, that is due in large part to Cofer Black.

I decided that a more aggressive variant on Operation Shockwave would be a good fit for my South African mission – especially since I had my own refrigerator-sized contact in Port Elizabeth, a former officer in the South African Police whom I'll call Russ. I rang him up and asked him to meet me in Johannesburg in a few days. I told him we had a job to do.

I still have a small scar on my leg from a bizarre African insect that burrowed into me on one of my previous visits to South Africa. I'm glad it hasn't disappeared: it brings fond memories.

I always loved visiting South Africa, especially the Western Cape. The climate is mild like my hometown's and the scenery is breathtaking. From the top of Table Mountain, I enjoy staring out at the expanse of the south Atlantic, nothing but blue ocean and white-caps between where I stand and the frozen deserts of Antarctica. The beaches are first class, too, though they come with a catch: waiting just offshore is the largest concentration of Great White sharks to be found anywhere in the world.

The city of Johannesburg, on the other hand, is a business-obsessed bore. The only excitement comes from its absurdly high crime rate. Things were so bad by the late 1990s that the police had more or less given up; most just sat in their stations, unwilling to risk their lives for the money they were paid. Whole areas of the city are off limits to people who value their lives. The former central business district, in particular, is a ghost town dominated by Nigerian drug lords and squatters. Some crooks carry AK-47 assault rifles – souvenirs from the days when the Russians and Chinese were eager to feed the revolutionary spirit of Africa's downtrodden. I always carried my GLOCK 19 handgun when I wasn't accompanied by armed security.

In and around Joburg, the highways are of excellent construction, but they're deathtraps, too. Instead of fighting Western imperialists and the apartheid regime, black gangs now stage roadside ambushes. A common trick is to set cinderblocks out on the highway; when an unsuspecting motorist hits one and stops to check out the damage, he finds himself at the gang's mercy. Carjacking in suburban neighbourhoods is also rampant.

Some have gotten very rich in the new South Africa – especially the businessmen who enjoy good contacts with the ANC. But poverty is everywhere. Driving around, listening to 94.7 FM ("Joburg's No. 1 Hit Music Station"), I'd watch small African children in rags hawking whatever they could at busy intersections to commuters in Mercedes and BMWs. I'd usually buy something – a comb, a harmonica, some trinket to take home. They were always so grateful and smiled ear to ear. I didn't delude myself into thinking that I was doing anything to alleviate African poverty: God knows what pimp-like figure would be pocketing these kids' money at the end of the day. I just liked to see their smiles. They were genuine and said everything about this colourful, dangerous, breathtaking continent.

The amazing thing about Africa is that no matter how poverty stricken or screwed-over the people are by their own leaders, they usually keep their heads. As far as I can remember, no African has ever donned a ski mask to attend a summer Olympics, or detonated himself in a school bus. In recent years, bin Laden's agents have had some success recruiting Muslims in Kenya, Tanzania, and a few other African countries. But so far, it seems an isolated phenomenon. I hope it stays that way; the continent already has more than enough problems.

South Africa's changeover to majority black rule in 1994 was a victory for racial equality and democracy. But it was not exactly a triumph in the more banal area of bureaucratic efficiency. Many of the functionaries in the new South African government were former ANC activists with little or no experience in government, some of whom hadn't lived in the country for many years. Exiled or jailed poets, writers, and guerrillas were being thrust into leadership posts at government ministries – the most famous among them, of course, being the country's new president, Nelson Mandela. The upper echelons of the security services were compromised by incompetents. The former white-run South Africa may have been racist and despotic, but the hard men who ran security made sure they knew what they were doing, if only out of a sense of self-preservation. In the new South Africa, things were chaotic, with different agencies and agents operating at cross-purposes and often with no shared communication. For my purposes, the chaos was perfect.

No spy, no matter how skilled, can function effectively without the help of good local people on the ground. The man who picked me up at Joburg's busy airport was very good.

"Howzit, China?" he invariably greeted me in the breezy South African way. *China* was short for "china plate," which according to the bizarre logic of white South African slang is a rough-and-ready approximation of "mate."

I'm five foot eleven. At six-five, Russ always made me feel like a shrimp. He also made me feel plain. He was handsome in a fair, classically Afrikaans kind of way, the sort of guy a movie director would cast to lead a safari. More importantly for my purposes, he was a rugby star and bush war veteran who knew how to take care of himself and any friends in the vicinity. Attired in a dark suit and Oakleys, he looked very much the man from the apartheid regime's feared and hated Bureau of State Security, known as BOSS. Russ was actually a nice Jewish boy and had never served in that hated branch of pro-apartheid state security. An Anglo South African who'd inherited his faith from a convert mother, he was genuinely ashamed of his country's racist past, as were most of the country's whites.

We went for a coffee in Sandton, Joburg's new white enclave, and I went over my plan. He eyed me closely. Nothing in his face suggested he was frightened or put off, but he looked concerned, I suspect about me. He had the good manners to keep his worries to himself.

We left, wandered around the mall in Sandton Square, found a sporting goods store, and bought some neoprene workout gloves, the kind weightlifters wear. Then I went back to the hotel and had a swim. I didn't sleep well that night, but managed a few hours.

Russ picked me up in the morning, both of us wearing our dark suits. We were trying hard to project the aura of uncompromising officialdom that translates as "We are from the government – do not fuck with us." I'd been with the Mossad for a decade by this time but I felt like a nervous rookie: this type of close-quarters engagement with the enemy isn't something that happens every day in the spy business. Russ looked cool, as if he did this sort of thing all the time. I suspect he had his own butterflies, but his innate South African stoicism and his sheer physical presence made him seem invulnerable. He winked at me and said, "This should be interesting."

We arrived at the three-star hotel, and Russ asked the drowsy reception clerk for house security with a tone of authority. She looked confused and Russ flashed a set of dated police credentials. The receptionist whispered into a telephone and a stunned-looking black man in a red suit jacket appeared. We'd obviously woken him up. Again, Russ flashed his expired ID and demanded that the man escort us to our targets' room. I kept quiet. Though I can fake a South African accent for non-South Africans, it wouldn't fool a local. Russ took the lead. He was in his element.

The security guard answered, "Yes, boss," pronouncing it *bass* like the fish. Like I said, old instincts die hard in Africa. This was one of those tiny daily clues that remind you it will take years before the psychological yoke of white rule is fully removed from this country.

We entered the elevator and the guard asked what the trouble was. Russ opened his notebook with a policeman's officious manner. He told the man that a certain Mr. Mortazavi and Mr. Nemati had overstayed their welcome. Russ then added that this was a confidential matter, one implicating "South African national security." In my impromptu role as the good cop, I offered a thin, vague smile.

Russ warned the guard not to discuss the matter with anyone else, especially the manager, who, Russ assured him, had also been sworn to secrecy. The guard just stared and said nothing. He looked burdened by this new secret, and was clearly anxious to get back into bed and put the episode behind him. We took his master key and told him to hold the elevator. I didn't want him in earshot.

We had no idea whether Nemati and Mortazavi would be awake, armed, or both. We opened the door as quietly as we could, eager to maintain the element of surprise. Our GLOCKs were drawn. We didn't plan to shoot anyone, but on the off chance it came to that, the two men would have to die and we would get out of the building quickly.

I was following Israeli weapons-handling procedure: my pistol was loaded, but not cocked, with chambers empty. Some Israeli military men grumble that the practice slows a shooter down, but I disagree. I've seen members of the Israel Security Agency put a tight cluster of twelve rounds down range in less than five seconds – including drawing and cocking. Walking around with a cocked pistol is unnecessary if you know how to handle it.

It's also risky. If a round is in the chamber, pressure on the trigger can set off the weapon. If it gets caught on something or a protruding object gets into the trigger guard, disaster can result. The Australian Federal Police – responsible for domestic VIP protection – had a cocked-pistol policy when I was in the Mossad (which I always found ironic, given the way they fussed about the risks involved with

Israel deploying armed agents to protect its athletes at the 2000 Sydney Olympics). Once, they almost shot their own prime minister, John Howard, on his plane. They also almost shot the former Israeli ambassador Gabi Levi in his blue Volvo S80. In both cases, the two were barely missed by accidental discharges that went into seats where their behinds had been parked seconds before.

A lot of rules go out the window when you're overseas. But not this one. And so I'd come prepared. Russ and I were using Fobus holsters, composite plastic paddles that sit inside your waistband, with the weapon secured on the outside. It makes for a cleaner draw, and is far more comfortable than having a weapon jammed into your pants. Israeli ingenuity in action.

Our two targets were in the same room – as we knew they would be. (The Islamic Republic is also a cheap republic.) The first thing that struck me was the smell, which suggested hygiene was not an operational priority. Mortazavi and Nemati were in separate queen-sized beds. The room was dark, but the intense early morning African sunlight was streaming through breaks in the curtains. Both men stirred vaguely as we entered. Russ followed me into the room and covered the groggy Iranians as they began to waken and mutter. I checked the bathroom and closets, weapon ready.

Nemati and Mortazavi didn't seem particularly surprised. I was wondering if this sort of thing happens to them a lot when they travelled, and then realized that they thought we were hotel staff. They brought us into focus, and the expression on their faces changed as it became clear we were not there to check the mini-bar and change their towels.

I asked who was Mortazavi and who was Nemati. I knew already – the dossier I'd been given included photos from previous visa applications. But I wanted to see how co-operative they were going to be.

They identified themselves correctly. Mortazavi was the better-looking one, mid-thirties, slim, with a trim beard and black shiny hair. Nemati was medium height, chunky, early forties, and had a huge forelock of wavy black hair. Neither was what one might call follically challenged. Nemati's beard was not as successful as his partner's, however, and I guessed it was Mortazavi who got all the girls.

Speaking English, I told them we were from South African security and that they had five minutes to dress and pack. After a few seconds of confusion, Mortazavi began protesting in whiny Farsi-accented English. His command of the language was pretty good, and I guessed he'd probably studied it outside of Iran. His friend began chiming in as well.

I cut them off quickly. "Shut your fucking mouths or it'll be a whole lot worse for you than it already is."

There was no telling if the guard would get curious and swing by again, so we couldn't let them stall us. Russ covered me with his weapon, and I threw a forceful kick into Mortazavi's midsection. He let out an *oooof* and fell backward onto the bed he'd just evacuated. I stood over him and pointed the GLOCK at his forehead.

I told him I was using 9mm Black Talon ammunition, which is banned by most Western police departments because it can penetrate a Kevlar vest. I added that when it enters the human body, it acts like a miniature buzz saw. Even if I aimed at an extremity, the least he could expect was amputation. Adding some local colour, I told him I'd make sure he was sewn up at a crummy clinic I knew in Alexandria township, where he'd get tainted blood or Ebola. It was all total nonsense. But if the increased volume of their blubbering was any guide, they bought it.

To a fly on the wall, all of this would have sounded like something out of a grade-B action movie. It doesn't happen often, but sometimes a real-life intelligence officer has a chance to spout off like a leading man in a Hollywood spy flick. I wasn't hamming it up for the hell of it, though; scaring these guys was the whole point of the mission. I wanted them to know we were enforcers, not negotiators.

They dressed and packed in a matter of minutes, while I examined their service passports and airline tickets. Russ took out disposable plastic handcuffs and cuffed them. We told them we had a car waiting outside and were heading directly to the airport.

Though I was trying hard not to show it, I was still nervous. My hands felt greasy and my throat was in a knot. There were a lot of things that could go wrong. The biggest risk was that someone – the guard, the hotel manager, some random bystander – would get on the phone and call in some real cops. We had prepared for this. I was on foreign documents, and our cover story was pretty good. Essentially, we'd try to bluff any locals with a complex story about a business deal gone wrong. But once local law enforcement gets involved, all sorts of things can happen. It wasn't a problem I wanted to face.

Fortunately, things went smoothly in the lobby. I asked the guard to help us with the Iranians' bags, and he proved eager to assist. Russ handed him a bundle of South African rand, and told him the government was grateful for his co-operation – and his silence. He also told him the hotel should check the men out on whatever credit card they'd put down when they arrived. I didn't want the Islamic Republic to get a free ride.

We all walked out calmly to our parked car. Russ and I shoved the pair in the back and I took the front passenger seat. I turned and pointed my weapon toward the back seat, wanting to give them another Clint Eastwood speech. But all I could think of was the scene in *Pulp Fiction* where Samuel L. Jackson shoots the informer by mistake. What a mess.

Russ drove cautiously to an industrial park off a freeway, where he'd secured a small, windowless warehouse space. The Iranians started to protest as we pulled up. They wanted to know what had happened to the airport. Then Mortazavi got a whiff of courage and demanded access to the Iranian embassy. I told him they were in the custody of the South African government and had no diplomatic rights. "The rules are different in Africa," I said. "We have our own way of dealing with things." I was making it up as I went along by this point. It was fun being on the other side of the fence. No wonder the domestic intelligence guys enjoy their jobs so much.

On arriving at the warehouse we took our charges inside quickly and sat them on two chairs in a plain room with no other furniture. On the floor was a black gym bag. I removed some duct tape, the quintessential multi-purpose Canadian solution to all nagging problems – leaks, tears, rips, IRGC thugs. I was careful not to let them see what else I had in there. I covered them with my weapon while Russ taped them to the chairs. They tried to resist, but a cuff from Russ stopped the chatter. His hand was like a catcher's mitt.

I removed my jacket and put on the gloves. I was breathing deeply, getting as much oxygen into my lungs as I could. I took out a small length of stiff black rubber hose about one metre long, and without any fanfare or foreplay brought it hard against Nemati's left upper arm. He howled, and then I brought it down on Mortazavi's thigh. They both started to yell and I told them to shut up. Russ stood back, impassive.

I started my speech. "Listen and listen well," I told them. "While the tinpot terrorists who run your country may think that they have a friend in Pretoria, they're mistaken." I told them that diplomats may say one thing, but on the ground, it was us – the National Intelligence Agency – who controlled access to South Africa.

It was all very puffed up and melodramatic. But that was the point. I wanted these two to think I was a sadistic cop – just like their friends back in Tehran – the sort of guy who gets off beating a defenceless foreigner tied to a chair. They had to take the message home that the South Africans are mean-assed bastards who were not to be trifled with.

"The NIA doesn't like foreign terrorists," I added with a snarl, pronouncing "terrorist" with that inflected pronunciation exclusive to the region. "We've been watching you. We know why you're here." Russ taped their mouths shut. They started to wiggle and their eyes got big.

And then I went kendo. I beat them with that rubber hose and my gloved fists like a crazed Samurai warrior. With each blow I yelled at them, "cocksucking motherfuckers" being my expletive of choice. It was a brutal frenzy the likes of which I'd never before unleashed. I beat them for Ron Arad, I beat them for my buddies in Lebanon, I beat them for the synagogue in Singapore, and I beat them for the anti-Semitic, terrorist hellhole they were sworn to defend. I also beat them for every shitty frustration that I'd endured since signing on with the Mossad.

Of course, by the standards of an Iranian interrogation room, my pummelling barely registered. Neither of them died, lost a limb, or even went unconscious. Russ, no doubt, had seen much worse. And so had these guys, albeit from the other side of the rubber hose. But I hadn't. This was the first time I'd beaten a man so severely. It surprised me how exhausting it was.

Once I was spent, I took out my GLOCK and shoved it against Mortazavi's nose as if I were going to screw the barrel manually into his face. His eyes were rolling back, and it seemed like he was going to black out. I heard a gagging sound from under Nemati's mask.

I pulled the gun away and stood back. I holstered my weapon. Russ was looking at me with a cocked eyebrow. When he signed up for the job, he knew there would be some rough stuff, but there was no way he wanted to be accomplice to murder. I nodded to him that I was okay. I took a towel from the bag and wiped down my accumulated sweat. I felt sick, but I was still angry. This had gone much further than I had originally intended, and I had been swept up in a homicidal rage that left me both nauseated and strangely elated. I wasn't done just yet.

The Iranians were moaning and crying in Farsi. I walked up and grabbed them both by the hair, jerking their heads up. "If you or any of your colleagues come back, I am going to take you to some friends of ours in Soweto," I told them. "They will put a tire around your neck, pour petrol on it, and light it. It's a very nasty way to die."

I asked them if they understood. They nodded and tried to say yes through the tape. Nemati was blubbering, and I thought the fat man was going to have a seizure. We took the duct tape off their mouths.

Though I'd given them both a solid beating, I never hit either of them in the head. I didn't want to drop off at the airport two guys who looked like they'd gone fifteen rounds with Lennox Lewis. I also could have killed them. Most people don't realize how vulnerable the head area is. A single solid blow to the back of the head, or even the brainstem area of the neck, can easily be fatal.

The four of us drove to the airport in silence. When we pulled up at departures, I gave them my final speech: "You will proceed to the nearest counter and take the first flight to anywhere out of South Africa. I don't care where as long as it's not here. We have cameras and security personnel inside who will be watching you." At this point, Russ started to have a fake conversation on his cellphone with our imaginary NIA colleagues in the terminal. We were both being careful. Airports, unlike hotels and industrial parks, are crawling with all kinds of serious security – not the sort of people you can bluff with tall tales.

I ended with a pledge that, should they deviate from my instructions, I'd take them to the veldt, shoot them in the legs, and leave them to the hyenas. (Apparently, the awakened sadist in me enjoyed thinking of ways to kill these two using local props.) At this point, Nemati kept praying over and over again in Farsi. "Your details have been circulated to our allies in other countries," I added. "Tell your superiors to stick to selling caviar and carpets."

With that, Russ cut their flex-cuffs with a quick jerk of his expensive Buck knife. The sight of Russ brandishing his knife at them probably scared them much more than all my antics had. The Iranians got out of the car, still blubbering. I thought they looked like sentimental airline passengers crying at the thought of leaving sunny South Africa. I guess a lot of the other departing passengers thought so as well because no one stared. "Have a nice flight," I said as they walked off.

We watched them go into the terminal and look around for a departure desk. My guess is they were headed for Lufthansa. (Germany is Iran's largest trading partner. The MOIS and IRGC both maintain large contingents in the country to watch over dissidents and spy on the West.) Russ and I drove to the warehouse. We cleaned it up, changed the car's licence plates, and went for a drink. I was exhausted.

"I thought you were going to kill them for a second," he said, cupping his beer.

"I really wanted to," I replied truthfully. He didn't ask me to elaborate, and that was just fine with me because I couldn't explain the cascade of anger that had been welling inside of me for so long. The frustration of working with Charles, the suicide bombings, the anti-Semitism had all been digging away at my calm for some time. Russ wasn't in the Mossad and hadn't seen the sort of things that I had, and any attempt by me to explain would have come out an incoherent mess.

We went down to Cape Town because I needed to decompress. We took a tour of the wine farms, and I got soundly drunk and did my best to forget about Mortazavi and Nemati. I flew back to Tel Aviv a day later and filed my reports. I didn't give them a blow-by-blow account of the rough stuff because I wasn't sure how far I was allowed to take the beatings. My division head, Itzik, had told me just to make it look very convincing. He left the details to me, but I have to admit that a big part of my omission in reporting the beatings was that I also didn't feel like lying on a couch talking to a Mossad shrink. I could only imagine the heavy weather they would have made of my emotional state and apparent anger management problem.

Later on, I heard that Tsomet, the Mossad's human intelligence division, was sniffing around South Africa, looking for sources to recruit – Iranians, Syrians, the usual suspects. But after a while, they shut down because there weren't enough targets. Apparently, the IRGC and MOIS contingent that operated out of the embassy had gone home. Somewhere in Tehran and Johannesburg, I hope there are still South African and Iranian bureaucrats trying to figure out what happened.

I had no illusions that Tehran had been scared out of South Africa permanently. It's been more than five years since all of this happened, and for all I know the country is now swarming with Iranian agents. With a country like Iran, the point isn't to land a knockout punch, but to play for time. Eventually, the people there will grow sick of being lorded over by a clique of aging theocrats, and the ayatollahs will go the way of the Shah. The Mossad's job is to ensure that day comes before Iran gets the Bomb.

Meanwhile, the fate of Ron Arad is still a mystery. During a quiet weekend at home, a couple of months after returning to Israel, I was catching up on the Israeli newspapers when I spotted an op-ed written by the pilot who had flown Arad's F-4 two-seater. He too had bailed out near Sidon. But once they hit the ground, the two were separated. The pilot was rescued in dramatic fashion – holding onto the landing skid of an Israeli rescue helicopter under heavy fire from Lebanese gunmen.

Writing under a pseudonym to protect his identity, he explained how heavily traumatized he'd been by Arad's fate – classic survivor's guilt. One of his coping mechanisms, he wrote, was to fantasize about Arad's safe return. In this fantasy, the two take off again in their Phantom. Only this time, they both land safely together at their airbase in Israel.

Arad disappeared two decades ago. But in Iran nothing has changed. It remains the brutal dictatorship Ayatollah Khomeini created in 1979. Even in Canada, you cannot escape it. In 2003, shortly after I returned to British Columbia, Zahra Kazemi, an Iranian-born freelance photographer residing in Montreal, was beaten to death in government custody during a visit to Tehran – punishment for photographing the outside of the city's infamous Evin Prison. The Iranians originally claimed the middle-aged woman had died of either a "stroke" or an "accident." But on March 31, 2005, Shahram Azam, a former staff physician in Iran's defence ministry, disclosed the results of his examination of Kazemi, four days after her arrest. Azam reported that Kazemi showed obvious signs of torture, including brutal rape, broken fingers, missing fingernails, a skull fracture, abdominal bruising, and marks from flogging.

Meanwhile, the country's president, Mahmoud Ahmadinejad, continues to maintain close connections with the IRGC. In fact, a former Revolutionary Guards commander, Ezatollah Zarghami, has been named to run Iran's state television and radio network. And the head of the country's judiciary, Ayatollah Mahmoud Shahroudi, named a former IRGC commander to be his legislative liaison. Not only is the Iranian government continuing to support terror in Israel, it is now doing the same in Iraq. In October 2005, a senior British official accused the IRGC of supplying infrared trip wires to Iraqi bomb makers through Hezbollah intermediaries. And, of course, we know that Iran supplied most of the sophisticated weaponry that Hezbollah used to kill Israeli soldiers during the brief Lebanon war of 2006.

Some readers may think I'm no better than these people. Admittedly, I may have sunk to their level for a few dark moments in that Johannesburg warehouse, and dark moments they were. Had Russ not been there to restrain me, I would have pulled the trigger, if only to let go of the murderous rage that had been snarling and pacing inside of me like an angry leopard waiting to be let out of its cage. I had a wife and two children in Israel and the constant threat by Israel's enemies to annihilate them had created a monster that surprised even me. But in the end, Messrs. Mortazavi and Nemati got to go home to their wives and children. My feelings have not softened since that muggy day in South Africa, and with each passing year since there are more days that I wish I had shot them than days when I am glad that I didn't. Perhaps that doesn't sit well with our sensibilities and indulgent Western value system, but as far as I was concerned all I did was administer a few well-deserved welts and bruises. If only Ron Arad, Zahra Kazemi, and the thousands of other victims of Iranian brutality had been so lucky.

19 | SECRET RELAY

A man should never be ashamed to own he has been wrong, which is but saying that he is wiser today than he was yesterday.

Alexander Pope

When I began work with the Mossad in 1988, my instructor Oren told me that each agent is like a box of matches. One by one, the matches are burned up, until there is nothing left but ash. Some of us may have more matches than others. But we all have a finite number.

It was in early 2001, while working as branch chief in Southeast Asia, that I realized my box was nearly empty. It wasn't a dramatic realization – certainly nothing resembling that trite set piece from spy movies in which the middle-aged protagonist barely cheats death, then tells his partner, "Man, I'm getting too old for this." I'd seen it coming for years: a gradual deterioration in job satisfaction brought on by stress and isolation. After the incident in Johannesburg, I knew that, like an old airplane, I was showing signs of metal fatigue.

The decisive moment came when my superiors asked me to attend a management course – a one-day test designed to evaluate an agent's decision-making and prioritizing skills through a series of simulated problems. Such requests were reserved for those being considered for command positions back in Israel, and most of my colleagues would have jumped at the opportunity. But not me: the prospect of gossiping over office politics around a Tel Aviv water cooler seemed even less appealing than fieldwork. I was forty years old, still young enough to begin a new career – but only if I acted quickly. It was time to leave the Mossad.

After giving notice in the summer of 2001, I stayed on the job for several months to help break in my replacement, Klaus. Having worked as a case officer for several years, Klaus already knew the basics of the spy trade. But I still needed to introduce him to my assets in Southeast Asia.

It was also important for Klaus to understand the nature of the Mossad's mission in this part of the world. Since the explosion of militant Islam following the Iranian Revolution of 1979, Southeast Asia had become a hotbed of fundamentalist terror groups – including al-Qaeda and its homegrown offshoots – seeking to target Israel and its allies.

Even before 9/11, terrorist organizations and their sponsors were finding it increasingly difficult to work in Europe. Asia's Muslim areas, including Malaysia, Indonesia, southern Thailand, and parts of the Philippines, provided a friendlier environment for attracting recruits and organizing attacks. And thanks to the links forged among jihadists who'd travelled to Afghanistan to fight the Soviets in the 1980s, as well as the explosive growth of the Internet in the 1990s, local terrorist cells had little trouble communicating with one another.

As well as briefing Klaus on such matters, I had to teach him the basics of operating in Asia. His previous experience had been gained in Europe, the agency's traditional hunting grounds. Things were less complicated there. Doing a surveillance detection route on the genteel streets of Paris is one thing; doing it amid the confusion and sweltering heat of Kuala Lumpur is quite another.

Finally, there was the sensitive issue of religion. Klaus, I noticed, had a habit of conducting his Orthodox Jewish rituals in public. This was a problem. Don't get me wrong. I have no issue with people of faith. But when Klaus started performing the morning *shachar* prayer in the waiting lounge of a regional Asian airport, complete with ceremonial *tzitzit* prayer shawl and *tefillin* on head and arm, I got nervous. Once his prayers were done, I explained to him – as diplomatically as possible – that not everyone had to know we were Jews. At Heathrow or Charles de Gaulle, that sort of thing wasn't a big deal. But in this part of the world, things were different. I urged Klaus to go talk to his rabbi. No doubt, he'd agree that a Mossad officer on assignment shouldn't feel guilty about missing a prayer or two when discretion was the wiser course.

But such quirks were few and minor. The important thing was that my assets seemed to trust Klaus, which meant they'd likely stay in our Rolodex. As my final trip as an intelligence officer wrapped up, I took comfort in the fact that my territory was being left in competent hands.

Then, with just days left in Klaus's training, al-Qaeda terrorists flew two planes into the World Trade Center, and a third into the Pentagon. In an instant, the reams of instructions I'd delivered to my replacement suddenly seemed obsolete.

Like everyone else, I remember exactly were I was on September 11, 2001: standing in my hotel room in a Southeast Asian city I'll leave unidentified, after a long day of meetings, freshly unknotted tie in hand, watching CNN, as I always did before going to bed.

At first, I thought some amateur pilot with more bravado than brains had miscalculated the height of the World Trade Center's North Tower. During the first confused minutes, in fact, that was what some news outlets were reporting. But then, as I kept watching, a second plane, United Airlines flight 175, plunged into the South Tower. It was obvious that I was watching a massive terrorist attack.

For anyone in my profession – and even many outside it – 9/11 didn't come as a complete surprise. Al-Qaeda and other terrorists had dreamed of humbling America for years. It was the scale and sophistication of the operation that astonished me. I'm not an overly profane man, but all I could say was "fuck" in a low, astonished whisper. I suspect millions of other TV watchers around the world uttered that same syllable at the same moment.

I began to speculate about the enormous planning that went into the attack. Even the relatively simple terrorist attacks that take place in Israel and Iraq typically require weeks, if not months, of planning, as well as the involvement of a variety of logistical and munitions experts. The 9/11 attacks took terrorism to another level, and I wasn't surprised to learn later that Mohammed Atta and his fellow ringleaders had been planning it since 1999.

Eyes still glued to the television, I made three phone calls. I called my family back in Israel and then my Dad in Canada. Finally, I dialled Klaus in his room. "Are you watching?" I asked.

"Oh, yeah," he replied.

"I'm calling the office. I suggest you get some sleep because we're not going to get any for a while. Barring any instructions from the office, I'll see you in the morning."

Almost immediately after hanging up, I heard the ring tone from my cellphone – a "sanitized" unit with an unattributable number, working off a SIM card I'd purchased through a local pay-as-you-go service. It was Etti, now the deputy head of my department.

"There's been an attack on the Twin Towers in New York," she told me. Her tone was matter of fact – as if planes smashing into skyscrapers were a common nuisance. "You need to get to an embassy. We will probably have further instructions at that point. It's going to be a zoo around here. The Americans are going to be at our gates very soon, looking for whatever information we've got."

I knew she had plenty of other calls to make, so I kept the chitchat to a minimum. After hanging up, I called a regional airline and secured two flights to Canberra, Australia – site of the nearest Israeli embassy equipped with a Mossad communication station that serviced the Mossad's regional Tevel officer. Then I slept – or tried to, anyway.

I'd started hearing the name Osama bin Laden as far back as the early 1990s, when he was a *mujahideen* leader in Afghanistan. (As 9/11 conspiracy theorists constantly remind us, he was then allied with the Americans, fighting his jihad against the Soviets with CIA backing.) When the Twin Towers fell, my thoughts drifted back to 1996, when I met with a gaunt low-level analyst from the CIA's Counterterrorism Center who asked us if we had anything on Osama bin Laden or al-Qaeda. This was shortly after the Khobar Towers attack in Saudi Arabia, which killed nineteen American servicemen. At the time, it seemed like a large death toll. Seen in retrospect, it looked like peanuts.

For obvious reasons, Israel's intelligence services have traditionally focused on Palestinian terrorist groups and other local threats. But in the 1980s, the Mossad had christened a new department, the World Jihad branch, to track global Islamic terror organizations then sprouting up in Southeast Asia, Kashmir, Pakistan, Central Asia, the Middle East, North Africa and Europe. It was a strange department, because up until the 1990s, most terrorist organizations were secular in nature. This new hybrid of Islamic extremism and terror was the tip of a very big iceberg that was headed in our direction.

Unfortunately, like the CIA, the World Jihad branch never cracked al-Qaeda. There's been a lot of speculation about whether anyone in Israel knew about the 9/11 attacks beforehand. Witness the stubborn theory – originally spread by Al-Manar TV, a Hezbollah-controlled Lebanese television station – that four thousand Jews stayed home from their World Trade Center jobs on September 11, 2001. As a former Mossad agent, allow me to set the record straight: we knew nothing.

During a visit to Mossad HQ in late 2002, about a year after my retirement, I caught up with Etai, the head of the Mossad's World Jihad branch. I remember putting the question directly to him: "Did you know a major attack was about to be perpetrated on U.S. soil?"

He looked at me squarely and replied: "We intercepted plenty of suspicious chatter. And sometimes, there were even references to this or that attack. But we didn't have a clue about 9/11."

At the moment the Twin Towers fell, I learned, Etai was in Poland on an intelligence exchange program, as a guest of that country's secret service. Al-Manar viewers take note: if the Israelis knew anything, I doubt the head of the branch mandated with covering al-Qaeda would have been sitting in Warsaw, suffering its lousy autumn weather and making polite industry chitchat about lord only knows what with his Polish hosts.

Most of the embassies in Canberra are located in a lush suburb called Yarralumla, and mimic the architectural style of their home countries. The Israeli embassy is a case in point, a small, tasteful structure built in the Mediterranean art deco style that's popular in Tel Aviv. It's a short walk from its more grandiose American counterpart, a large red-brick colonial mansion that sits imposingly on a hilltop.

As our taxi neared Turrana Street, Klaus and I were met by a roadblock manned by the Australian Federal Police (AFP). In the background, I could see buses evacuating U.S. embassy personnel. Despite flashing my diplomatic passport to all and sundry, I could not convince the AFP to allow us into the diplomatic neighbourhood. Being unaccredited, I didn't have the necessary ID card that is supposed to accompany the diplomatic credentials. I told the driver there was a fat tip in it for him if he circled around to the other side of the U.S. embassy. He immediately complied. (No doubt, it was the most exciting fare he'd ever received: Canberra is quite possibly the most boring capital city in the world.) After being dropped off near the Polish embassy, just one hundred metres from Israel's, Klaus and I made a dash for it as the AFP scanned for traffic in the other direction.

The Israeli embassy in Canberra has a Mossad liaison station, complete with a "strong-room" – a small chamber, secured by a bank-style vault door, that contains classified material, as well as facilities for transmitting and receiving encrypted communications. When we arrived, the building was officially closed because of the 9/11 attacks. But the security officer and the ambassador, Gabi Levi, were onsite.

I went into the ambassador's office to brief him on what I knew. I didn't have much to tell him, but the mere act of sitting down for a conversation was an important courtesy, something I did with every Israeli ambassador when I was visiting a diplomatic mission. You never knew when such small acts of kindness would need to be repaid. We were travelling on diplomatic documents, after all, and if I got myself into trouble, I'd be relying on the ministry of foreign affairs to deal with the official fallout.

Unlike some of my Mossad colleagues, I had a lot of respect for the diplomatic side of Israel's overseas operations. Yes, they spend a lot of their time performing eye-glazing protocol functions. But being Israelis, they also face a lot of danger – and unlike most intelligence agents, they don't have the benefit of operating undercover.

Even low-level employees at Israeli embassies and consulates are potential targets for terrorists, neo-Nazis, and anti-Semites. When overseas Israeli diplomats are taken to task for the Israeli Defense Forces' allegedly heavy-handed counterterrorist tactics, I always wonder how they can resist responding to such lectures by asking, "And which one of us checked the underside of his car for explosives before driving his kids to school this morning?"

I'd met Levi on a few previous occasions. He was a smart, solidly built, compact man with a head of thick white hair. He also struck me as kind and generous in that gruff Israeli manner, offering up the use of his chauffeur-driven armoured Volvo S80 whenever he wasn't using it.

This was just half a day after the 9/11 attacks, and Levi still looked shaken as he watched CNN on the big-screen TV in his office. "How did this happen?" he asked me as I walked in.

Obviously, it was a question I couldn't answer. On September 12, 2001, who could? And yet my immediate reaction was to find something meaningful to say. As an intelligence officer, I felt embarrassed to stand there and tell him I hadn't a clue. (I can only imagine how much more acute the embarrassment was for my CIA counterparts, who were at that moment presumably enduring more pointed variations on the same question.)

After mumbling something about al-Qaeda, I told him I needed to check the cable traffic, but that I'd be out of his hair by the next day. I went back to the liaison station, where Klaus was waiting for me, and we headed to the communication room in the basement. On a normal day, there would be a cipher clerk to handle communications. But today being 9/12 and all diplomatic missions having been evacuated, the room was empty. We would have to improvise.

It was hard to make head or tail of the various computers and beeping, blinking peripheral devices laid out before us. But eventually, after a few tries, we managed to send a cable to my desk officer and department head at Mossad HQ. We then spent the afternoon and most of the night reading classified updates about the attacks on the Twin Towers. All told, it didn't add a lot to what we'd already learned from CNN.

We were given our mission by Etti and it was simple: meet with established assets in the region and see if there was intelligence of any kind pointing to another impending terrorist attack. We were also asked to press our assets for any information they had on known al-Qaeda cells.

I knew this would probably be a waste of time: if any of our sources had known anything about people crashing airplanes into buildings or anything similar, they would have come to me long ago. But we went about our business anyway on the theory that doing something was better than doing nothing – and that maybe, just maybe, after the enormity of 9/11, some of the rats would go scurrying for cover and inadvertently reveal themselves.

So my days after the 9/11 attacks were consumed by travelling around Southeast Asia, where Klaus and I were responsible for a region that spanned millions of square kilometres. Over two weeks, we flew from city to city, meeting with assets plugged into the Islamic communities, as well as checking the security status of potential targets such as synagogues in Singapore and Hong Kong. As predicted, we learned nothing. But we still had to write long reports for HQ. This did little but give already busy people extra sheaves of paper to read. But we had no choice. Every business has its bureaucratic protocols, and spy work is no different.

The only real lead I had was an al-Qaeda money-laundering ring that one of my assets who worked in the Thai banking industry had uncovered a year earlier. My contact had noticed that a small group of Middle Eastern men were transferring funds to a Jordanian Barclays Bank account believed to be controlled by Hamas. I asked my asset to photocopy all the available documents relating to the suspicious transactions. At great risk to himself, he gave me everything, which I sent home for my colleagues to analyze.

They eventually traced the money to Afghanistan, but that's where the snooping ended. In the pre-9/11 world, there were a lot of leads like that. In retrospect, they seemed tantalizing, but at the time, following them didn't seem like a useful investment of resources. Jihadi financiers moving money from "Afghan Arabs" to Asia and the Middle East were common creatures. In any case, we didn't have the manpower to follow the cell around, and we couldn't pass the details on to the local secret service as we wanted to protect our assets. (If you don't take care of your sources, its difficult to recruit others. Even in the post-9/11 era, the Mossad wouldn't have passed the intelligence I'd gathered on to the local security services until it was "whitened" – that is, sourced to a fictitious third party.)

During the weeks that the world was still reeling from the Trade Towers attacks, I wish I could say that I was single-mindedly devoted to my professional investigations. But the truth was that the screwed-up state of the world was competing for my attention with the screwed-up state of my own life. While this book is about the former, I would not be giving readers a complete picture if I didn't at least mention the latter.

For one thing, I was in the midst of a divorce. Things had soured with Dahlia, the dog-walking kibbutznik who'd been such a big part of my settling in Israel in the first place. As well, I was leaving my job, and had nothing lined up to replace it. I was experiencing what I now recognize as your standard and banal midlife crisis – compounded by the not-so-standard occupational stress that goes along with the spy trade.

There was something else gnawing at me as well: after almost two decades of being away from my native Canada, I missed it. In recent years, I'd travelled with my family back to Victoria when on leave, and each time I found it tough to return to Israel. One reason was that my father's health began a steady decline in the late 1990s. I hadn't spent much time with him after my parents divorced when I was three, and I wanted to make up for the lost decades as best I could.

Though the romantic attachment I'd developed to Israel in my younger years hadn't vanished entirely, I now saw the country's flaws as well. I was tired of the endless traffic jams, the scorching heat, the low wages, and the confiscatory tax rates. And, of course, I was sick of the terrorism. I'd seen the results of a suicide bombing up close in 1997 while working as a counterterrorism liaison officer. Ironically, we were escorting two agents from the FBI who'd flown in for an intelligence exchange relating to U.S. citizens killed in a previous attack on Israeli soil. While out with our Shin Bet hosts, we were notified of a bombing at a pedestrian mall in Jerusalem. We arrived at the scene shortly thereafter and bore silent witness to the carnage that resulted in four deaths and almost two hundred wounded.

"Wounded" doesn't sound so bad in news reports. But when you see the destroyed limbs, the missing eyes, and the horrific burn injuries, it somehow seems worse than death. I'll always remember the sight of the intact head and shoulders of one of the Hamas suicide bombers propped on an auxiliary light junction box against a stone wall some eight metres above the street. This sort of thing takes its toll.

(As a footnote to this story, I returned to the scene of the bombing about a month later with two different FBI agents dispatched from Washington and a jovial Shin Bet officer from the Israel Security Agency's Jerusalem office. The FBI is mandated to investigate terrorist incidents in which American citizens are involved outside of the

United States. We toured around and I described the scene to the FBI agents while our Shin Bet host talked us through the attack. You'd never have known that there was carnage and death at the pedestrian mall just a few weeks before: the shops and cafes were doing a brisk trade. According to our host, the suicide bombers had disguised themselves as women in an effort to avoid suspicion amidst the crowd of shoppers and coffeehouse patrons. He kept referring to them as "transverters," and our FBI guests were doing their best to keep a straight face. I couldn't bear it anymore and told the poor fellow that the term was "transvestite." His English was without accent, but his vocabulary was at times bizarre. The strangely comic and completely human moment was a wonderful respite from my memories of the chaos, gore, and death that had occurred on the same spot.)

Such scenes shouldn't have affected my decision to leave Israel: in an ideal world, we'd all ignore the threat of suicide bombings in order to ensure we weren't "letting the terrorists win." But in truth, everybody thinks about it. Whatever they tell you about the low statistical likelihood of getting blown up, you still can't help but let your mind ponder worst-case scenarios. I didn't want to end up that way: my arm on the sidewalk and my torso sitting on a mailbox and no one knowing which pair of legs belonged to me.

I filed my reports, submitted my expenses, and returned to Israel in late September. My official retirement date was October 1, 2001. I didn't hang around for the retirement party and stayed in Israel only long enough for my divorce to come through.

The timing of my retirement was ironic. For almost two decades, I'd helped Israel fight terrorism and the Middle East's rogue powers during a period when the Western world's attention was focused elsewhere. And now, in late 2001, at exactly the moment when this campaign had become the central front in the great clash of civilizations – with terrorism and jihad suddenly the topics *du jour* among journalists, authors, academics, and government officials – I was withdrawing from the fray. I suppose part of me wanted to stay on for this reason. But whenever those second thoughts came to me, I remembered what Oren told me: When the matches are gone, they're gone.

After I arrived back in Canada, I continued to follow Israeli news closely. Living in a Western country, I got a different perspective on events in the Middle East. Despite the cliché about how 9/11 "changed everything," I found that many Canadians, like many Europeans and even many Americans, didn't really understand the threat from militant Islam. The people I spoke with seemed upset by the 9/11 attacks – but then, in the same breath, went on to say that America had it coming because of its "arrogant" foreign policy. Even those who denounced 9/11 without qualifications typically found some way to distinguish that attack, in moral terms, from the Palestinian suicide bombing campaign that was then going strong. According to the standard left-wing view, the "humiliation" of living under Israeli occupation made Palestinian attacks inevitable. Of course, even when I was living in Israel, I was aware that this was a common view in the West. But it was distressing to hear – especially after 9/11 made it clear that the world's jihadists regarded Israel as just one battleground of many.

The worst came in April 2002, when Israel invaded the Jenin refugee camp, at the northern end of the West Bank, and the Western media parroted Arab-invented tales of mass murder. In European newspapers, Ariel Sharon was casually compared to Adolf Hitler, and Israel to Nazi Germany. In Canada, meanwhile, the government was resisting attempts to list Hezbollah as a terrorist organization, and the Canadian prime minister sat next to the group's leader at a conference of the Organisation internationale de la Francophonie in Beirut.

To someone who has been on the front line in the fight against global terrorism, such attitudes are distressing. One senses that the jihadists will have to hit each Western nation individually before they wake up to the threat, and stop trying to blame democratic nations such as Israel and the United States for bringing the violence on themselves. This struggle is not about oil, or about Palestinians who feel they've been cheated out of this or that parcel of real estate. Militant Islam is a totalitarian ideology. The fanatics who embrace it see liberal democracy, religious pluralism, equality between the sexes, the separation of church and state, and all the other values we hold dear to be deadly sins that must be expunged – along with the sinners. It is a point the jihadists hammer home with every bus, disco, hotel, and restaurant they blow up in Indonesia, Jordan, Egypt, Iraq, Britain, Afghanistan, Saudi Arabia, and – yes – Israel.

That is not to say that no progress has been made since 2001. Afghanistan has been liberated. Libya, long an implacable foe of Israel, has given up its weapons of mass destruction program and sought to rejoin the community of civilized nations. And Saddam Hussein, the very epitome of brutal Arab tyranny (not to mention a generous financier of Palestinian terrorism), has been hanged.

Yet terrorist havens remain – none more dangerous than Iran, whose president proclaims the Holocaust a hoax and embraces dark messianic fantasies of Israel's destruction and Iran's emergence as a world superpower. Syria, though weakened, continues to be ruled by a cabal that embraces the same Baathist creed as Saddam Hussein. And then there is Lebanon, a country so hollowed out by decades of civil conflict and occupation by Syrian troops that it has essentially given up its southern region to the control of Hezbollah guerrillas.

I think it was the comedian Dennis Miller who proclaimed that Israel lives in "psycho cul-de-sac." Not very poetic, but I couldn't have said it any better myself.

20 | LOOKING FORWARD

*A dreamer is one who can only find his way by moonlight,
and his punishment is that he sees the dawn before the rest
of the world.*

Oscar Wilde

Long before I took up spying as a profession, I loved reading J.R.R. Tolkien's *The Lord of the Rings*. Tolkien abhorred allegory in all its forms, and like any good story, his masterpiece can be easily ruined if one tries to read too many real-world lessons into the narrative. But at least one basic theme from the book has helped me make sense of the challenges this world faces, and the way we must respond to them.

Like the Hobbits in Tolkien's shire, many young Westerners today grew up largely oblivious to the modern-day Mordors of North Korea, Saddam Hussein's Iraq, and Taliban-controlled Afghanistan. The period between the Cold War and 9/11 was one in which we collectively retreated into our own safe, prosperous societies. As Canadian columnist Mark Steyn wrote the day after 9/11, "From the end of the Gulf War to September 11th, 2001, the world's only superpower took a long weekend off, loaded up the SUV, and went to the mall."

But the deaths of 2,973 innocents on that day tragically communicated the message that we cannot remain holed up in such places. In this global age, jihadist terrorists are but a cheap plane ride away. And unless we go out and fight them where they breed, they will come attack us where we live.

My active role in this fight is now over. But I worry about my two sons, who both still live in Israel near their mother. They come to visit me in Canada regularly. And it's always a hard moment when I have to put them back on an airplane. Every parent who has a child serving in Iraq, Afghanistan, or any of the other fronts in this strange new war knows what I'm talking about. I wave goodbye and simultaneously say hello to a rush of memories that lead me along the path that brought me to where I now stand in 2007. When I think of my children, I cannot help but feel a twinge of guilt. I have projected my fight against Israel's enemies onto my children: my eldest has fought Hezbollah as a member of the IDF, and his younger brother will have to do his military service in three more years.

The world is a very different place from the one it was on that fall day in 1982 when I departed on what turned out to be a two-decade-long adventure. In 1987, only a few years after I finished my military service, the first intifada erupted. Then came the Oslo Accords, the emergence of Yasser Arafat's corrupt Palestinian Authority and, finally, Israel's complete withdrawal from Gaza. As the Palestinians have gained more autonomy, the area has descended into anarchy. Many areas in the West Bank are now ruled by violent clans, with the Palestinian Authority the government in name only. And Gaza, as I write this, is teetering on full-blown civil war. Which is better: chaos and autonomy, or occupation and order? I still don't know. When it comes to the seemingly intractable Arab–Israeli conflict, I'm still not sure I have a better idea than anyone else of how a permanent settlement can be achieved.

There have been other changes in the Middle East. Iraq is now free but wartorn. Iran is sponsoring conferences for Holocaust deniers. Hezbollah has more or less taken over Lebanon. Palestinians are doing their best to destroy the state that Israel has given them. And everywhere, Muslim extremists are blowing themselves up in the deluded belief that killing innocent civilians is the path to holy salvation. This path upon which the Muslim world now finds itself evokes the place the poet John Milton imagined over three hundred years ago: "To bottomless perdition, there to dwell."

There's another difference, too: the very nature of war has changed. In 1982, wars were still fought with tanks and planes, and you could draw the battle lines on a map. Nowadays, you're more likely to get blown up on King George Street in Jerusalem than you are hiking along the Syrian border. Moreover, the Israeli generals who fought the 1948, 1956, 1967, 1973, and even 1982 wars never had to deal with round-the-clock news channels, including saturation coverage of every civilian killed in the fog of war. Until the creation of the International Criminal Court, Israeli generals never had to worry about being arrested abroad as war criminals. Nor did conventional war provoke in Western societies the wrenching trade-offs we are now making between security and civil liberties.

But from an Israeli perspective, perhaps the biggest difference I've observed in the last quarter-century is the re-emergence of bald-faced anti-Semitism as a mainstream ideology in many parts of the world. The phenomenon is confined mostly to the Muslim world, but it is encouraged by the international community as well – the most glaring example being the UN's 2001 World Conference against Racism, Racial Discrimination, Xenophobia and Related Intolerance, at which the imprimatur of the United Nations was hijacked by bigots who want to see Israel wiped off the map. Left-leaning NGOs have been an active partner in this process. This is one area in which nothing has changed since the Cold War. Then, as now, the bleeding hearts who lecture the United States and Israel have a curious willingness to overlook the far greater abuses committed by the Robert Mugabes, Mahmoud Ahmadinejads, Fidel Castros, and Hassan Nasrallahs of the world.

The fight between Israelis and Palestinians has long been a media obsession in the West. But now, thanks to the emergence of Arabic-language satellite television stations seeking incendiary footage, the problem has gotten worse, and skewed, lurid coverage of Palestinian casualties is being used as a terrorist recruiting tool. Even in the early days, when I lived on my kibbutz in the 1980s, I was stunned by what I saw on the English-language television channel that broadcast from Jordan. It was as if there was no other news on the planet worthy of being reported except Israel's latest purported outrage. And Jordan is considered a *moderate* regime in the region. The Syrians, Saudis, and Egyptians produce programs that would make a Nazi propagandist blush.

Despite all the threats facing Israel, however, I am at least optimistic that the men and women protecting the country remain highly motivated and competent. Since my retirement, I have visited my former Mossad colleagues on several occasions. Although they cannot share with me the sort of information I was privy to as an active agent, I've learned enough to know that the organization is in good hands. True, I had many trying, frustrating moments during my career. Yet I have nothing but admiration for this small, secretive organization that has been so often misunderstood and maligned. I know that on more occasions than I can count (or am permitted to describe), it took measures to eliminate threats against not only Israel, but other countries that were oblivious to the fact.

As for me, I am happy in retirement. After so many years of being someone else, I am at this point in my life ready to live within my own skin. I have paid a personal cost for my actions and, more importantly, have forced others close to me to pay a cost as well. That is the hardest part of the equation and one that I must wrestle with as I lie awake and think myself into endless scenarios of "If I had only . . ." My neglect of my personal life resulted in divorce and a lot of long-range parenting. I think for every success I had in my professional life, there were two failures in judgment concerning my personal life.

I know that the biggest question that I'll be asked is "Why did you write this book?" My answer is simply that part of me being myself is putting what happened to me in my previous life down on paper. I also like to think that this world will be a better, safer place if more people understand the lessons I've learned in my service to Israel. In this age of global jihad, the threat Israelis have been dealing with for decades is becoming a reality for the whole world.

I owe the Mossad much. They took care of my family as best as they could during my frequent and long absences, and they looked after many practical things for me, including my university tuition. I am sure that they will not exactly relish the fact that I have written this memoir – no intelligence service encourages such undertakings by its former officers. They will react in their best interest, as they have when other ex-agents have written their own accounts, and that's all I can say on the matter.

Whatever they say, however, I believe that the world needs to hear these stories. A storm is coming, and it would appear that those of us who cherish life, liberty, and the goodness in our way of life will have no choice but to endure it.

As for me, I decided not to wait for the inevitable. I volunteered.

| ACKNOWLEDGEMENTS

I'd like to thank and acknowledge the assistance, support, love and friendship of the many people who guided my way to seeing this book published:

My friend and collaborator, Jonathan Kay, the smartest man I know, whose integrity and editorial skill are outmatched only by his superlative wit.

My agent, Michael Levine, a true *mensch* who believed in me and, despite all the reasons in the world to turn me away, embraced *The Volunteer* with an open heart and open mind.

My publishers at McClelland & Stewart, Doug Pepper and Chris Bucci, for their foresight and enthusiasm and for simply being what every writer could ask for out of a publisher. Special thanks to my editor, Trena White, who laboured over the manuscript and only reinforced my belief that writers are not quite as smart as editors.

My publicist, Ruta Liormonas, for her hard work and creativity.

Evan Solomon for listening when I was probably at my least coherent.

George Jonas for very good advice. I think I owe you a lunch?

My friends at the Mossad and CIA, who continue to make personal sacrifices that will forever go unnoticed. I won't forget.

To Dave, Arthur, Mike, and Robert, who helped in ways that can never be mentioned.

My family both near and far for their patience and many kind offerings of encouragement and support.

My ex-wife for being there when I wasn't and for continuing to be there when I can't be.

My mother for thoughtfully tethering the civilities and good form required of every young gentleman with the survival skills needed to weather the unforeseeable.

My father, who passed away in 2004, for his encouragement and humour, which saw me through some dark days.

And especially my wife, Shannon, who not only supported and nurtured the concept of this book throughout, but through whose experiences I realized what real strength, courage, and love are. Each day with you is a gift.